THE ALLEGORY

OF THE

Faerie Queene

THE ALLEGORY

OF THE

Faerie Queene

BY

M. PAULINE PARKER
I.B.V.M.

OXFORD
AT THE CLARENDON PRESS
1960

Oxford University Press, Amen House, London E.C.4

GLASGOW NEW YORK TORONTO MELBOURNE WELLINGTON
BOMBAY CALCUTTA MADRAS KARACHI KUALA LUMPUR
CAPE TOWN IBADAN NAIROBI ACCRA

PRINTED IN GREAT BRITAIN

PREFACE

IT is extremely difficult to trace the formation of critical ideas and impressions. Probably, therefore, I am even deeper in debt than I realize. Where I was aware of a debt I have tried to acknowledge it in the text; but besides expressing my general gratitude to all, known and unknown, whose good things I have used, I ought also to emphasize how much, even when sometimes differing in conclusions, I owe to the works of Professor Renwick, Professor Lewis, and Dr. Spens. Only to the de Selincourt preface could one owe more. I owe much also to the suggestions and criticism on the part of the Clarendon Press itself, and I have to thank the Cambridge University Library for the courtesy with which I was allowed access to the books.

I wish very specially to express my gratitude to Miss Helen Darbishire, without whose encouragement this book would never have been begun at all, and to Professor A. M. D. Hughes, without whose constant patience and wise criticism it would never have been completed.

M. P. P.

CONTENTS

I

INTRODUCTORY

IN what follows I do not attempt to make a contribution to Spenserian scholarship. Numerous valuable books have been written on Spenser in the last thirty years, more it would appear than in the three preceding centuries. In these, far more competent persons have discussed every detail of Spenser's biography, have considered the evolution of his text, have indicated sources whence he drew material or suggestions, have estimated his character, his theology, his poetic personality, his historical place and importance. In particular Spenser's allegory has received an attention which proves that critics are no longer deluded by the notion that his genius is for description, and that his 'dark conceit' may safely be ignored.

It may then be fairly asked what remains for a Spenserian critic to work on. The answer is that Spenser remains. For textual, historical, biographical, and social criticism, though admirable, though essential, is preliminary. And though there are excellent and most helpful essays towards the understanding of Spenser's poetry, such as will not easily be superseded, there is much difference of opinion, and there has not yet appeared that full, final, authoritative appreciation and interpretation which one of the best of Spenser's critics long ago desired. There is therefore still room for a humble commentary which shall strive to remove, as is now necessary, the difficulties which Spenser's contemporaries did not perceive, and to give the explanations which they never required. And first the objection of obscurity.

The Faerie Queene is not obscure because it is differently spelt or because it is allegorical and 'we have outgrown allegory'. T. S. Eliot's allegory is contemporary, and much more difficult than Spenser's, while allegory can in any case never be outgrown. This age in particular, even when unaware, is an age of allegory, especially in painting, and there is moreover little evidence of any intellectual advance such as should render any earlier literary form outmoded. But the question of symbolism, type, and allegory will be treated more fully later. The length and the language of the *Faerie Queene* are equally unreal objections. For language, Chaucer is more difficult, Shakespeare often no easier, and if length be considered, the *Faerie Queene* is much shorter than the huge novels, the immense serial autobiographies, which have been in vogue in the twentieth century. These are not the reasons why Spenser is admired without being read and, when read, so often misunderstood.

The poetry of the present day is a poetry of mood, and of personal reaction to sensory and emotional stimuli. It may range therefore from the cry of a bird to the yelp of a dog when his toe is trodden on, for it comes from the same source. When it is descriptive the reader's response depends on his having had the same experience of incident or spectacle, and having reacted to it similarly. But Spenser's poem is a work of organized imaginative thinking, which uses both mood and emotion but which does not depend on them; which draws immensely on sensory perceptions but which does not consist of them, and which, appealing to human experience, is indifferent to individual biography. Besides all this, and more vitally even than this, the *Faerie Queene*, like the *Divina Commedia*, presupposed an intellectual system and a mental background which, though it still exists and is still operative, has not possession of the school textbooks or the examination syllabuses, and is therefore unfamiliar to a large and ever increasing number of persons who derive their culture principally from these sources. Spenser and his earlier readers shared an experience to which many of his modern ones are strangers. In fact, the modern reader of Spenser is much like a man who, expecting to enter a crematorium, should find himself in Lincoln Cathedral. The builders of that cathedral, though they might have differed from Spenser on many points of dogmatic theology, would have had no difficulty in understanding his poem, and in sympathizing with its general tenour for, like the poet himself, they were Christians, and their art derived from their Christianity.

The singular diversity of opinion which exists among the

critics who have so much elucidated Spenser in recent years is another proof of the absence of the ancient common factor of Christian culture. That diversity is indeed striking. Every book of the *Faerie Queene* which has been especially commended by one professor has been decried by another, and most of the passages which have been cited by one to prove that even Jove can nod, are cited by another as evidence of the supreme decorum with which the poet adapts his style to his subject; the passage which to one is full of meaning is an excrescence to another. One regards him primarily as a poet of sensory experience and appeal, another praises his 'concepts' and attacks his descriptions; one admires his structural genius, another denies it. But nearly all, at least in passing, condemn the poet for not having done what he never intended to do. And while all this may be as much an illustration of Spenser's genius as a similar experience was to that of Apelles, yet it also shows that each critic is looking at Spenser's world from his own point of view. This is a perfectly legitimate proceeding. But it leaves room for one Saul among the prophets who will try to see things as Spenser saw them, as his contemporaries saw them, as the ancient cathedral builders saw them, as the heirs of Christendom see them today. In saying this I distinguish. It is perfectly possible to hold certain beliefs as a personal and private matter and yet, in the judgement of art, literature, politics, science, to prescind from those beliefs, and judge according to a culture which has not been formed by them. It is also possible to be guided practically by a belief which is supported on so little positive, doctrinal knowledge that it cannot be used as a key to problems outside those of daily concrete experience. But in Spenser's day, as Professor Tillyard has well shown,[1] the belief in a world order which was governed by the God of the Christians, and in which each being had its place, an objective place in an objective order, still held good, and was assumed as a common basis of thought and judgement. It is the contention of this book that the *Faerie Queene* is primarily and fundamentally a Christian poem, and that it cannot be interpreted unless by reference to that fact, but that most of the alleged inconsistencies,

[1] E. M. W. Tillyard, *The Elizabethan World Picture*, Chatto & Windus.

redundancies and obscurities fall into place and into proportion when the poem is thus regarded from within. It would be possible to argue longer on this point; but there is one final and absolute test of a key: whether it opens the door. To that test the chapters devoted to this interpretation must submit.

For the purpose of trying to see the poem as Spenser saw it the poet's sources matter much less than his use of them. That he gathered freely from earlier writers, that he even translated at times, every examination candidate knows. Shakespeare and Chaucer did the same; the idea that books constitute a property from which nothing may be taken without payment, and that it is a merit not to take anything, is the product of a later age in which money is both more important, and much more dependent on simple buying and selling. Biographical detail also is usually irrelevant unless it throws light on the poet's character and mind. It is the use Spenser made of what he took from Ariosto, Malory, Lydgate, and the rest of them, which is important to his poetry, not the fact that he took it, in which he was only doing what everyone did. Biography, not literary criticism, is concerned with the name of his first wife, or the remarriages of his second one, and so forth. Yet a knowledge of his career in Ireland may do something to remove the popular misconceptions about him as a typical 'romantic' poet with his head in the clouds and his feet in a ditch, composing dreamy fancies only comprehensible to those whose heads are equally in the clouds; or, a more recent idea, that he was a hard-headed careerist whose poetry was simply instrumental to his purpose of 'go-getting'. Spenser's career in Ireland confutes both errors for, on the one hand, he held offices which were given him in troublous times because of his proved military and practical capacity, and, on the other, though he did indeed seek court favour to try to establish his family, which last it was clearly his duty to do, he also remained faithful to his friends when they were out of favour, like Lord Grey de Wilton, or could no longer help him, like Leicester. Moreover, he retained the friendship of those for whom a careerist, however brilliant, would have had no attraction. The steady friend of Gabriel Harvey was not vain or profiteering, the friend of Sidney could not have been unworthy, he who stood by the unfortunate, who wrote *Mother Hubberd's Tale* and *Colin Clout's Come Home Again*—to say nothing of certain passages in the *Faerie Queene* itself—held other things dearer than worldly ambition, and did not fear to show it.

Another problem might also appear to be relevant, namely the possible part played by the differing theological views of Cartwright, Grindal, or Bishop Young of Rochester, in forming Spenser's mind and religious character. But it hardly seems possible to determine this exactly, though something may be inferred from the favourable references to Algrind and Roffy in the *Shepheardes Calender*. But the fact is, that it is not dogmatic theology but ascetic and moral which really offers us the key to Spenser's thought in the *Faerie Queene*. Obviously the second presupposes the first. But ascetic theology does not depend essentially on any dogmas that were controverted at that time, except the important issue of justification by faith or by faith and works, and here the whole plan of the poem, besides passages in Book One, demonstrate that Spenser was neither Lutheran nor Calvinist on this point. The primary relation of creature to Creator, the special one brought into being by the Incarnation, the obligation of the human being to live by the help of divine grace, as one who has a heavenly destiny, the further possibility of being able to walk with God even in this world, Grindal would have denied no more than St. Pius V, and Thomas Young believed equally with Thomas Aquinas. Spenser assumes no more than this. But he does assume this, and his Faerie land can be entered more easily through the Thebaid desert than through the Elysian fields, or even the wood outside Athens, though this latter certainly lies near by. Professor Whitaker in *The Religious Basis of Spenser's Thought*,[1] has ably argued that Spenser's doctrine tended rather to what later centuries would call 'High' than the contrary. This would not mean that he was not quite definitely a Protestant, loyal to the Church of England as Elizabeth and Burleigh understood it.

Spenser's Christianity, his Christian experience, is not

[1] Stanford Univ. Series, vol. vii, 1950.

simply an element in his thought or work, as material taken from Malory or Ariosto might be, nor is it an influence such as that exerted by Aristotle, Plato, or Plotinus. It is the stuff itself of which, and for which, the poem is. The *Faerie Queene* without Christianity is *Hamlet* without the prince of Denmark. This is the simple explanation of much that has otherwise seemed puzzling. Spenser's Platonism being generally admitted, why do we not find the 'Platonic ladder' in Spenser? It is because he is a Christian Platonist and believes in the Incarnation. Like St. Augustine, himself a Platonist, he ascends from body to soul, from matter to spirit, from earth to heaven:

> These thus in faire each other farre excelling,
> As to the Highest they approch more neare,
> Yet is that Highest farre beyond all telling
> Faierer than all the rest which there appeare . . .

It may be true that the *Hymne of Heavenly Beautie* from which these lines are taken, is a failure. In fact it must be true for, 'Eye hath not seen nor ear heard . . .' and St. Paul himself could not utter it. Nevertheless in it the poet makes clear that, deeper than all the knowledge of Greek that Bryskett ascribed to him, there lay in his mind the knowledge of the Bible. However much Platonic doctrine may have appealed to his imagination, he knew St. Paul's teaching of the redemption of the body which was to be 'like the body of His glory'. Hence for him, there could be no Platonic ladder in the usual sense, terminating in the love of beauty in itself, freed from the limitations and impurities of matter. Spenser cannot hold this. His ascending scale, rejecting none of the rungs on which it did ascend, rises through all the degrees of creatures to that Most Fair who originated all: 'For the first author of beauty made all those things',[1] and upon the throne of the heavens sits 'the most beautiful of the sons of men'. By the same line of reasoning light may be thrown on the apparent inconsistencies of Spenser's use of Aristotle.

After acknowledging that Spenser's Christianity is to be reckoned with, our next step to understanding him must be

[1] *Wis.* xiii. 3.

to believe what he tells us of his own intention in writing the poem, namely, that: 'The generall end therefore of all the booke is to fashion a gentleman or noble person in vertuous and gentle discipline. . . .'[1] All the critics of Spenser quote this. But most of them seem to assume in what follows, that he did not mean it, or not seriously enough to remember about it, and that, in any case, he meant what they would mean by 'a gentleman or noble person'. But without going into the present connotation of the words, it is quite clear what Spenser meant; he meant 'prince Arthur before he was king', who moves through the poem seeking true glory, 'Whose beauty fills the heavens with her light', and he meant those who, like that 'clownish person', could wear the armour which Truth had brought, 'that is, the armour of a Christian man specified by St. Paul v. Ephes. and wearing it, would seem 'the goodliest man of that company'.

However far it may be from the present practice that a poet should avowedly devote his chief work to a moral purpose, and that without direct psychic relief or complaint, there can be doubt that in Spenser's time, when 'psychic release' (except in the case of love poetry which followed an acknowledged convention) would have been regarded as a matter of purely private concern, not of public interest, the purpose he proclaimed was the very one that critics agreed upon as that most worthy of their greatest poet. Indeed it is precisely that of Sidney's ideal poet in the *Apologie for Poetrie*, he who excels the moral philosopher because he not only sets forth what is good but, by the beauty of the examples he gives, allures men to follow it. It will therefore be assumed throughout this interpretation that Spenser meant what he said about his intention, that he found in this the unifying principle necessary to organize the mass of material he had gathered, and that he understood it in the light of the ascetic discipline with which he was familiar, together with his first readers who, like himself, had no idea of a 'gentleman' who was not also a Christian.

Spenser's minor poems are equally impregnated with his sense of moral and spiritual values. However, though he was always an artist, these works derive their present interest

---

[1] 'Introductory letter to Raleigh', Spenser's *Works*, Oxford Ed., p. 407.

very largely from their relation to his greatest creation, so much is his whole poetic being incorporated in it. His vision of the world, of life, of what it is, and all it means, his thought, the knowledge acquired through his own spiritual experience as he followed the path opened in the Thebaid a thousand years before; all that he had seen and learned of the hidden forces that lie behind human conduct in Cambridge, in the Bishop of Rochester's household and in Leicester's, amid the struggles and intrigues in Ireland, or at Elizabeth's court, the people he had known, the places he had seen, the substance of much of his earlier thought and writing—they all had their place in this one synthesis. It was as though from his own mount of contemplation, he had looked first at the heavenly city: 'Whose walls and towers were builded high and strong', and thence down to the kingdoms of the world and the glory of them, and had seem them as indeed the regions of fayerye; or as if, like that Langland who is in some ways so near to him, he had stood on the Malvern hills and had seen the field full of folk and the tower of truth: or as if, like Bunyan, but with a saner, purer, further, vision, he had seen both the unending pilgrimage to the celestial city and also the perpetual assault round the walls of Mansoul, inexpugnable if not betrayed from within. But the poet's gaze, not yet contracted by the limits assigned by Bunyan's fugitive and cloistered virtue, has perceived that Christian fleeing alone from the City of Destruction, hastening onward driven by fear, seeking his own salvation only, is manifesting but half of the whole Christian character. As Bunyan too had come to learn, when he imagined Standfast and Greatheart, Spenser knew that the fates of all humanity are bound together, and that Arthur will never find Gloriana in herself if he has not sought her in her servants. This is one reason for the structure which makes Arthur so often the helper, even the saviour, of the other knights.

But if Arthur is not human in the usual sense of partaking in human frailty but is rather a kind of earthly providence, neither are his fellow knights to be judged by the psychology of a novel writer. The allegory itself is the reason which justifies Spenser against the common complaint that in certain episodes, Guyon and Artegall, to take two frequent examples, do not behave like human beings. To this there is only one answer: 'They do not. They behave like Justice and Temperance.' It may not be according to the schoolboy notion of fair play that a human being should be assisted in battle by an iron man such as Talus, though he may be helped by an atom bomb if he can get one, but it is highly desirable that unshakeable justice should be attended by irresistible strength. It is a tribute, unconscious perhaps, to the poet's power as a story-teller that the reader should find the human semblance so convincing as to demand even those traits which are inconsistent with their equally real allegoric character. For many there is another consideration also, that, even when they are not virtues, they are elves or elvish bred; but, more immediately relevant to the psychology of Spenser's allegorical heroes, what relation have they to the virtues considered in the *Ethics* of Aristotle to which the poet seems to appeal?

No one can fail to remark—few critics have failed to remark—that Spenser's six virtues have not much apparent connexion with those of Aristotle. Nor can it be supposed that Spenser did not know this. He could not be unaware that Holiness is not on Aristotle's list and that, even if it may be thought to appear on Plato's, it could not have there the meaning that he gives to it. He must have known that Arthur, whom he himself calls 'Magnificence', was not the magnanimous man, and he could hardly have given Guyon his name without admitting tacitly that there is more in him than the Greek ideal of exquisite moral balance. The famous phrase: 'As Aristotle hath devised' has perhaps been taken too narrowly. 'I labour', he says after citing Homer, Virgil, Ariosto, and Tasso, as examples of allegory, 'to pourtraict in Arthur before he was king, the image of a brave knight perfected in the twelve private morall vertues, as Aristotle hath devised; the which is the purpose of these first twelve books . . .' and then, significantly for the rather enigmatic figure of Arthur himself, he explains that his characteristic virtue is that of Magnificence, 'for that it is the perfection of all the rest, and containeth them all. . . . Therefore in the whole course I mention the deeds of Arthur applyable to that vertue which I treat of in that booke'. That is, Arthur shows in each book, the perfect exercise of the virtue, the acquisition or perfecting of which, is the subject of the book. From this it would appear that, however much he may have wished to use the great name of Aristotle as a defence against Gabriel Harvey and his like, and however much he may have been conscious that Aristotle had exercised a real influence on his thought, Spenser did not intend his expression 'as Aristotle hath devised' to define the list of virtues, but to apply to the whole passage; meaning that, like Aristotle, he was expounding an ethical system in which the virtues, though being treated separately, would also be shown resumed in a single typical figure, Arthur's, bearing the same relation to his virtues as the magnanimous man does to Aristotle's. If so, the figure of Arthur, the pattern of chivalry, perfect in every virtue, veiled also in something of mystery and even of mysticism derived from his association with the Grail legends and with those of Wales, together with his own strange coming and going, becomes a sort of criterion which shows how the other knights too should be judged.

In point of fact Spenser, a Christian Aristotelian as he is a Christian Platonist, does include many of the virtues mentioned by the Greek philosopher. He could hardly fail to do so. Thus courage and liberality must be assumed in all the knights, since no virtue can be exercised without courage, and no knighthood without liberality. Temperance, Magnificence, in Spenser's sense, Truth, all hold principal places; gentleness and urbanity are comprised in Calidore's perfect courtesy. But they remain part of a synthesis in which, just as the ultimate heavenly beauty is identified with Him 'whose sceptre is the rod of righteousness', so holiness is placed in the forefront of all the virtues. What other virtues the poet meant to introduce in the books which he did not live to write, we cannot of course know, though some guesses may fairly be hazarded. But in those which he has written, he has kept very close to a list which was common property, and which is divided into two parts; the first including the 'theological' virtues, faith, hope, and charity, which are most clearly exemplified, apart from Arthur, in the Red Cross

Knight, Calidore and some minor characters; and the second, the 'cardinal' virtues: Prudence, Justice, Temperance, and Fortitude. For prudence and temperance may be regarded as different aspects of the same thing, and it is to be suggested later that the Constancie of the fragmentary Seventh Book must be understood as Fortitude.

Here, then, are Spenser's principal personages; characters governed by a master-virtue instead of a master-passion yet, in their concrete form as imagined, reviving for an instant the ideal of Christian chivalry without fear and without reproach, which Chaucer had known, which Malory had depicted, which breathes through the very name of the popular tales of the 'Seven Champions of Christendom', and which had recently been summarized in Hawe's lines:

> For knighthood is not in the feats of warre,
> As for to fight in quarrel right or wrong,
> But in a cause which truth cannot defarre:
> He ought himself for to make sure and strong,
> And no quarrel a knight ought to take
> But for a truth, or for a woman's sake.

Yet deeper than all episodic debts to Malory or others, is the value expressed in Caxton's introduction to the *Morte D'Arthur*: 'For herein may be seen noble chivalry, courtesy, humanity, friendlyness, hardyness, love, friendship, cowardice, murder, hate, vertue and synne. Do after the good and leave the evil, and it shall bring you to good fame and renown.' It is a guess, but a reasonable guess, that when Edmund Spenser read these lines it came into his head that he himself might some day write such a book. But when he came to do so, he of a set purpose, introduced a new element into his knightly virtues. For all save Britomart are either elves or elvish bred. Arthur himself has been brought up by a faerie knight and does not know his own origin, and Britomart, whose birth is no mystery, is the daughter of King Ryence of south Wales, a country certainly bordering on 'faerie lande' as local folk-lore placed it, and rich with elvish gifts.

The word fayerye retained in the sixteenth century the fundamental meaning it had in medieval times, that is, connoting glamour, the illusory appearance, sometimes of attraction more than human, which can invest earthly things, and which certain beings can command at will. Thus Chaucer in *The Merchant's Tale*, speaks of the old man's young bride as so fantastically lovely: 'That to behold it seemed faye-rye.' And in the same sense Gower, speaking of Constance, says:

> The god of her hath made an ende
> And fro this worldes fayrie
> Hath taken her into companie . . .

True, the idea of place was also included. Sir Launfal,

> That noble knyghte of the round table,
> Was take yn to the fayrye,

Thomas Chestre tells us, and of his bride, 'Tryamour that hyghte', he says, 'Her fadyr was kyng of fayrye.' The perilous forest where Huon of Bordeaux meets Oberon, is perilous precisely because by the power of the fairy king, it is under the glamour which can fall on any place, and will make it fairy land as long as it lasts. People too may be 'fayerye' either by birth or adoption. This manifold significance, shifting like the pictures reflected in a dewdrop, informs the word as Spenser knows it and uses it.

The Elizabethan understanding of 'faerie' laid upon Spenser an exigency which he complied with by creating the Spenserian stanza, and the Spenserian diction or poetic language. When writing to Harvey in 1580, he had claimed for poets 'the kingdom of our language', and he here exercises his privilege.

Spenser had always been an experimentalist in prosody, imitating, inventing, adapting. His *Shepheardes Calender* advanced, one may say, as the old guild apprentices advanced their piece of unaided craftsmanship when they claimed to pass to the rank of master, is a collection of experiments, some of which suggest that he understood more about Chaucer's *-e* final than might have been imagined, and all his minor poems are interesting for their technique quite apart from their more essentially poetic achievement. He would not seek to evade the special call on his resources that the evocation of 'faerie' would make.

If Spenser was to project into the imaginative perception of his readers, that world of his poem which was at once popularly traditional, romantic, Platonic, and Christian, he would need some distinctive poetic form, a metrical arrangement and a diction which should be at once familiar and remote. The images it would create ought to be recognizable and yet elusive; as near to us as the stories that delighted our childhood, and yet with an Orphic light, not that of common day. Spenser's faerie land is, simultaneously, the scene of the Christian adventure within the soul, the earth of the ancient ballad where the maidens were buried 'to keep the red rose company', and the phantom which fled before Ulysses, the 'untravelled world' of the Castle of Carbonek which receded for three days as one advanced towards it. It needed therefore a language of its own. It has been suggested[1] that it is a world of the heroic dead such as Virgil shows us in *Aeneid* VI. But this seems impossible, principally because it is still a place of struggle and achievement, and also because both in Book One and Book Two, persons leave it to visit an underworld where the spirits of the dead dwell.

Spenser's diction, then, must be strange because it is faerie; but familiar because it is ours. We are moving in our own world and yet in another. The same language is spoken in both but it is spoken with a difference. The colouring of the northern dialect, the demonstrative 'thilke', the past participle in '-ande' (regional dialect was still in honour and Mulcaster had spoken like that) would give a feeling of reality, of common air and earth, to the form of English which Spenser, the university man, spoke with Sidney, Raleigh, or Bryskett, and still it would not be the language of the streets. And the old words from Chaucer and the romances, forms like 'bene ybrought', 'haberion', 'ventayle', 'encheason', 'warray', 'prowe', or words passing into disuse like 'whilom', were in the first place necessary, many of them, because he was speaking of the things of which they were the vocabulary, jousts, castles, chivalry, but also they gave just

[1] i.e., Rathborne, *The Meaning of Shakespeare's Fairyland,* chap. 1, Columbia University Press, 1937.

that touch of difference which made it a language of beyond the arch:

> For all experience is an arch where through
> Gleams that untravelled world whose margin fades
> For ever and for ever as I move.

A language Spenser's readers could understand, yet not spoken as they spoke it; this was what he required and this he created. He was not unaware, for he follows Tasso's *Discourses on Heroic Poetry* also on other matters, that that poet, recommending the style he considered proper for heroic poetry, includes uncommon words and those taken from the use of distant peoples, provided they are sufficiently akin to be understood.[1] He might also have retorted Ben Jonson's criticism that he 'writ no language' by saying that he certainly did not write the speech of Sir Epicure Mammon, but that his Christian allegory might be none the worse for that.

On the whole Spenser prefers archaic or dialect words to foreign borrowings, though he uses these freely to make proper names. Thus Grantorto, Pastorella, Orgoglio, are Italian, Perissa is Greek, Turpine is Latin, Bruncheval is French. He often uses Italian forms for the names of minor personages like Decetto, Despetto. Other foreign sounding names are genuine, such as Placidas, Serena, Blandina. Tasso also recommends a sustained sentence and stanza as being more dignified. Doubtless the English poet was glad to have the support of the great Italian on this point but it is clear from his prosody in general that his natural genius led him the same way.

Spenser's names have a familiar yet elusive ring. They are recognizably human names as Sumerian ones, for example, are not to us. We accept them as the names of persons, but we do not expect to meet persons called by those names, some invented, some collected from legend, romance, or martyrology, and this is quite apart from the moral significance which many of them have. On the other side, actual ethical names, like Despair, do not strike one as unnatural or too abstract, because the poet has given us the picture of

[1] Tasso, *Discorsi dell'Arte Poetica e del Poema Eroica*, Venice, 1587, no. iii.

despair as our unconscious knows it, and we recognize that this is really the name of that nightmare image.

Yet if Spenser assumes the kingdom he claimed from Harvey, he is not an unreasonable sovereign. He created a special diction to serve a special purpose, and he was master of it. But he did not deal in difficulties and obscurities for their own sake; his sentence structure, though often prolonged, is much more lucid than that of many a writer who had not the excuse that he was writing in a difficult metre. And the language of his time was still so fluid, its vocabulary being daily augmented, its grammatical forms being still unstable, the delight in linguistic feats being so general, that he was doing much less violence to usage than those might think who glibly repeat the clichés of the moment without knowing the wealth locked up in the dictionaries and in the older writers. Even some of the spellings, which might seem just an easy way of making a rhyme, may be more nearly phonetic than we now suppose. Foreigners, taking dictation in English, sometimes reproduce Spenserian spellings in their attempts to write down the sounds they hear.

That Spenser, commanding a vocabulary drawn from various sources; accepted usage, dialect, reading, invention, foreign languages, drew on the whole of it in order to say what he wished to say as it ought to be said, needs no explanation and no excuse. That he was too disciplined an artist to do this without knowing it, is also clear; though we need not suppose that he explained himself to himself as it may be necessary to explain him to later readers. He achieved his purpose by devising a diction which would be understood, and yet would not dispel the fayerie glamour by any untoward realism. A momentary vogue may require its adherents to call a spade 'a damnation shovel'; but they may still recognize that that is not the name it would bear in Faerie land.

Spenser adapts this diction to his purposes. In dialogue and reported speech, he is often remarkably simple and straightforward; as when Guyon, speaking to Artegall of Braggadochio, says:

> . . . Sir knight it would dishonour bee
> To you, that are our judge in equity,

> To wreake your wrath on such a carle as hee:
> It's punishment enough that all his shame do see. (v. iii. 36)

When reporting the conversation of Phaedria and Cymochles, the poet is concise and businesslike:

> . . . Cymochles of her questioned
> Both what she was, and what that usage ment . . . (II. vi. 9)

This simplicity is conditioned both by the occasion and by the person. Evidently it is proper to a passage of familiar conversation, but it also displays character. When Una rejoins her knight after he has killed the dragon, she must have been at the highest point of joy, relief, and satisfaction. But her words are few and briefly reported:

> Then God she praysed, and thankt her faithfull knight (xi. 55)

But Fidessa-Duessa's Letter in the next canto is highly rhetorical, full of alliteration, elaboration, antithesis, all the tricks of the trade: 'The woeful daughter and forsaken heire?' 'Vnto another loue and to another land', 'sad mayd, or rather widow sad',

> Therefore since mine he is, or free or bond,
> Or false or trew, or liuing or else dead. . . (I. xii. 26, 27, 28)

The Red Cross Knight himself tends a little to rhetoric in his indignant defence: 'There did I find, or rather I was found' but Una's speech has the energetic plainness that usually characterizes her:

> Ye shall him Archimago find I ghesse,
> The falsest man aliue; who tries shall find no lesse.

Tasso, in the work already cited, gives a list of the figures of speech that he considers proper to a heroic poem, of which the style should hold a middle place between the tragical and the lyrical (note, however, that to an Italian, the word lyrical connotes a mood rather than a form). He names particularly amplification, hyperbole, prosopopeia, meiosis. But Spenser, who diverges from the Italian master on other points also, is not specially attentive to him on this. The description of the dragon might be an example of hyperbole, and the Salvage Man's unarmed slaughter of Arthur's enemies, but on the whole Spenser, with all his imagination, was too essentially sober-minded to take much pleasure in this device unless when some very special occasion called for it. In an allegory, prosopopeia and personification are part of the material. They cannot be distinguished as devices. The texture of Spenser's style is not made and put together as the Italian poet seems to envisage it. But alliteration is an essential to its structure as to that of pre-Conquest poetry. It is to be found everywhere, linking the adjective and the noun, or other connected words, and it affects not only initial letters of words but also those of accented syllables. Thus in the first verse of the last canto in Book One, though the obvious alliteration is on *h, s, w, v,* the *v* and *f* sounds are taken up right through the stanza:

> Behold I see the hauen nigh at hand,
> To which I meane my wearie course to bend;
> Vere the main shete, and beare vp with the land,
> The which afore is fairly to be kend,
> And seemeth safe from stormes that may offend;
> There this faire virgin wearie of her way
> Must landed be, now at her journeyes end:
> There eke my feeble barke a while may stay,
> Till merry wind and weather call her thence away.

This habitual art is better seen in quiet passage than in one where he might be thought to be making a special effort.

Almost as frequent as alliteration is the simile. These appear everywhere, and are usually taken from nature, the more elaborate ones being developed into little pictures like those in Homer: the following refers to the 'troublous rout' that assailed the Castle of Alma (ii. ix. 16):

> As when a swarm of gnats at eventide
> Out of the fennes of Allan do arise,
> Their murmuring small trompets sounden wide,
> Whiles in the air their clustring army flies;
> That as a cloud doth seeme to dim the skies;
> Ne man nor beast may rest or take repast,
> For their sharpe wounds and noyous injuries,
> Till the fierce Northern wind with blustring blast
> Doth blow them quite away, and in the Ocean cast.

Allegory itself has been called nothing but extended metaphor; but the metaphor itself Spenser uses much less often
than the simile. But sometimes his metaphors are very
striking, as when of Amavia he says:

> . . . That sad pourtraict
> Of death and dolour lay half dead, half quick. . .

But what he enjoys very much is a device which, misused,
produced the aureate diction Wordsworth disapproved of;
the substituting the names of classical deities for the natural
objects they ruled over. In such cases he amplifies in the
traditional way with parallelism, or possibly, kenning. The
use of alliteration with amplification is well seen in the
following three lines:

> Scarsely had Phoebus in the glooming East
> Yet harnessed his firie-footed teeme,
> Ne reard aboue the earth his flaming creast. . .

Or again, of sunset instead of dawn:

> Now gan the golden Phoebus for to steepe
> His fierie face in billowes of the west,
> And his faint steedes watred in Ocean deepe,
> Whiles from their iournall labours they did rest. . .

The continuous pictorial pattern which the use of such
means produces is in part the reason of Spenser's great
reputation as a descriptive poet.

Critics seem now rather divided about this reputation.
Some call him a master of descriptive poetry whose diction
suits itself to the occasion with unfailing propriety, enabling
him to set before us the loathsomeness of Error's children,
the hideousness of Gluttony, the loveliness of Shamefastness,
the grotesqueness of Malbecco, the sudden radiance of
Britomart's hair, all with equal vividness. Others, admitting
this, concede him hardly any other poetic quality; others
still, while praising the melody of his verse and the structure
of his poem, deny him any great measure of descriptive
ability, and some think he has none at all. A single book[1]

---

[1] *That Soveraigne Light*, ed. Muiller and Allen, a commemoration of Spenser's
quatro-centenary, Baltimore, 1952, *passim*.

may contain an essay by one professor showing with numerous illustrations, that Spenser's command and use of colour are to the last degree sensuous and even sensual, so that everything else is overwhelmed in it; and an essay by another professor showing, with numerous illustrations, that Spenser has in fact little or no sense of colour or visual imagery, the merit of his poetry depending entirely on his extraordinary command of sound and rhythm. Another tells us that the poet can describe very well when he chooses, but that he does not often choose, and only on state occasions, noting that most of his famous descriptions are of pageants, processions of sins, of rivers, of seasons, months, and so forth, as though the processional movement of his verse had transferred itself to the eye; but that Faerie land as such is never described. Though indeed that processional movement is essentially faerielike.

In Spenser's art of description suggestion plays as great a part as direct statement. There is a passage in Raleigh's book on Shakespeare where the great critic remarks that whereas writers vie with one another in admiring the pastoral beauty of the Forest of Arden, its Arcadian loveliness, its sunlight and green glades, the poet himself only says it had a palm and an olive tree, a lioness, and a green and gilded snake. Yet if some kindly wizard should transport us to the Forest of Arden as it then was, we should know it at a glance. What does he, the greatest wizard, tell us about the wood of Oberon and Titania in itself? The Duke's oak is in it; there is a hill somewhere near and a bank where wild flowers grow; cowslips may be found there; the ground is dank and dirty. Yet who does not know the wood near Athens better than Bushey Park? Similarly, no one has read even one book of the *Faerie Queene* without seeing far more of its plain and forest than the poet ever mentions. Besides the art of description, whether in full-length passages, or touches given in passing, there is an art of suggestion, which set scenery on the Elizabethan stage, which by subtle atmospheric touches, created the Forest of Arden for us, and a hundred other places now on our secret map. It is thus that the whispering branches of Fraelissa's and Fradubio's trees multiply themselves into Spenser's forest country.

It would be a curious study to examine the psychology of this. Perhaps that common ground of the unconscious, where are buried those images which are shared by all, contains also images, or visual memories, going far back, nearer the trunk of the racial tree, and the poet's art, by some magic of sound or rhythm, recovers from that dark backward and abysm the picture of an earlier world, our first heritage:

> Like that strange song I heard Apollo sing,
> When Illion like a mist rose into towers . . .

However, Spenser undoubtedly possesses the power to make a vivid waking picture when he chooses, whether by the accumulation of detail as in the famous set-pieces, or by an evocative selection: Britomart's blush at Merlin's recognition of her, Malbecco's crooked claws, or the happy isle of Venus where Scudamour finds Amoret and sees Cheerfulness with 'eyes like twinkling stars in evening clear', or Sanglier taking up the head unwillingly, 'as rated spaniell', or the broad black wings of Eventyde (Night is always an enemy), or the frightened Turpine rising from the ground like a troubled ghost; the lips of Enuy, 'like raw lether, pale and blew', the false Florimell vanishing like a rainbow, Diana gathering her robe about her when Venus unexpectedly appears, all these, and many more, are evidence of the poet's power to call up a picture in passing, leaving the roused imagination of the reader to complete the scene so vividly as hardly to be aware afterwards how little the poet had actually said. But Spenser uses this art as Shakespeare uses it, not for its own sake but for that of the action, that we may see vividly what is passing, and yet not be delayed or turned from the immediate purpose. His longer, more elaborate, descriptions are either required by the circumstances, as when he creates the environment of Despair, or they cover a pause in the action, as do the various processions, or, like Japanese carvings, they cover a weak spot with decoration.

Some of the most often-quoted passages of Miltonic description have their origin in that Spenser whom he so much admired, as in the case of Sin. Satan's moon-broad shield hung first on Radigund's shoulders:

And on her shoulder hung her shield bedeckt
Vpon the bosse with stones that shined wide,
As the faire Moone in her most full aspect,[1]

But the difference between Satan's shield and Radigund's is the difference between epic and romance.

In Spenser's longer descriptions, he has an aid which is almost entirely absent from the detached phrases which have been quoted to show his mastery of the art of suggesting a picture by one significant detail. The music of language can play relatively little part in short phrases detached from their context. But the imagination is touched almost as readily through the ear as through the eye, in some cases possibly more readily, and Spenser, like his own Calidore, commands an enchantment

. . . that through both the eyes
And both the eares did steale the hart away.

This at least, has never been disputed even by those who, while calling him a great poet, deny him all the qualities but this that a great poet should possess. Not even Keats, and not even Tennyson, still less Thomson, or another, has drawn the bow of Ulysses, or caught the authentic sound of the Spenserian stanza as Spenser himself used it; though both the Introduction to the *Lotos Eaters*, and the *Eve of St. Agnes* have something of its dreamlike lulling quality.

In devising a metre for the *Faerie Queene*, Spenser had the same problem before him as when he created a diction to be the language of faeries as of men; he needed a verse pattern that should be an enchantment in itself, placing us under the glamour and evoking by its rhythms that country, so much our own, which yet like King Fisherman's castle, recedes from us as we advance towards it; or like the fairy horse which Ossian rode, and King Herla, which would keep the rider from age or death unless he touched the ground. We must not ask such a horse to gallop like a battle charger, or leap about like a show-jumper; it is a pacing steed, yet even the omnipotent camera cannot catch its movement, and the land it moves through, though our own, is yet inviolate.

---

[1] But Homer too describes Achilles' shield like this.

Television will never see it, nor the radio catch the rhythm of its motion.

The slow complex movement of the Spenserian stanza with its eight ten-syllable lines, its interlaced and repeated rhymes, its long, rolling ninth line, is not suited to rapid motion or violent action. Byron achieved a *tour de force* in that respect in the Waterloo passage in *Childe Harold*, but only by sacrificing all the special charm and virtue of the stanza, which is no more meant for such a purpose than an organ is meant for dance music, even though you can play dance music on an organ. Doubtless, the author of *Mother Hubberd's Tale* could have composed in a straightforward quickly moving narrative style if he had wished; and if he had done so the persons of his poem might have been Elizabethans as realistic as the Fox and the Ape of that fable. This is as much as to say that if he did not want to write the *Faerie Queene*, he need not have written it. But if he did wish to write it, then he needed such a stanza as he invented, and he did not need such a one as would be requisite if a Scott were narrating the Battle of Flodden. For 'our warfare is not against flesh and blood but against principalities and powers and against spiritual wickedness in the high places'.

For this reason the narrative must be held at a little distance from our too literal eye and ear. The Red Cross Knight, for instance, is not knocked down by an outsize prize-fighter; he falls, by frailty, not malice, to a temptation to spiritual pride. Guyon, to take a less-obvious example, is not led by Mammon into the cellars of a bank to do a little expert safe-breaking; he is being tempted to lust after superfluous possessions for their own sake; and Calidore, when he gagged the Blatant Beast with an iron chain, was not applying a muzzling order, but using Christian charity to master evil-speaking, which in this world can be checked but cannot be destroyed. The *Faerie Queene* as a story is at two removes from material realism; it is an allegory, and it is a fairy story. Spenser's stanza, with its wave-like roll, is admirably designed to effect, and express, this removal, though even now there are readers who persist in confusing the events of the soul with those of the body.

The stanza has another advantage; it is sufficiently long

and varied to carry its own music independently of any statement it may make. Hence it supports the inevitable moments of flatness of a long narrative as no quick simple metre could do, without requiring any such inflated diction as Wordsworth was to condemn. The interlaced rhymes, which Spenser always loved, contribute much to this sustained flowing effect without abrupt transitions, and so does the length of the stanza; while the long closing lines makes a natural stopping-place when one is wanted, and varies the rhythm, which might otherwise become too even; it is the ninth wave rolling farthest up the beach.

It is this musical accompaniment which makes the reader pass so smoothly and flowingly along a narrative full of curves and convolutions, never allowed to forget that it is no common daylight that brood over that country, and that the trees may shed blood if their boughs are broken.

The onomatopoeic power of the stanza has always been recognized; as witness the frequent citation of the lines about the dwelling-place of Sleep, and those spoken by Despair. Yet these are not isolated passages. With the Despair passage one might compare, both for sound and picture, the lines describing the descent of Night's iron charet to Avernus:

> By that same way the direful dames doe drive
> Their mournful charet filed with rusty blood,
> And doune to Plutoes house are come bilive:
> Which passing through on every side them stood
> The trembling ghosts with sad amazed mood,
> Chattring their yron teeth and staring wide
> With stonie eyes; and all the hellish brood
> Of feends infernall flocked on euery side,
> To gaze on earthly wight that with the Night durst ride.

(I. v. 32)

Here is the same play on the sound of *d* to produce what the Elizabethans appropriately called 'doleful dumps', as in the Despair passage. But whereas that is static, and the poet therefore proceeds with other thudding consonants, in this the chariot is moving silently forward, and the *g*'s of the 'greedy grave' are exchanged for *f*, *p*, and *b*, lighter and smoother. To illustrate the combined effect of visual and auditory images depending largely on vowel sounds, few

examples could be better than that of the trembling ghosts:
'Chattring with yron teeth, and staring wide With stonie
eyes. . . .' But here is an example where there is no visual
imagery, and the thought and verbal melody are all. It is
one that Milton certainly remembered, just as the preceding
one suggests a famous Shakespearian passage:

> It is the mynd that maketh good or ill,
> That maketh wrecche or happie, rich or poore:
> For some that hath abundance at his will,
> Hath not enough, but wants in greatest store;
> And other, that hath little, askes no more
> But in that little is both rich and wise,
> For wisedom is most riches; fooles therefore
> They are: which fortunes doe by vowes devize,
> Sith each unto himself his life may fortunize   (VI. ix. 30)

Here it should be noted that this very difficult metre pattern
has not in any way impeded the clear expression of the poet's
thought, and that the musical flow of the lines, rising and
falling, is no less than before. But it is now serving another
purpose, that of carrying the concept smoothly forward to
its conclusion. One might fairly ask how much Milton's
famous verse paragraphs owe to the Spenserian stanza;
there is in both the same art of sustaining the thought on the
melody till both are complete.

The formula for the Spenserian stanza is easy enough to
put down; eight decasyllabic lines, the accent normally
falling on the second syllables, followed by one of twelve
syllables having a strongly marked caesura, most often near
the middle, and rhyming: *ababbcbcc*. The difficulty of re-
peating the rhyme as often as is done in the *c* group, is
specially marked in English, where the proportion of rhyming words is much lower than, for example, in Italian; while
the smooth forward surge and flow only Spenser himself
fully achieved in a long passage. Tasso had recommended
a stanza form, and it has been suggested that Spenser was
influenced by the *ottava rima* which both he and Ariosto
used. There is nothing inherently unreasonable in this
suggestion, seeing how intimately Spenser knew the *Orlando
Furioso*. But the resemblance is not really very close; the
ottava rima is simply two alternately rhyming quatrains

followed by a couplet; the two features which makes
Spenser's verse, the interlaced rhymes, and the final alexan-
drine, are absent, and the effect upon the ear is quite different. Moreover the interlaced rhymes are one of the special
marks of Spenser's prosody throughout; it is by them that
he varies upon Surrey's form of the sonnet. Not Ariosto but
Chaucer would seem the real source. Both his rhyme royal
and the stanza of the *Monk's Tale* have the interlacing and,
more than that, he always has the smooth melodious flow.
Spenser is the master both of his stanza and his style; he
does not alliterate only from habit, when no other purpose is
served, and just as the mature Shakespeare would not allow
unpoetic characters to speak in poetry, so Spenser refrains
from using poetic devices to make faked poetry of what is not
poetic in its own rightful character. Keats, if he had not been
too much a child of the second romantic generation, might
have learned from him, as he did learn other things, not to
use language as a pretty embroidered coverlet to hide what
it would be uncomfortable to look at. If we compare the
later poet's dodging of the ugly, repulsive, or frightening in,
for example, *Isabella*, with Spenser's straightforward description of Error and her spawn, or the interior of Orgoglio's
castle, or the realism of Winter in the procession of the seasons,
we see how remote the young romantic revivalist was from
the Elizabethan's vision of things as they are. Wordsworth,
who also knew his Spenser, was in this much nearer to him
than Keats, who had followed Coleridge into a path of
subjectivism which has led English poetry further and
further away from the great Elizabethans and the great pre-
Kantians.

Subjective writing has led to subjective reading, and this is
peculiarly unsuited to Spenser's poetry. This poet's prosody,
his diction and his thought, are so inextricably interdepen-
dent that they must be taken as one whole. The Jack Horners
of criticism, who only look 'for what they like' in a poem,
may indeed pull out a plum, but they lose the Christmas pie.
Thus those who read Spenser for his imagery, or his melody,
or his descriptions, or anything else which appeals to them,
are gaining for themselves a perfectly legitimate pleasure. But
they are not reading Spenser, nor will they understand him.

The essentially non-rational, subjective, method of reading and writing, increasingly prevalent as the twentieth century progresses, sets a deep gulf at the turn of the nineteenth century, a much deeper gulf than that which separates medieval literature from the Renaissance, a deeper one than that which divides the 'romantic' period from ours, as long as it, rejecting much else, retains this. In becoming primarily individualistic and emotional, and in conceding an exaggerated importance to details of technique, poetry has become limited and local, has set a 'thus far and no further' for itself which our classics never knew. Poetry, like painting, tends to be regarded as chiefly a mode of psychical release, and since the possibilities of emotional response are very limited, the scope which this allows to 'art' becomes progressively narrower. But in any case, those who compose from this motive, or who read from it, are following a therapeutic process not an aesthetic one. The extrusion of foreign matter from the organism, which process, when not physical, is dignified by the title of psychic release, is natural, is healthy, is only not praiseworthy because not voluntary; but it is not artistic save by accident. When a pailful of used water is flung away its drops may sparkle in the sun, but he who flung it cannot claim to be an artist because of that. On the other hand, he who seeks in the study of an art, only the pleasure of the ear or eye, however complex, is in need of our Divine Master's warning to those who 'look after a woman....'.

Spenser's poetic style, his incomparable melody, form the outward seeming of his whole conception, and if his readers will make it a garden of Acrasia to their own hurt, it is not the poet's fault, for he both set it in the garden of Adonis, and warned them of their peril.

II

ALLEGORY, SYMBOL, SIGN, AND TYPE

> Omnis mundi creatura
> Quasi liber et pictura
>   Nobis est in speculum,
> Nostrae vitae, nostrae sortis,
> Nostris status, nostrae mortis
>   Fidele signaculum.[1]

SPENSER's legacy from the Middle Ages included the ability to perceive visible things both as they were in themselves, and as they represented other things in the mind, thus existing on two planes of reality at once.

To the Middle Ages, as the verse quoted above suggests, all created things were both themselves and pictures of something else. Sometimes the correspondence between the two series of realities might seem forced and arbitrary, like that story in the *Gesta Romanorum*, used by Shakespeare, in which the identification of the virtuous and faithful princess with the soul of the sinner, seems distinctly far-fetched. At other times it was as natural, as almost inevitable, as that between human life and a journey, or a conflict, which has been the soul of nearly all allegorical narrative.

The long popularity of the *Roman de la Rose*, the general use of allegory in medieval poetry and drama, both bear witness to a habit of mind in which it was perfectly natural to consider any story enriched by being capable of an allegorical interpretation; and any series of moral truths increased in attraction by being given corporeal existence in a story. To us, the setting of Gower's *Confession Amantis* seems cumbersome; we should prefer to read his stories absolutely, so to speak, not relatively to the sins against love which the Lover is confessing to Genius. But this is because the focus of our attention is changed; we judge the story from our personal reaction to it, irrespective of any more

---

[1] R. F. F. Raby, *History of Christian Latin Poetry in the Middle Ages,* 1st. ed., p. 355. The quotation is from a hymn by Alan of Lille.

universal meaning it may bear, and we even resent the ascription of such meaning, partly lest the story might have been manipulated on that account, and for that reason correspond less exactly with our conception of life, and partly because we should regard the writer's attempt to impose it on us as an unwarrantable liberty. If there is to be a meaning it shall be ours.

The mental attitude associated with humanism, and prevalent after the Renaissance, assumed that what was interesting was the thing itself on its own factual plane, what it looked like, what it was made of, how it behaved, what use could be made of it. In the literary field this is demonstrated by the rise of the 'real life' drama, by the novel, and even by the importance given to visible natural phenomena; for though it is an age when artists have abjured the quest of beauty, it is still held meritorious to be an admirer and lover of 'nature', that is, of animals and scenery.

But this was not yet the attitude of Spenser's age, in which the older tradition still held good, and allegorical interpretations were given as a matter of course, even to such works as those of Ariosto and Tasso, as Spenser himself points out. To the people of that time, there was no difficulty in perceiving allegorical correspondences. We can still perceive metaphors with the same facility.

While the poet was a child in London Queen Elizabeth I went through the city on her coronation procession. In Little Conduit Street, Time, with his daughter Truth, presented the Queen with a Bible. (She had already seen Pure Religion treading down Superstition and Ignorance.) Here was an animated metaphor. By natural correspondence an old man may stand for Time, and a beautiful girl for Truth. A simile may be the first step—Time is like an old man. Then follows the metaphor, Time is an old man. Now set the image in motion, let the old man move along a road, leading a mule on which is loaded all the riches of the world, for all falls to him, and let him be waylaid by robbers, three young men, Strength, Lustyhood, Youth, and let them fall before one touch of his icy fingers, and be led captive behind his mule. There we have an allegory; it is as simple as that.

Such simple allegories would easily have been found in the England of Spenser's day; he would have met processions containing such groups as that, in his own part of London on some festal occasion. On his daily way to Merchant Taylors' School, which the learned and original Richard Mulcaster was then conducting in Suffolk Lane, near the river, and not far from the Tower, he would have seen shops carrying outside some sign or symbol denoting what was to be found within. In the bookshops, he would have seen those Emblem books, full of little allegorical pictures, which were having such a vogue at that time. If his careful parents allowed him to enter a theatre, or if he witnessed his school plays, he would have seen the strangest medley of allegorical, typical, and realistic personages jostling one another on the stage of that transition drama which filled the gap between the interludes and the University Wits. The old allegorical mood, moreover, continued to influence the drama even when its name and form were lost. Marlowe and Ben Jonson both conceived of human character in a mood so near that of the morality as almost to make them allegorists, at certain moments, even in spite of themselves. Their personages are often nearer to universal types than to individuals, and if Tamburlaine were called Everyman, Volpone, Avarice, Mosca, Flattery, some earlier ghost, wandering back into the theatre, might well remain almost unaware of the change that had taken place.

It would be pleasant to speculate whether the edition of *Piers Plowman* which had three impressions in 1550, and was reprinted in 1561, fell into Spenser's hands. The two poets have much in common. He who placed the Tower of Truth as the goal of his pilgrims' journey, who sent Lady Meed to London, who insistently repeats: 'When all treasures are tried Truth is the fairest', a line which might well have been printed on the title-page of the *Faerie Queene* so exactly is it in Spenser's spirit, would certainly have found the later poet congenial. The insistence of both poets on truth, to say nothing of lesser parallels, may really be more than coincidence. Such friends as Camden would be likely to know and mention the book, even if it had escaped Spenser himself. Yet it is doubtful logic to argue that resemblance must be caused by contact. If we find deep buried in the soil of one-quarter of the world, shards of pottery adorned with a red circle, it may be rash to assume colonization from another quarter of the world where also red-circled pottery is found. Colonization indeed is possible. But it may also be that a second man perceived independently how much his wife's pottery would be improved if he painted a red circle round it. Two great poets may have independently understood the essential role of truth in their picture of human life. Yet it is a pleasing and not an unreasonable fantasy, granted the popularity of the poem in the generation before him, which shows us Spenser puzzling out the difficult pages of *Piers Plowman*, and realizing with a growing excitement that Langland was a kindred spirit.

It is not surprising that Spenser should have conceived his greatest work as a 'continued allegory or dark conceit'. That was the traditional and well-approved way of expounding moral truth. But also the *Faerie Queene* had to be an allegory. There is no other way of making a story about immaterial things. Even a spiritual 'human document' like the *Confessions* of St. Augustine cannot escape the necessity altogether and, when writing in the third person, the law becomes stringent. Professor Lewis has pointed out that when medieval writers turned their glance within they began to write allegory.[1] For if spiritual realities are to be presented to the mind as acting, this can only be through the senses, and then figurative speech is inevitable. A divine voice demands of the prophet: 'Son of man, can these dry bones live?' A divine voice begins a story: 'A sower went forth to sow his seed.' An apostle speaks of a wild shoot being grafted into the parent tree. For Boethius Philosophy is a beautiful woman, for St. Francis so is Poverty. Plato is full of allegorical myths, black and white horses, chariots, processions; Guillaume de Lorris cannot write the *Roman de la Rose* otherwise, nor the dramatist, *Everyman*. In modern idiom, and for the modern mind, another imagery prevails, mulberry bushes become prickly pears, and Tarot cards enter; but T. S. Eliot is as allegorical as Spenser and much more difficult; so connatural to the human is allegory.

[1] C. S. Lewis, *The Allegory of Love*, O.U.P., 1936, p. 60.

Allegory is not a literary device which can be outgrown or superseded. As soon as a statement is to be made about immaterial realities, figure of speech must enter and is accepted as a matter of course. St. Paul speaks of being caught up to the third heaven; but no one imagines that he made an aerial journey, or counted the celestial gateways. He was telling a truth for which there are no words, by means of an image. This in itself is not allegory. But it is the stuff of which allegory is made. Allegory implies a narrative. But the agents and the adjuncts will include images, personifications, types, symbols, and by their means the mind, which can seldom apprehend anything which has not first been presented to the senses, will grasp the writer's conception far more strongly than if it were stated directly, but in abstract terms. Thus it becomes a correct, if a paradoxical, expression to say that sometimes in order to tell the truth distinctly, one must tell a lie, in the sense of affirming that to be so which is not so in fact.

In an allegorical narrative every detail will not necessarily have itself an allegorical significance. The drizzling rain that falls in the abode of Sleep in Book One of the *Faerie Queene*, need not stand for anything; it need only be appropriate 'background music'. But the unstable palace of Lucifera has an evident interpretation. It will always be a matter of some delicacy to decide what is scene-setting, what is imposed only by the narrative, and what is figurative in its own right, especially where inanimate objects are concerned. Some eyes will perceive significance hidden from others, perhaps not specifically intended even by the poet himself. But, whatever doubt there may be about details, the meaning of the allegory as a whole should be capable of coherent statement, and should underlie the whole composition even though less apparent in some places than in others.

Much of what I have said would apply to allegorical paintings, such as, in words, Mercilla's castle is, and which represent the branch of allegory that I should call 'static' because it does not admit of change or development. That this may be deeply significant to some minds one need only read Ruskin to acknowledge. There are background descriptions in written allegory which are of this character.

Narrative allegory itself presents special difficulty. The story must be interesting and well constructed, the personages reasonably convincing independently of their special significance, and yet never so much so as to overwhelm the allegorical meaning which, for the poet and those for whom he intended to compose, is the most important element in the whole. And while such poets are often blamed for the slow movement of the story, it is clear that, if it went at the pace of Scott, the reader would not have time to see it completely and penetrate its depths.

Yet while the two 'subjects' should both be capable of separate statement, they should both lose by the separation. The human soul without its body even though blessed, is still imperfect as human; the human body though retained in animal life and physical beauty, would without the soul, become a horror to us. In a less degree the allegorical poem is like that. Left with 'meaning' alone it is but a ghost of itself, reduced to the level of the scientific formula. Left with the literal story it may still have interest, but it is impoverished and crippled. *Hamlet* with a commonplace hero would still make a good murder story of its kind and would soon have been relegated to the dusty shelf which holds *Arden of Feversham*. The allegorical romance necessarily contains passages the function of which is to keep the two elements in accord. Sometimes these are incidents which are not allegorical at all; but which are required by the story. Or the allegory itself may impose its requirements on the narrative. Thus in Book One Duessa saves the life of the Red Cross Knight when he is struck down by Orgoglio, not that in her character of Falsehood she could desire his survival, but because Spenser, as story-teller, must explain why Orgoglio did not kill his enemy when he had the chance. Calidore, to take the opposite case, muzzles the Blatant Beast when the story required that he should kill it, because Slander—Evil speaking—that tongue which, St. James tells us, is a raging flame, cannot be killed while human malice lives, and that will be to the end of the world.

Besides such incidents there will be characters who are not in the strict sense allegorical, though they have a real place in allegory. Thus Pastorella should probably be

interpreted as representing Simplicity, as attractive to Calidore as Perdita to Florizel, and for the same reason. But
Pastorella's father is a type; that of the man who has known
the attractions of the world and has withdrawn from them un-
stained, the ideal of the virtuous peasant, the true Arcadian.
In the striking episode of Malbecco and Hellenore, we are
even present at the transition whereby Malbecco, type of
the jealous curmudgeonly husband, is transformed into
Jealousy itself, symbolized by an owl, a dweller in the dark
with a deadly grip.

Even among the chief personages of the books there are
these distinctions. Arthur represents 'Magnificence', we
have the poet's word for that. But this is only because the
word magnificence connoted for him, as it does not connote
for us, the sum-total of qualities which make up the ideal
man, the perfect type of Christian gentleman whom he had
set out to portray. Artegall, though not without his human
traits, is much more nearly Justice in the abstract. Hence the
iron man who has given so much offence to critics; themselves like-minded with the child who wept for 'the poor
lion that hadn't got no Christian'. For they blame Artegall
for his ruthless use of the brute force of the invulnerable
Talus. Yet have they never wished that in this world such as
they know it, Justice might have strength enough to impose
its order on men's chaotic wills? Artegall is doing precisely
this; and since he is Justice itself not one could fall by the
hand of Talus, who should not have fallen:

> For, in the course of justice, which of us
> Should see salvation?

Britomart, with the spear of perfect purity before which evil
cannot stand, or even lesser virtue, is the right mate for him:
'We do pray for mercy.' Yet, when we look forward to another world, is it not mainly because there justice will prevail?

But if we consider the literal story, ignoring the allegory
for a moment, we must recall that it is a fairy story, and that
therefore Spenser has a perfect right to give his heroes
magic weapons and the help of grotesque creatures of
strange gifts. Huon of Bordeaux encountered two iron men
who were guarding a castle, Perseus had a whole armoury of

enchanted weapons, Long, Broad, and Sharp-eye saved the princess from the sorcerer.

Qualities like those who are called Artegall, or Guyon, are relatively pure and unmixed. They are like the spirits in the prophet's vision who go forward as the impulse is, and turn not when they go. But others, Calidore, for example, move up and down along the scale which measures the degrees leading from allegory through type to individual, and pass all the shades between being Courtesy or Natural Virtue, and being courteous or honest men. They stand for the types of these virtues much as Abraham stands for faith, and Bayard for chivalry. Indeed all of the principal characters, even Guyon and Artegall, are individualized as persons, though not all the time. It is a procedure which facilitates the poet's method of using interwoven stories to bring out special aspects of the virtue in question. Satyrane, Tristram, the Salvage Man, all illustrate different aspects of natural virtue, just as different aspects of chastity are represented in the love-stories of Britomart herself, but also of Amoret, Timias, Florimel, and, later, of Calidore and Pastorella, fraternal charity appropriately mated with simplicity.

In an allegorical narrative the necessity of combining an abstract quality with a certain concrete individuality may also be met by introducing figures from mythology. Venus, Cupid, Mars, &c., are often so used. They have the advantage that they can sometimes act in their literal characters, and at others as the quality which marks the field of their mythological divinity without any need of transition or explanation. Some may be always, or almost always, only mythological as, in Spenser, his sea-nymphs, like the mother of Marinell, usually seem to be. Moreover, these personages can act in their own persons without risking the dream setting as fully human beings would do. In the special case of the *Faerie Queene*, too, they probably enabled the poet to convince Gabriel Harvey, and other such readers, that all the correct classical names were present—though sometimes they may have been used for beings who would hardly have been recognized on Olympus.

Narrative incidents too participate in all the shades possible to personages. Some are direct allegory, some may be mingled with mythology, some may be typical romance, others are good fairy-tale, others may be most of these things simultaneously.

There is also what may be called the allegorical innuendo; where the poet uses phraseology which must necessarily suggest an allusion which he does not directly intend, yet does not repudiate. Thus a strange perspective opens, as when mirrors reflect mirrors. For example, the successor of Spenser in narrative who most resembles him[1] speaks of 'ents', the giant shepherds of the trees, themselves treelike. The description cannot but carry with it a fugitive gleam, a breath of fragrance, borne on the air of that first moment when men were seen as trees walking; and the whole conception is deepened and enriched by this, however little direct relevance the reference may seem to possess. In this particular instance no allegory would seem to be intended; but the possibilities for allegory are evident.

Such allusive allegory is, in fact, seen in Spenser's description of the seven-headed dragon which Orgoglio gives Duessa to ride on. The poet obviously did not mean to import the Apocalyptic Beast himself, with all his implications, into Faerie land, especially with so minor a function. But he equally certainly meant to allude to him, to invest the monster servant of Pride and Falsehood with an atmosphere of terror and evil borrowed from the vision on Patmos, just as Duessa herself has the attributes of the Scarlet Woman. It is not the apocalyptic dragon himself but spawn of him, it is. Thus, too, the hill where Calidore sees the Graces is called Acidale, and the name casts an added gleam on that figure for whom alone Colin Clout is playing.

But we should in any case be mistaken if we supposed that allegory can be confined, so to speak, in rows of bottles, one labelled chastity, and all the chastity is there; one labelled friendship, and all the friendship is there, and so forth. Allegory can be written like that, the late Bishop Wilberforce did so in a work entitled, *Agathos, or the Rocky Island*, and Bunyan, whose personages are usually types, as his names reveal, is inclined to this practice, but not Spenser. His allegory is pervasive; the seal of Solomon has been

[1] J. R. R. Tolkien, *The Lord of the Rings*, Allen & Unwin.

broken and the djinnee, huge and cloudlike, has escaped from the brazen vase. In other words, though minor qualities may be represented by only one figure, appearing in only one incident, or one book, the main themes are illustrated again and again, in different aspects and relationships, through various persons and episodes, and in several, or sometim sin all the books. The adventures of the protagon-ists ot each book, though indeed illustrative each of its proper virtue, are also related to the underlying theme of the poem as a whole.

This underlying theme is first and most frequently seen as the conflict of truth and falsehood. In Book One it is illustrated in the concrete when Archimago, representing one form of falsehood, hypocrisy, masquerades as Holiness and Duessa as True Religion, and these are contrasted with the Red Cross Knight and Una. But the same contrast is repeated again and again in various forms. Archimago in his disguise as a hermit 'unholy of works' is set against the true hermit on the Mount of Contemplation, and also, more remotely, against the healer in Book Six. The sham mag-nificence of Lucifera, her court and castle, is set against the dignified, plain house of Celia with its hint of that heaven from which Lucifer fell. Orgoglio's claim to power and dignity is equally sham; his castle is a ruin dwelt in by Ignorance. Dragon, witch, and giant all together cannot protect it against one man, whereas the brazen tower of Mansoul, the house of Truth, is impregnable, unconquered if not conquering. The contrast reappears in other books; there is a true Florimell and a false one, Braggadochio, the false knight, the boaster, is contrasted with the true ones. Acrasia, mother of nothing, stands against Venus, mother of Amoret, and her garden against that of Adonis. Busyrane's power, too, is in deception; the false lovers of Book Four are contrasted with the true ones. It should be noted that the enemy of love and true friendship is not hate, though hate and discord both enter, but lesser or evil parodies of love, with insincere or interested friendship. Similarly Courtesy is contrasted not, primarily, with discourtesy, but with flattery and false politeness; exterior 'manners' only, where no good will is within. Even Justice and Chastity are not exempt from the general law that the real enemy, whatever be the appearance, is Falsehood. Artegall is trapped and deceived by Radigund and Clorinda; Britomart mistrusts Artegall, and when later hastening to rescue him, is at first deceived by Guile. So true is it that, for Spenser as for Langland, 'When all treasures are tried, Truth is the fairest.'

The identification of evil with falsehood, the devil 'is a liar and the father thereof, is the central theme of the whole allegory, and it is in harmony with this conception that the poet's frequently repeated contrasts of physical light and darkness, life and death, are so significant: 'For everyone that doth evil hateth the light, and cometh not to the light . . . but he that doth truth cometh to the light. . . .'[1] Light is a natural symbol of truth, and Spenser shows his realization of this even in such a detail as Arthur's veiled shield borrowed though it be. Like Shakespeare, who also associates the coming of night with moral evil, Spenser uses the chequer of light and darkness which is a feature of his descriptive art throughout the poem, to suggest to us, visibly, the unending struggle between good and evil, truth and falsehood, which is the dynamic element in his conception of the training of 'a gentleman or noble person'. It is a psychomachia far more deeply conceived than in the morality plays where perhaps he had first seen it.

In Book One Error dwells in thick gloom where she can neither see nor be seen, and it is the 'armour of a Christian man', not the veiled face of truth, which gives light for the contest. Yet light that face can give, as in the famous description of Una unveiling under the tree. The portrait of Arthur, the perfect man, whose virtue of Magnificence includes all the others, is touched in with the brightest colours, and seems radiant with sunshine. His shield is covered because of its dazzling brilliance, and it flashes like lightning when the stress of conflict reveals it. Evil beings live in darkness, either that which they carry with them, as Night in her iron chariot does, or that of caverns and pits under the earth, like the subterranean regions where Mammon treasures his heaps of unsunned gold, or the dens where the Brigantes imprison Pastorella, or the night in which

[1] John iii. 20.

Serena was to be sacrificed. The whole tribe of Duessa's kindred, who are her allies, are descendants of Night and of Aveugle, darkness and blindness, and Superstition's appropriate name is Blindheart, Corceca. But, to the Red Cross Knight's purified vision, the heavenly city shines in light inaccessible, and the brightest terrestrial thing is the crystal[1] tower of the good city Cleopolis, the earthly home of heavenly glory. Florimel, white and gold, passes like a beam of light through the forest gloom, and into the witch's cottage, and though Britomart strikes the traitor knights like 'levin', she has waited till daylight to do so.

Belphoebe too is a creature of brilliance and energy, 'excellently bright', imagined as Artemis the virgin huntress, but otherwise with little of the moon about her save the name. Indeed Spenser is no moon-lover, despite Wordsworth's famous comparison; for him she was rather Hecate, goddess of witchcraft, than the associate of heavenly powers. The moonlit night of the later romantics has no place in Spenser's faerie land save briefly in Book Seven; the nights there are dark and dangerous, even the bravest knights seek the shelter of the nearest castle and, if treacherously attacked in it, they still do not leave it until morning:

> . . . Light thickens and the crow
> Makes wing to the rooky wood:
> Good things of day begin to droop and drowse:
> While night's black agents to their prey do rouse.

This is Shakespeare's night; but Spenser's is no less dismal and dangerous. Even the Maske of Cupid takes place:

> . . . when as cheareless Night ycouered had
> Fair heauen with an universall cloud,
> That every wight dismayd with darkness sad (III. xii. 1)

And Night itself is thus addressed by Arthur:

> Night thou foule Mother of annoyance sad,
> Sister of heauie death and nourse of woe,
> Which was begot in heauen but for thy bad
> And brutish shape thrust down to hell below,
> Where by the grim floud of Gocytus slow

---

[1] Crystal is the almost invariable romance material for a specially magnificent palace, and it also appears in Celtic legend.

> Thy dwelling is, in Herebus black hous,
> (Black Herebus thy husband is the foe
> Of all the gods) where thou ungratious,
> Halfe of thy days doest lead in horrour hideous. (III. iv. 55)

Milton too describes a misshapen being, conceived in heaven, and thrust down to hell, the enemy of God, and he names her outright, Sin. After completing the description of Night, bringer and protector of evil, Arthur makes the contrast:

> For day discovers all dishonest wayes
> And shewth each thing, as it is indeed:
> The prayses of high God he faire displayes
> And His large bountie rightly doth areed.
> Dayes dearest children be the blessed seed
> Which darkness shall subdewe, and heauen win:
> Truth is his daughter; he her first did breed,
> Most sacred virgin without spot of sin.
> Our life is day, but death with darknesse doth begin. (Ibid.)

The reader will notice the thudding alliteration on *d* with which the poet has emphasized this last line.

Thus, in Spenser's hands, Nature herself takes part in the conflict which earth sustains on her bosom between those whom the poet calls 'the blessed seed', and embodies in such forms as those of Una and her knight, Guyon, Britomart, Artegall, Scudamour, Satyrane, and so forth, and those he enumerates in a verse following that quoted:

> Light-shonning theft, and traiterous intent,
> Abhorred bloudshed and vile felony
> Shameful deceipt, and daunger imminent;
> Foule horror, and eke hellish dreriment:
> All these I wote in thy protection bee,
> And light doe shonne for feare of being shent:
> For light ylike is lothed of them and thee,
> And all that lewdnesse loue, doe hate the light to see.

The Gospels have hardly been given their due place as inspirer of Spenser's thought and language, but the source of this is too obvious to require the parallel citation.

The primal division between light and darkness is then Spenser's chief symbol of the spiritual struggle he is narrating.

But it is not the only one. Evil and its allies not only live in darkness, they are themselves ugly, misshapen, and sick. Those who are good are beautiful, well-formed, essentially happy, whatever their immediate trouble, and the better they are, so much the more are they strong and vital. Deliberate association with the people of darkness is the only thing which weakens and injures them, and this weakening may come about even when the association arises from an honest mistake, as that of the Red Cross Knight with Duessa-Fidessa, or, in a less serious degree, that of Guyon with Phaedria. Still more is this the case when he plays with Mammon's temptations, even though never consenting to them. This is reasonable. The absence of intention lessens or removes the moral guilt, but it does not affect the natural consequences. He who drops a paper into the fire accidentally is not guilty of its wilful destruction. Nevertheless, it will burn. Those who, not originally bad themselves, yield to the bad association, may be destroyed by it, as are Fradubio and Fraelissa, Mortdant, Hellenore. If they then continue to live it is on a sub-human level. In this too the great poet saw clearly, Fradubio, through fear, remains with Duessa even when he knows what she is, and by so much is he less a man and nearer to the animal-like tree which he then becomes; Hellenore, without change of shape, declines interiorly to the level of the satyrs, whose life she has chosen and while still looking like a woman, has become no better than a beast, and therefore much worse than a real beast. Serena and Timias, wounded by the Blatant Beast, can be cured by no external means, however skilful; they must minister their own healing, by restoring the control of reason in which they had failed.

Spenser is skilful in turning his folklore to use to express these ideas. Duessa, in her own person, is a witch, 'a filthy foul old woman', hideously deformed, subject to the limitations of witches; Archimago is old and feeble when not disguised, easily overthrown by Sansloy, but still he has strange powers, especially the characteristic one of unpredictable movement, on the north, the witch's wind. Error is hideous too, an unnatural monster, Ignorance is 'an old, old, man', with 'creeping crooked pace', wrinkled, blind,

distorted: Alma's castle is attacked by 'a monstrous rabble-
ment of fowle misshapen wights, deformed creatures with
hideous shapes'—'But the fift troup most horrible of hue'—
'vile caytive wretches, ragged, rude, deformed'. Yet these
last, however terrible in appearance, were significantly
enough, only 'ydle shades': 'For though they bodies seeme,
yet substance from them fades.' Such are the immediate
enemies of the soul, and they are led, again significantly, by
Maleger, Disease itself. 'Few are improved by sickness',
says Thomas à Kempis from the depths of his experience,
and Spenser here shows it attacking the soul, not, primarily,
the body, by means of a whole host of fears and phantasms
who fight, and can fight, only by terrifying the imaginations
of those who are not captains of their souls. It is almost
startling to see that perhaps the only time when Arthur
comes near defeat is in his encounter with Maleger and his
attendant hags. Maleger, however, like his similars, illustrates the real ugliness and inferiority of evil. Malbecco,
through self-consuming, loses the form of man; Busyrane
the enchanter is strong only against the weak. Mammon and
Florimell's witch are hideous and very largely helpless unless
their enemies help them. Orgoglio himself was really only
a bladder.

That sin or moral weakness should be symbolized by
bodily wounds or illness is not extraordinary. But Spenser's
persistence in this is remarkable. The most obvious example
is that of the Red Cross Knight after his encounter with
Despair; but there are many others. Amoret's inordinate
yielding to the pleasurable element even in a pure and lawful
love, is represented by a wound in the breast, and Scudamour is burned by the flames round the castle which symbolize his uncontrolled passion, and which sink before
Britomart. The defects which give rise to scandal are shown
by the poisoned sores inflicted on Timias and Serena by the
Blatant Beast; Cymochles, yielding to his passion, is scorched
by a raging fever which water cannot refresh. For evil
things have a quality which illustrates both the sanity and
balance of Spenser's mind, and the traditional character of his
ethics: they are less living and less real than the good are. It
is not the Garden of Acrasia which is fecund, but the Garden

of Adonis, and the descriptions of the protagonists of virtue have a solidity and brilliance which the others lack, except when they are falsely disguised as good.

Professor Lewis has perceived that in Spenser's contrast of art and nature, art is considered inferior and corrupt.[1] This contrast might seem curious in such an artist as the poet; nor had puritanism in his day developed so far as to disapprove the fine arts unless when they could be shown to serve a practical end, as in portraiture. Shakespeare who had little sympathy with puritanism, expresses views very similar to Spenser's through the lips of the exquisite Perdita, a most Spenserian figure, who will not grow streaked gillivors:

> For I have heard it said
> There is an art which in their piedness shares
> With great creating nature.

And though she admits the validity of Polixenes' defence of the process, her instinct remains against it:

> I'll not put
> The dibble in the earth to set one slip of them;
> No more than, were I painted, I would wish
> This youth would say 'twere well, and only therefore
> Desire to breed by me . . .

The illustration brings out the force of the objections. To Perdita, as to Spenser in this connexion, there is falsity in art if its end is imitation, that it may replace the original. In the Garden of Acrasia the falsity goes much deeper than in the case of Perdita's flowers. For there, art is regarded as a substitute for nature; the painted golden ivy is used where the real plant could have grown and should have grown. Acrasia has tried to conceal the transience of the joys she offers, by adorning her pleasure ground with that which cannot die because it never lived, and in the same way, the pleasures themselves are false, and fail of their natural purpose. Archimago's miscreated sprights, and the false Florimell, are in the same category. If art, as in the cant phrase of the day, consists in imitating nature, then Spenser seems to say, it may become a sort of hypocrisy.

Hence it is clear that Spenser's symbolism is consistent

---

[1] Lewis, op. cit., p. 324.

throughout. Being, in his faerie world, is as hierarchical as that order of being which, in common with his predecessors and contemporaries, he held to be the system of the real world. But his hierarchy depends on degrees of being in this sense that, as we descend the scale, which is a scale of moral values, the creatures on each step become not only less good but, in virtue of that less good, less real, less substantial. Highest of all, of course, is that God, the source of being, to whom he always refers with so much reverence, '. . . highest God, the Lord of life and light'. Then come the angels, always carefully distinguished from the natural powers, such as Venus, or even 'Natura', and, associated with these, are such figures as Coelia and her household, Una, Gloriana herself. Close to these follow the other virtues with the knights their representatives, who differ from them chiefly in being still in the state of trial: then come their enemies and their helpers, always losing life, substance, beauty, happiness and being, until we reach the lowest and the last, false Florimell who vanishes like mist, and Maleger and his army:

> . . . which fled asunder and him fell before
> As withered leaves drop from their dried sticks.

Their leader is

> of such subtile substance and unsound
> That like a ghost he seemed whose grave-clothes were unbound.

Finally, lurking behind and beneath all, visibly represented perhaps by the figures of the deadly sins, is 'Great Gorgon, prince of darkness and dead night' of whom Archimago himself is only the catspaw.

There is, however, something else in Spenser's allegory which cannot be fitted so precisely into this table of oppositions, despite my recent mention of 'Natura'. This is nature and the earth itself. What part do these play in the story? Associated with these are three other rather enigmatic figures, Florimell, Marinell, and Satyrane.

The texts which allude to the opposition between Earth and Nature are neither as numerous nor as clear as those which oppose truth to falsehood, light to darkness, health and happiness to sickness and misery, and nature, in another sense, to art. Nevertheless, from a study of the allusions, it would seem to emerge that Spenser thinks of earth rather as, according to some mythologists, Irish Celtic myth thought of the sea, the home of the misshapen Fomorians, that is, as dark, chaotic, lawless. All the evil things have their home under the earth, 'low in a hollow cave', is a typical expression, and many are her children. Orgoglio is the child of Earth and Aeolus, Maleger too is born of Earth, Argante and Ollyphant are sprung from her by an unlawful union with Typhoeus; she brought forth the grape in order to fire men against the gods, the defenders of Geronio are 'children of earth', Grantorto too falls on 'his mother earth' and in the Mutability cantos the Titans are 'earth's cursed seed'.

As against this, nature, mentioned much less often except in these latter cantos, seems to stand for the generating power which imposes order on chaos, and makes things bring forth according to their kind. This power seems, in the description of the Temple of Venus, and also of the Garden of Adonis, to be equated with Venus Genetrix, the life-giving mother.

Beautiful persons and things are called 'the goodly workmanship of Nature'. Nature walled the temple of Venus, though art, in a good sense, is allowed a secondary place. Concord harmonizes everything in that order of nature and of being which was still so real a conception in Spenser's day, while the power of Venus vivifies the 'daedal earth'. Mount Acidale, the haunt of Venus, contains: 'All that ever was by nature's skill devised to work delight', and the Mutability fragment refers to:

> All that Nature had establisht first
> In good estate and in meete order range,

In the account of the Garden of Adonis we are shown that 'meete order' in operation drawing forth the material required from the subjected earth:

> For in the wide womb of the world there lyes,
> In hateful darkness and in deepe horrour
> A huge eternal chaos, which supplyes
> The substances of nature's fruitfull progenyes.

In the Mutability fragment Nature is shown as a person,

familiar to readers of Alanus,[1] a semi-deified being, associated perhaps with the demiurge of Plotinus that mediates the exercise of the divine power upon matter. She is a power above and behind Jove, Pluto, Cupid, and so forth, who are all part of the fairy world of myth, holding their due place, however, and yet she is still a creature, far below Almighty God and His angelic hierarchy.[2]

> This great Granmother of all creatures bred
> Great Nature, ever young yet full of eld,
> Still moouing, yet unmoued from her sted;
> Unseene of any, yet of all beheld.

She decides the appeal from Jove and Mutabilitie, and, having said her say:

> Then was that whole assembly quite dismist
> And Nature's self did vanish, whither no man wist.

The famous lines on the eternal Sabbath follow so closely on these as to suggest that over Spenser's own mind at that moment there had flashed another vision: 'Thou in the beginning, O Lord, didst found the earth: and the works of Thy hands are the heavens. They shall perish, but Thou shalt continue, and they shall all grow old as a garment: and as a vesture Thou shalt change them and they shall be changed: but Thou art the selfsame and Thy years shall not fail.'[3]

Among the minor characters of the *Faerie Queene* there is a group which seems to stand in a special relation to nature, understood in a more restricted sense. This group includes the satyrs, Tristram, the Salvage Man, Sir Satyrane, and also the mysterious pair Florimell and Marinell who alone have been permitted to complete their story within the limits of the allegory as we have it.

In Book One the satyrs, who protect Una and gladly accept her instruction, in the context in which they appear, seem to represent in the allegory the innocent superstition of folk-belief, legend, and myth, which is erroneous certainly,

[1] Alan of Lille, *De Planctu Naturae*, text in T. Wright, *Anglo-Latin Satirical Poets* ii. 458, Rolls Series, London, 1872.
[2] But cf. *F.Q.* VII, vii. 9.
[3] Heb. i. 10.

but not in itself evil or opposed to truth; but rather like the legends which have gathered round the childhood of Our Lord as narrated in the apocryphal Gospels, or those village fancies which Puck alludes to, or Bishop Corbett in *Farewell Rewards and Fairies*. The less innocent element, the nymphs, fled away as soon as Una appeared. These satyrs are harmless; Una is never in danger from them. Yet later, Hellenore, abandoned by Paridell, finds the appropriate refuge of her unbridled desires amongst the satyrs with whom she too takes shelter very differently. The 'salvage nation', who capture Serena seem, like Hellenore, to be human beings who have sunk to a beast-like level. Children of earth, they are idolators and eaters of human flesh.

It is not too fanciful to see in these conceptions no inconsistency, but the representation of wild nature under three aspects. First comes earth-nature playful and innocent, as it seems on a spring day, and as Wordsworth describes it at the beginning of the 'immortality ode', when

> the young lambs bound
> As to the tabor's sound,

which yet, though innocent, is not virtuous, since the apparent goodness is impulsive only. Then we see these same earth beings fierce and in a literal sense brutish, the animal which satisfies natural and proper appetites by the nearest way, bestial, if you will, but still innocent, because unreasoning. Hellenore, and the 'salvage nation' are, thirdly, representatives of the degradations of human beings who are living, by their own will, at the animal level. Of these Hellenore is clearly the worst. It may be too, that monsters like the one which pursues Florimell, show this earth-nature when its action seems purely destructive, 'red in tooth and claw' like Blake's Tiger. The context of the Book on Courtesy would suggest that the 'salvage nation' are almost on the lowest step of a scale which illustrates all the diversities of conduct between a man and his neighbour, from Calidore, all inward goodness and outward grace, at one extreme, through Blandamour, Blandina, Paridell, and others, outward manners with no virtue within, on through Briana and Crudor, where the selfish rudeness is barefaced, and ending

in the Brigantes and the salvage nation, superstitious, utterly
selfish, eaters of others, as many are today who would not
call themselves cannibals. These are below the satyrs, for
they are undoubtedly human in the sense of lacking the good
qualities of animals and possessing only the bad ones of men,
but they have no homes except dark underground dens
which they have no means of lighting, and they are not able
even to herd cattle. This description, incidentally, together
with that of the salvage man who was a food-gatherer, and
had no articulate speech though he could use gestures, make
one wonder what Spenser knew, or had guessed, about man
in the ages we have learned to call prehistoric, though we try
to write their history.[1] Shakespeare too, perhaps drawing on
Spenser, has given us a picture of a savage who had not
originally any power of speech, a step below even Spenser's
Brigantes, for Caliban is evil:

> You taught me language, and my profit on't
> Is I know how to curse—

Spenser, then, shows us two processes, one of degeneration
from a false civilization only such in appearance to savages
far below the level of Una's lion, and another, passing by
Meliboe and the other shepherd friends of Calidore, through
Tristram to the Salvage Man with his soft inarticulate
murmur, spontaneous kindness and loyalty, and his wild
strength when aroused, and ending with the satyrs, innocent
because irrational.

Satyrane, Florimel, and Marinell are in a different category. To discuss them fully now would lead to repetition
when the stories in which they bear a part come to be treated.
But it is clear that they too illustrate the theme that the
creatures from Nature's ordering hand are seen by Spenser
as good and fair, in contrast with the children of 'Great
Earth, great Chaos child', who are corrupt, misshapen, dis-
ordered, dying.

This brief study of Spenser's symbolism indicates that,
beneath his expressed intention of illustrating allegorically

---

[1] There were already books in which ancient Britons and Red Indians were
somewhat fancifully described and depicted: cf. T. D. Kendrick, *British Antiquity*,
Methuen, 1950.

the training of a noble person in virtuous discipline, there lay a more universal conception, which came naturally enough to one who was still familiar with the idea of man as the microcosm, and who perhaps realized that, as Professor Bowra tells us, all the literary epics are didactic after Dryden's pattern: 'The design of it is to form the mind to heroic virtue.' The absolute conflict between heaven and hell, good and evil, is fought out relatively in every human soul, is fought out then, all through Spenser's poem, and marked by the symbolic opposites referred to. But, being a Christian, he cannot be a dualist, and therefore that conflict is not:

> Between the pass and fell incensed points
> Of mighty opposites . . .

who may be considered equal, but between enemies related as light to darkness, truth to falsehood, health to sickness, beauty and joy to deformity and misery, living nature to its dead imitation, order to disorder, the *is* to the *is-not*. There is a deep gulf fixed between Spenser and his great follower Milton, a gulf caused by the breach with traditional spirituality which had by then been made. Spenser stands with Dante, and the medieval artists, painters, or carvers, in regarding sin, and the Arch-Sinner, as ugly, degraded things, abhorrent to man when seen as they are. But when beauty was no longer regarded as an attribute of the Most High and the Most Fair, but had become one of the pomps and vanities of this world, it could also become, because merely earthly, diabolic, and Milton can lavish his genius in making a magnificent figure of sombre tragedy out of that demon whom Dante, and the sculptor of the Lincoln imp, had seen as hideous, and the tellers of folk-tales, with a true insight, as stupid as well. If we compare such passages as Milton's famous description of Satan which begins:

> He above the rest
> In form and stature proudly eminent . . .

with the Spenserian pictures of the procession of the Seven Deadly Sins, or the unveiling of Duessa, or the person of Malengin, we may well doubt which is the better poet; but we cannot doubt which was the deeper thinker, the better theologian, or the nearer to the universal common sense of humanity.

Spenser's Faerie land is itself a symbol, standing, by means of the special connotation which the word faereye still had, for this transitory world with its chances and changes, subject to the mutability of which the poet had so strong a sense, and contrasted with the eternal heavens of which the Red Cross Knight is vouchsafed a glimpse.[1] These heavens we are not allowed to forget since the poet, by his frequent allusions not only to God, but to the angels who are even actors in his narrative, constantly reminds us of the reality which lies unchanged, unchanging, behind the pageant of contingent being. It is this contrast which gives its significance to the lines, so often quoted, which form the last verse of the Mutability fragment:

> Then gin I think on that whicl. Nature sayd,
> Of that same time when no more Change shall be,
> But stedfast rest of all things firmely stayd
> Upon the pillours of Eternity,
> That is contrayr to Mutability:
>   For, all that moueth doth in Change delight:
> But thence-forth all shall rest eternally
> With Him that is the God of Sabbaoth hight:
> O that great Sabbaoth God, graunt me that Sabaoths sight.

Spenser would have found his imagery confirmed by that of Plato with his vision of the immutable Ideas eternal in the heavens.

The poet's indifference to details of time (sometimes the time of one part of a story seems to be inconsistent with that of another part, as in the account of Marinell's fall) is to be partly explained by his feeling that that does not really matter; it is all part of the general illusion. Spenser could only work at his poem at intervals, these intervals may sometimes have been long, and there is little that is more vexatious than looking back over old work to make sure that there is no disagreement with the new that is glowing before the mind. It would be no wonder if Spenser procrastinated and

[1] Doubtless, as the realm of Gloriana, it is in a certain sense a 'land of fame'. But I think I. E. Rathbone in *The Meaning of Spenser's Fairyland* exaggerates this into a non-Christian and therefore non-Spenserian conception.

in the end, knowing the strange ebbings and flowings of fairy-tale time, and that all this is, as I have said, illusion, left it altogether.

It would be exaggerated to try to find a special significance in every picturesque detail scattered through the poem. Some are needed by the literal story, others are part of the poet's art in harmonizing the outward scene with the inward event, as when he describes the abode of Sleep or the surroundings of Despair. Others are allegory properly so-called, like Phaedria's Idle lake, or the languorous fountain of 'white melancholy', accidie, nervous depression after a strain might be the present day diagnosis, which takes the strength from the Red Cross Knight; or the crumbling foundations of Lucifera's palace. Others are more exactly symbolic, for example, the chalice with wine, water, and a snake which is carried by Faith in the House of Coelia. The snake is found again twined round the feet of Venus Genetrix in her Temple. Spenser seems to observe the heraldic distinction between the wormlike dragon which stands for evil, and the shorter, taller one which stands for strength and vigilance, therefore he has no need of the snake as a symbol of wrong. He is thus free to remember that the snake is also used as a symbol of eternity and that, even more to his purpose, it may stand for wisdom, the wisdom which, in fact, the Christian is recommended to possess. The symbol of snake and cup is found in modern Christian imagery, where it is associated with the Sacrament of the Holy Eucharist. In Fidelia's hands it will have had a more general sense, the wisdom which believes what faith reveals beyond the power of reason. In some cases Spenser adapts the common properties of folk-lore to his purpose, the magic weapons, the gift which reveals chastity, the wise animal, the healing well or plant. Some of these will perhaps be more relevantly discussed when the virtue with which they are associated comes to be treated in detail.

The names in the *Faerie Queene* fall into several categories. These are first, straightforward abstract labels denoting one aspect of one quality, like 'Despair', 'Error', Womanhood', 'Concord', 'Awe', 'Reverence', and so forth. These have no more personality than their one quality can give them, and they are only seen in relations which illustrate it. Sometimes, as at the Court of Mercilla or the Temple of Venus, their presence is chiefly decorative, like the pictures on the wall of Love's garden in the *Roman de la Rose*. Next come names which can, owing to their disguised form, be accepted as personal ones even though they really indicate a quality. Acrasia, Cymochles, Medina, Adicia, Corceca, Atin. These characters are more developed as persons and may play more than a momentary part, but they do not carry with them a hint of any further significance greater than themselves. Then comes the class of those who are more fully realized as persons, who bear names which are appropriate, but not labels; but who are types also, persons that is, who do carry with them a greater significance, like the figures in Vergil, or even in the Bible; Aeneas who is not only himself, but the dedicated Roman; Abraham, the faithful man, or Job the patient one. Such as these are Scudamour, Amoret, Satyrane, Florimel, and these shades into the class to which most of the principal persons belong, who have real names, sufficiently in keeping, but who add a significance to them which they did not originally possess: Arthur, Britomart, Calidore, Tristram, Blandina, even Una, Guyon, possibly Gloriana. Some of these names may have had the additional merit of suggesting associations which would enrich them, like Arthur, or like Britomart, classical in itself yet, in its form hinting at Bradamante; or Tristram, a name full of romantic colouring from Malory. Besides these there are two associated groups, the personifications like Night, Sleep, Nature, the Earth, the mythological figures, definite, as in Venus, Cupid, Proteus, Neptune, indefinite as in the witch, the satyrs, the Brigante chief, nymphs, who carry about with them, from their very names, a sort of romantic aura which gives them a certain luminosity even when their function is something entirely secondary and subordinate.

Then there are two characters, at opposite ends of the scale, who are conspicuous by being treated in detail, and yet having no real names of their own. These are the Red Cross Knight and the Salvage Man. The old hermit on the Mount of Contemplation who, inspired by heaven, reveals the early history of the Red Cross Knight and predicts his future, tells him that the peasant who found him as a baby lying in a

furrow in Faerye land, named him Georgos, which is, after
all, a purely functional designation, but that he was to be
called St. George. But, in fact, the Red Cross Knight never
is called by either name in the poem, the first has been outmoded from the time he ceased to be either peasant or
natural man, which is before he appears in the poem, and the
second he will not obtain until the seven years of his earthly
quest have been completed. In the meantime it is the red
cross which distinguishes him, the crusader badge, put
forward on all occasions to impress on us that this sign of
our redemption is the seal on the whole poem, and that all
interpretations are false which do not take this consistently
into account. The Red Cross Knight has no name such as
the encounters and exchanges of earthly life would have
thrust upon him, because, in these encounters and exchanges
he has no part. It is essential to his character as representing
Holiness, that, though he bears a part in this world, he has
no place there. To have overcome evil here on earth is not an
end for him even though he must do it. To be united here
with Religious Truth is not an end. He is to the others as
Galahad to the knights of the Round Table, and, as with
Galahad, the Round Table, the justice and equity attainable
in this world, are not enough; his fulfilment lies beyond, in
the heavenly city. There he will receive the new name,
having won the victory and received 'The white stone, on
which stone a new name is written, known only to him who
receives it.' The virtues of the other knights can reach
perfection in this life, the Red Cross Knight can attain it only
in the other; together with the

> Soldier saints who, row on row,
> Burn upward each to his point of bliss;
> The end of life being manifest,
> They have burned their way through the world to this.

The others are heroes, but the Red Cross Knight is a saint.

The Salvage Man is in the opposite condition. The Red
Cross Knight has transcended his natural name, and has not
yet received his supernatural one. The Salvage Man, solitary
and without language, has not yet attained even a natural
name. Spenser's conception is an interesting one, an imagina-

tion of what natural man, if he were alone, might have been like before any sort of civilization had been developed. The Salvage Man does not cultivate the soil, nor does he hunt, though 'swift as any bucke in chace'; he has not even built a shelter for himself; he carries no weapons, though when he is roused he fights 'like to a tygre that hath mist his pray' and is so terrible in aspect that the evil knight Turpine, is terrified even to shrieking, 'a thing uncomely in a knight'. He is deeply moved by compassion, generous and hospitable, having, however, only fruit to give his guests:

> For their bad stuard neither plough'd nor sowed,
> Ne fed on flesh, ne ever of wyld beast
> Did taste the bloud, obaying nature's first behest.

But he knows the healing herbs, and can dress wounds though he is himself invulnerable. Moreover, when Serena has lost Calepine, not Calidore himself could have attended and protected her more loyally than the Salvage Man does. When this duty is fulfilled, and he meets Arthur, with a true instinct he attaches himself to that which is highest, and obeys his least sign. This wild figure, in conceiving whom Spenser had nothing to learn from Rousseau, has a link with Artegall when the latter disguised himself in moss and forest ✓ leaves, and enters Sir Satyrane's tournament on his side as the 'Salvage Knight'. His motto, *salvagesse sans finesse*, is in the context best translated as 'Nature, not art'. Here is again the contrast between the real and the sham which underlies the opposition of nature and art in Spenser. Turpine and Blandina knew all the forms of civilized life, but they are false and savage within; whereas the poet's strange vision of primitive man inarticulate and untaught, is loyal, compassionate, generous, a lover of goodness. This arrow drawn at a venture, has struck near the mark, for the earliest human settlements seem to have been without walls, as he without weapons; but when what we call civilization began, so also did war. The Salvage Man, too, roots up an oak to defend his sleeping friend and master from the treachery of civilized enemies.

There is much affinity between Artegall and Calidore. Justice gives everyone his due, Courtesy treats everyone as he ought to be treated: the Salvage Man, with the courtesy that springs from real goodness, not from acquired 'manners', stands also for a sort of natural justice, a spontaneous righteousness, as though the first image of Eden were still living in his heart.

After two persons without names comes one name without a person, Gloriana who, often spoken of is, in these six books, never seen. The poet says that by her 'I mean glory in my general intention' (and of course Elizabeth on the factual plane). Critics on the whole have assumed that fundamentally Spenser is thinking of glory in the same terms as Milton in *Lycidas*:

> Fame is no plant that grows on mortal soil,
> Nor in the glistering foil
> Set off to the world, nor in broad rumour lies:
> But lives and spreads aloft by those pure eyes
> And perfect witness of all-judging Jove. . .

True glory, as against the false, worldly, 'fame' represented by Pride and Ambition, Lucifera and Philotima, is what only God, who knows all, can justly give, and that only the Christian, who seeks God as his end, can justly seek. But in I. E. Rathborne's *Meaning of Spenser's Fairyland*, a work characterized, among other things, by all the incredible industry which marks American scholarship, argues ably in favour of the view that Gloriana stands only for such deserved earthly fame as virtue may honourably attain. Of such fame Gloriana is the goddess. But that cult of fame marks the pagan aspect of humanism rather than the Christian, for which Spenser stands, and the Red Cross Knight could certainly not have a prior duty to serve such a Gloriana rather than dwell at once with heavenly Truth seeking in prayer the celestial city. A reconciliation is possible. All the action takes place on three planes, that of the spiritual allegory in which Gloriana 'of heavenly seed' is heaven's glory and Cleopolis the kingdom of God upon earth, St. Augustine's *civitas Dei*. Historically, the service of the Virgin Queen is a type of that higher service, and her capital city of the Jerusalem above. But as far as the poem is a fairy-tale, that is, in its literal meaning, the fairy queen may well be the dispenser of the chivalric honour that Hotspur sought and Henry V coveted, the honour of the romances. Gloriande appears in various romances as a powerful fairy's name, for example, both in *Huon of Bordeaux* and in its sequel (and Arthur, like Huon, receives a fairy kingdom from Oberon) so that it may have suggested a suitable name for the fairy mistress whose quest was the visible aspect of the dark conceit of the poet.

Though Spenser's use of his various categories of names seems to be specially connected with the degree to which the personage is to be developed, and the frequency with which he will appear, another distinction may be traced. Furor, Occasion, Dolon, and so forth, owe their being to moments of crisis. They are furious ghosts who vanish with the situation which produced them, and their character might be missed if they were not clearly labelled. More solid than these, seen, one might say, in relief, are those, good and bad, who are more enduring, who represent fixed habits and permanent dispositions. Pyrochles and Cymochles, the passionate brethren, are such as these. Anyone may be seized by Furor once in his life and, when the storm has passed, there need be little permanent trace of its passage. But Pyrochles is the habit of yielding to anger, as Cymochles is the habit of yielding to bodily passion. This is shown by their behaviour. So too, the three brethren in Book One: they also represent permanent mental states, not passing crises; that is why they are dangerous. Between these two groups there flickers another, phantoms which we all carry imprisoned, thrust far back in the imagination where it merges with the unconscious, so that like the iceberg five-sixths of these grisly images are invisible. Despair, Maleger, Malengin, perhaps also the misshapen monsters, like the ones which pursue Florimell, these are Spenser's bogeys, the 'things that go bump in the night', or 'the business that flyeth in the noontide', visual images of fear, and dangerous only because frightening. For if some of Spenser's mythical beings are the familiars of Olympus, others come from dark corners behind thatched cottages, from fairy rings, and from haunted buildings.

Such a classification as has here been attempted, must not,

of course, be pressed too far. It would easily become merely fanciful, and seem to attribute to the poet a hard-edged systematization which is far from being his method. The distinctions do not depend on the predecided headings of a catalogue but on the shifting focus of attention. Our consciousness is a stage, and our attention works the lime-lights. The spot-light focuses now on one figure, now on another. Those on whom it falls become suddenly bright and three-dimensional, while those from whom it passes, lose colour and substance, and slip into the mist which veils every-thing which we are not immediately thinking of, though we have not, and cannot, entirely forget it. Spenser was obviously a man of sane and balanced intellect; this is evident from his writings and from the whole course of his life. His mental processes then, were not abnormal even if his powers were extraordinary; there is no insane fixation, no hysterical wavering, his images move forward or retire as occasion and his purpose suggest. Some, of course, are always central if they are on the stage at all, some are always near the edge of the light, some never quite pass the edge, remaining always as figures darkening the penumbra. These groupings correspond more or less with the poet's use of proper names, but it will have been an artistic intuition rather than philosophic or psychological considerations that guided him.

The Tudor age, true to its love of colour and display, was delighted to make use of the possibilities of heraldic orna-ment. Indeed this was carried so far that the crest, for example, became far too heavy to be of any use for its original purpose, the distinguishing of the knight in the field. Arthur's crest was distinctively royal, English, and Tudor, apart from any other significance of the dragon. Spenser could safely assume that his readers would under-stand the bearings he is sometimes careful to give, for it was still a necessary part of a gentleman's education. He knew this from his own experience. The Spencers of Althorp, with whom the poet claimed cousinship, had sprung from that rising merchant class which, having made money, attained social security and recognition by rooting itself in the land and obtaining coat-armour. These Spencers, in due time, applied to the proper authority to recognize their kinship with the ancient Despencer family, and thence permit the use of its coat-armour; this claim was allowed. Probably the College of Arms was not inclined to make too many difficulties; the new-old Spencers were prosperous, cultivated, and generally accepted. As they, for their part, acknowledged the poet's relationship, he, like Scott, could please his imagination with the glamour of an old line, 'a house of ancient fame', to use his own expression. Interested in history too, as he was, he clearly meant more than a piece of 'period' colouring, when he was so careful to give the arms and mottoes of some of his persons. However, he uses his heraldry like a poet, not like a pursuivant, he only mentions the arms when they serve a purpose, and when it is convenient, he uses the knight's name as a motto, and prints on his shield 'Sansloy', or 'Sansfoy', as the case may be. Most of his coats of arms are simple and their meaning would have been evident at a glance.

One of the most interesting cases is that of Arthur. Of his crest I have said sufficient, but there is still something to be observed about his bright, blank shield. There are reasons for its blankness. In each book Arthur manifests a different side of his character, namely the stable perfection of the virtue therein treated. There could hardly be a better symbol for this than the stainless shield itself, light to the good, and destruction to the evil. And, from the point of view of the historical allegory, which certainly exists from time to time, though always of secondary importance, there would have been a practical difficulty. Arthur, destined to wed Gloriana-Elizabeth, and thus, in a certain way, standing for England itself, but not yet king or husband, could hardly assume any real arms. However the poet has another way of making up for this. Arthur, when he is first described, is a brilliant figure. Among his jewels appears his special personal badge, attached to his baldric. It is a 'precious stone Of wondrous worth and eke of wondrous might, Shapt like a ladies head', the symbol of that glory which he sought. This crest is enough to mark him while he is still going about as it were incognito, a figure mysterious if bright. Britomart bears 'a lion passant on a golden shield', and a silver lion passant was really the arms of South Wales, the kingdom of Ryence, her father. Britomart's lion could not be silver if the field were gold but, disguised as she was, she could hardly bear her national arms without any difference. Satyrane's usual shield, a satyr's head, is a canting one, punning on his name, but at the tournament for the Golden Girdle he changes this for a 'maiden-headed shield' in honour of Florimell. Other knights, Scudamour, Paridell, Pyrochles, bear arms which are a clue to their character. Scudamour, for example, carries a winged Cupid. The wings are significant. Cupid in Spenser usually stands for lawless love, 'cleaving but to dust', but Scudamour stands for the love of a faithful husband who has been weak only where no man, without heavenly aid, can be strong. Braggadocio's blazing sun is also well suited to his ostentation; it also, by some subtlety, seems to make him more absurd.

The Red Cross Knight's arms are the most significant of all, the cross of St. George, the cross of England, the cross of the crusades, the cross of Christ. He bears it in 'dear remembrance'; it marks him out among all the knights because his role is not primarily ethical but spiritual and religious.

Closely associated with the subject of heraldry is that of the orders of chivalry. Gloriana's knights belong to her Order of Maydenhead, this is natural enough. Spenser already had Malory and the Arthurian legend in mind and would require an equivalent for the Round Table. Indeed, in the 'prose Merlin' the Queen has her own order, pledged to help all who are in need. But in choosing the name it would seem that, apart from the compliment to Queen Elizabeth which he very likely intended, he was thinking more of works like the *Roman de la Rose* than of the *Mort d'Arthur* or the *Merlin*, of works which maintained the convention that the husband and the lover could never be the same. The older romances, and the same thing was implied in the fashionable Petrarchan love of Spenser's own day, assumed a sort of chivalric order of Cupid in which all lovers were bound together in the service of the god of love, which service they refused at their peril. There is a hint of this in Spenser's story of Mirabell and her penance. In this convention the whole structure of *Frauendienst*, of the lady and the *cavaliere serviente*, was based on the assumption that chivalric or 'courteous' love, must always be outside marriage. Spenser's Order of Maydenhead would seem a deliberate ✓ contradiction of this idea and all that lies behind it. He makes the dedication Virginity because it is the Order of Gloriana, still a virgin-Queen; but his ideal is not virginity alone—Belphoebe is treated as a lovely exception—but chastity 'according to one's state', as the phrase goes. Thus there is but one Knight of Chastity, who purposes marriage in due time, but there are three books in honour of chaste love, in marriage and out. The poet did not give the name *Amoretti* to his love sonnets without adverting to the name of Amoret, the type of the chaste and faithful wife. Though it is true, as Professor Lewis points out, that Spenser's thought on love goes far beyond the distinction of lawful and lawless, it does nevertheless insist on that distinction, and to that which is lawless the poet would even deny the name of love. But not even the Knight of Temperance refrains from love altogether. Indeed the nature of his love proclaims at once that Spenser's conception of temperance is something very different from the modern notion of a dry and bloodless virtue. Sir Guyon loves the Faerie Queene herself, bears her image on his shield, and thus speaks of her whom, like a real troubadour, he loves without hope:

> She is the floure of grace and chastitie,
> Throughout the world renowned farre and neare,
> My lief, my liege, my Souerane, my deare,
> Whose glory shineth as the morning starre,
> And with her light the earth enlumines cleare;
> Far reach her mercies and her prayses farre,
> As well in state of peace as puissance in warre. (II. ix. 4)

How did Spenser reconcile his classic mythology with his Christian figures, whether knight or angel? It must first be observed that, though there are beautiful allusions to God and His loving providence in the poem, He is nowhere made directly an actor in it. Angels do appear and do act, but they are never shown together with pagan deities. In the first, the most doctrinal of the books, the mythological figures are reduced. Hecate becomes Night, Morpheus becomes Sleep,

Hades becomes Hell, and the Classical god Aesculapius becomes the damned soul of a skilful physician. But in other books this procedure will not serve, for the poet needs Venus, Cupid, Neptune, Proteus, to say nothing of the river deities, in their own proper persons, and he evidently feels no serious incongruity since, just after the beautiful apostrophe to the guardian angels, he compares that of Guyon to Phoebus and to Cupid.[1]

The difficulty, in so far as it is a difficulty, which the Milton of *Lycidas* does not seem to have admitted, was not new. It would be extremely interesting to know certainly whether Spenser had read the *Lusiad* of Camoens. The dates of composition would easily allow it, the *Lusiad* having been published in 1572, and since the union of the crowns of Portugal and Spain under Philip II, the trade relations of the two countries with England were sufficiently close to make it reasonable to suppose that the Portuguese epic could have been known through Spanish contacts; it would not have been the first time that Spain had influenced the literature of England. Fanshawe's translation is, of course, some time after Spenser; but if the poet could read Tasso, as apparently he did, in Italian, it would not be impossible for him to make out the *Lusiad* in the Spanish translation of 1580. Probabilities are not proofs but, whether it were by coincidence or by influence, Spenser and Camoens found the same solution of a problem both had in common, that of introducing pagan deities, as the epic idea required, into a Christian poem. Both for the Portuguese and the English poets the great gods of the classical pantheon become personifications, or even rulers, of certain departments of nature, the sea, the planets, generation, but they are not, in the strict sense, gods, they are more in the position of Uriel, Lord of the Sun, Milton's adaptation of the same theme. Yet this does not answer the whole question for Spenser, who brings into his poem a multitude of lesser supernatural beings who cannot all be explained in this manner. I believe the answer is to be found in the fact that Spenser's universe did allow an organic place for beings who are not angels and who are not men. They are far below the angels in the hierarchy, but

---

[1] He is here diverging from Tasso who objected on other grounds, op. cit.

they are not intruders, and there is no antinomy in their presence as there would seem to be in Milton's world, where the same person is at once a saint in heaven and the genius of the shore, a Puritan clergyman and drowned in a sea whereon 'sleek Panope and all her sisters played'. An indication of Spenser's scheme is to be found in the Mutability cantos (VII. vii. 4). Besides, in *Huon of Bordeaux* Christianity is the religion of Fairyland.

The critic must, as always, restrain himself from projecting his twentieth-century mentality back to the first Elizabethan age. The whole conception of faerie was a living one in Spenser's time. There was a place for it in this hierarchy of being; nor need there be anything strange in the idea that the world might contain other than human and animal inhabitants. The belief in such beings persisted far later, and indeed has even now rather changed its shape than disappeared.

That Spenser, to some extent at least, equated the lesser deities of classical and other, mythology with the fairies, is clear from the famous episode in the sixth book in which Calidore surprised the Graces dancing in a ring round Colin Clout's bride to the music of Colin Clout's playing. When he shows himself, they disappear in the best fairy tradition, and not even Colin Clout can recall them:

> Much wondered Calydore at this straunge sight,
> Whose like before his eye had neauer seene,
> And standing long astonished in spright,
> And rapt with pleasaunce, wist not what to weene;
> Whether it were the trains of beauties Queene,
> Or Nymphs or faeries or enchaunted show,
> With which his eyes mote have deluded beene.
> Therefore resoluing what it was to knowe
> Out of the woods he rose, and toward them did go.

The reader will have noticed the reference to druid illusion in this verse.

> But soone as he appered to their vew
> They vanisht all away out of his sight
> And cleane were gone, which way he neuer knew—

So appear, and so vanish, such faerie trains as Tamlin rode

in, or such revels as belated peasants surprised by an open hillside. Of such a beauty as these graces was that queen who came riding down by the Eildon-tree, and bore off Thomas the Rhymer. Spenser can still use the charm by which a medieval writer had transformed Pluto into a black-haired fairy king, and Hades into Fairyland. And he wielded that charm precisely because, like his predecessor and contemporaries, he recognized in the Latin and Greek supernaturals with which school and university had made him acquainted, the same beings as he had met under other names, in popular legends and stories whether native or of that world of Celtic myth of which he seems to have known something. French, English, Welsh, Irish, or Greek, they were all part of the same world and, as a good neo-Platonist he could account for them satisfactorily. (Shakespeare makes the same equation in *A Midsummer Night's Dream*.) Archimago and Duessa come and go shifting their shapes like druids, and the former frightens Braggadochio by vanishing on the north wind. Spenser knew that the north was the quarter of witchcraft, and that the north side of the churchyard was the more haunted and perilous.

The Mutability cantos give the clearest picture of the Spenserian system. Mutability, a Titaness, child of Earth, claims from Jove the throne of Olympus which carries with it the sovereignty of the lower world. It then appears that, like the Saturn of Keats, himself a good Spenserian, Jove is not the first of powers. He is supreme over the world of matter. Under him are the other gods, even Pluto, demigods, nymphs, graces, fairies, men, and satyrs. Only Neptune exercises a certain independence as he rules the sea-nymphs, and also the lesser sea-gods, such as Proteus. Yet Jove is not the ultimate power even over matter. Above him is Nature, to whom the Titaness appeals, who seems a creative spirit, able to act on matter, and to appear visibly, but is not material. It was she who imposed order upon chaos. She has a function, then, like that of the Demiurge in the hierarchy of Plotinus. Such an apotheosis of nature had already appeared in literature, though neither Spenser nor his predecessors would have conceded it the position which this personification holds today. All Spenser needed was to take over the earlier poets' 'Natura' who was greater than the gods. But neither is she supreme. At most, she is no more than a Platonic demiurge. Indeed, she is hardly even this, for above her are the angels Spenser loved so much, more beautiful than the Idalian Cupid, those whom the privileged may sometimes hear:

> Singing before th'eternall Majesty
> In their trinal triplicities on hye.

These are never put into immediate contact with the half-material beings, lords in the lower world, whom Jove rules over; they appear only as ministers of Divine justice and mercy while above them, how far above, is only 'heavenly God', 'Him that is the God of Sabbaoth hight', the God of the Christians. Thus comes about the synthesis in which Spenser, really the celestial thief that Raleigh called him, carries off all the pagan pantheons, and all the beings of popular imagination, and arranges each in his rank as servant of the Most High:

> In sight of whom both Sun and Moone are darke,
> Compared to his least resplendent spark.

It is now easy to abstract from their quality as heathen idols even when, like Venus and Isis, they have temples, and treat them as dignitaries rather than as divinities. They then become personifications of a special kind. Venus, for example, represents the lawful and ordered love found in marriage and issuing in parenthood, and also, in a wider sense, the force of generation and reproduction in the world, the organizer of life. Cupid, almost always, stands for the unlawful and disorderly? (inordinate would be the technical term), passion which aims at pleasure for its own sake. It is not for nothing that the pageant of Cupid is shown in the house of Busyrane, protected by raging flames, yet flimsy as a house of cards. And though this contrast did not originate with Spenser, it forms another of those opposite pairs in which, as we have seen, he delights, and which make so integral a part of the structure of his poem.

It is not necessary to seek an allegorical meaning for every mythological being who appears. For, after all, the poem is also a fairy-tale, and though Marinell, for example, most likely has a meaning which must be sought in its due place, Cymoent, his mother, need be no more than the mermaid or nixie who makes a human marriage in so many legends and ballads. There are many trees in Spenser's forest, and only two of them are called Fradubio and Fraelissa.

Single actions, particular situations, may be symbols as much as people or objects. We all remember the prophet Agabus who bound his own feet and hands with St. Paul's girdle to symbolize the saint's approaching imprisonment. There is one situation in the *Faerie Queene* which recurs so often that it cannot be without significance, and, to save repetition, it may be dealt with here. All the poet's knightly heroes achieve their quests, but none of them is allowed to enjoy the fruits of his victory. The same is true of other prominent personages. The Red Cross Knight is indeed married to Una, but he leaves her immediately to complete his term of service in the Order of Maydenhead; while his vision has already suggested that he will never know peace upon earth. Britomart finds Artegall and gains his love; but he too must complete his quest, and though he does so the poet does not narrate their reunion. Calidore wins Pastorella, but he also leaves her, and they do not meet again in the poem as we have it. Guyon destroys the Bower of Bliss, but he is still a wandering knight; and though Cambell and Triamond with their brides could not illustrate the virtue of friendship without remaining together, they are still errant, we meet them on journeys and fighting in tournaments, never in a settled home. Of the others whose stories are made much of, Calepine rescues Serena in the dark, and neither has recognized the other when the poet leaves them, while, most striking of all, Spenser, who had restored Amoret to Scudamour in his first version, divides them in his second, so that they too are left unfulfilled. Of the leading characters of the poem, only Florimell and Marinell are made happy at the natural end of their story. This must be more than coincidence, and more than the taking a trick from Ariosto.

No doubt the poet may have meant to bring all his personages together at the great climax when Arthur achieved his quest for Gloriana; but when we consider how careful he is about everything which affects the structure of his poem,

we are forced to realize that he must have had a grave reason
for adopting a plan which would oblige him to leave so
many stories with their climax suspended. At this point we
may remind ourselves of two things. This is the land of
fayerye, of illusion, the insubstantial pageant of Prospero's
vision. Nothing in it can be lasting; those who fight the good
fight, even if victorious, cannot enjoy their reward here.
Cleopolis itself is transcended by the shining towers of St.
George's vision, and there is no permanence in this world
even for the good. It is a place of struggle, and attainment
lies beyond. Certainly Spenser himself had found it so. If
Florimell and Marinell have another lot, it is because they
belong to another dispensation, as I shall hope to show. But
this faerie land is not only the outer world, itself destined to
perish, which is the scene of the human adventure; it also
stands for the inner world which man, the microcosm, carries
about in his own soul, and within which the exterior actions
have their only permanent effect. In this inner world too,
there can be no standing still, until the tree falls as it will lie.
Virtues are not things that one possesses as one possesses a
sword; they are habits which must be maintained so. Dolon
and Malengin, Orgoglio, Duessa, or the Blatant Beast, they
cannot be defeated once and for ever. Spenser narrates it
only once, but a thousand times has Guyon uprooted the
Bower of Bliss, and will a thousand more. Justice will still
be tempted by bribes, Courtesy must still put a bridle on
evil speaking, the flames round Busyrane's castle will be
burning again when Britomart passes there next, 'but those
who persevere to the end, they shall be saved'.

III

HOLINESS AND TRUTH

THE tracing of Spenser's narrative from book to book with the idea of interpreting the allegory step by step, would be attended by several inconveniences though, in the first book, fewer than in any other. The six books are not self-contained like, for example, the various divisions of the *Idylls of the King*. Themes run from one book to another; that of chaste love, for example, is introduced in Book Two, developed in detail in Books Three and Four, reappears in Book Five, and is a leading motive of Book Six. The various personages, too, disappear and reappear; no one really ends his story in the book which belongs to him. The attempt, therefore, to interpret each book separately would necessarily mean that either significant episodes must be omitted, or repetition must be inevitable. But, besides this, such a plan would do less than justice to Spenser. He did not write six poems tenuously connected by Arthur's presence in each; he wrote one complex narrative, in which several themes are interwoven, attention being concentrated now on one, now on the other. The more one reads the *Faerie Queene* the more one realizes that Spenser could quite well have completed his full plan of twelve books, and even of twelve more, if only he had had the time. As Chesterton says of Dickens, an immense pageant of story passed by him unendingly, and he wrote down as much as he could while it was going on. He was taken from it, and never saw the end. The sense of this continuous flow is lost when we make too much of the divisions between book and book, and the unavoidable similarities become unnaturally evident. This is less true of Book One than of the others. Its principal characters appear but little in the subsequent narrative, Una not at all, and it differs from the others in that its theme is not really an ethical one. Holiness is not a virtue, but a state; Truth is not a virtue either, though truthfulness and sincerity are, for these are habits of the will, disposing always to act in a certain way, whereas truth is objective, and holiness is a complex state.

A holy man possesses virtues; but a virtuous man will not be holy unless the love of God's will is his motive. He is not holy, for example, whose ruling motive is the fear of hell; he is only a man who, under God's mercy, will save his soul. The fear of God's justice is the beginning of wisdom, but the love of God begins holiness. So teach the Fathers. Truth also is not a virtue, and in its most general sense, it has no direct connexion with morals as such; though it remains a fact that immorality in its widest sense, if persisted in, affects the power of apprehending truth. Truth is related rather to being in itself than to modes of behaviour. Spenser, however, is clearly not thinking of truth in its most abstract and philosophic sense, but in reference to religious doctrine, more especially as this may be embodied in a divine revelation, or enounced by a Church. This is clear from the historical allegory where the main theme, which underlies the whole, is the conflict between England, the Protestant power, and Spain, the Catholic one, and from the fact itself that Una appears as the guide of Holiness. There is, however, an apparent inconsistency in the character of Una which requires comment.

Una in the story is the daughter

> of ancient Kings and Queens that had of yore
> Their sceptres stretcht from East to Western shore

and, more particularly, of a 'godly King and Queen' who seem to stand for Adam and Eve as typifying the human race 'captived' to sin (the symbolism of the dragon is obvious). Their kingdom is Eden (1. xii. 26), the human world as it ought to be if sin were absent. But Coelia, the heavenly one, whose children are the supernatural virtues Faith, Hope, Charity, thus addresses her, 'Most vertuous virgin borne of heauenly berth', and regards her visit as a singular favour. Her white attire, and the brightness of her veiled beauty, are other signs that the daughter of Adam and Eve was also the daughter of heaven. Her name too is significant. She is the One, as opposed to Duessa the Double, double-minded we still say, who is Falsehood, and more particularly deceit, that being the form her falsity generally assumes. Una's own special personal enemy, however, is not Duessa but Sansloy, Lawlessness. When she is wandering alone in search of the Red Cross Knight, she encounters 'blind Devotion' and her daughter, and is safe with them, however uncomfortable; but their friend Kirkrapine is a danger to be met only by brute force, the lion. She is also deceived by Hypocrisy imitating Holiness, and protected by Satyrane who, as in other contexts, seems to stand for natural virtue. Moreover, the dwarf attendant of Una seems to represent natural reason. The Red Cross Knight takes him for guide when he believes Una false, and though he does not recognize Duessa, who, after all, is Deceit itself, he perceives the dangers of Lucifera's Castle (the folly of worldly pride was recognized even by pagan philosophers); he warns his master, helps him to escape thence, and himself escapes later, from Orgoglio. He then brings Una and prince Arthur to the rescue, after which his task seems to be done for we hear no more of him. Yet, in spite of this effective action, when Truth and Holiness are together, the dwarf lags behind; he is Una's servant but he cannot keep pace with her. All this suggests that Una is indeed, as Coelia calls her, of heavenly birth; that she is, in fact, revealed religious truth. This interpretation is confirmed by her being always veiled when with others until she is finally restored to her own home. Natural reason is surpassed by revealed truth, that is why it is veiled. And there is a further reason. When Moses received the revelation of the Law, we are told in the Biblical narrative, his countenance became so radiant from his intercourse with God that when he at length descended the mountain side, his followers could not bear the brightness, and he was obliged to veil himself. It is not too far fetched to suppose that Spenser remembered this when he described the radiance of that 'angel's face' which usually she 'did hide under a veil that wimpled was full low'.

But if this be granted, how can Una also be the daughter of an earthly king and queen even if they typify the human race itself? The reason is that she does not stand for divine truth in the abstract, but for divine truth as revealed to men, and left as a sacred charge among men. It is thus that she

stands also for the true Christian Church, the repository of
the divine revelation to man, which would have been co-
extensive with Adam's descendants had he never sinned, as
Eden would have been equated with the inhabited world.
That Spenser in his own mind identified this true Church
with that 'of England' at that moment of history is certain,
but his allusion to the original kingdom would suggest that
he also, in the moral allegory, intended the ideal true Church
in itself. In this connexion the name Spenser has chosen for
her has a special significance. He might differ from his
contemporary, the Dominican Pope St. Pius V, in his idea
of what God has revealed; but he did not differ in supposing
that that revelation could be only one self-consistent whole,
and that any other belief was heresy, foul, horrible, engen-
dering in controversy further errors even more hideous and
unnatural than the first. But he had too much poetic judgement to allow him to yield to the temptation to enter upon
doctrinal discussion or definition himself. Like Langland,
whose picture of Holy Church may well have influenced
Spenser's conception of Una, it is enough to show us a
vision, which a greater than he had seen already: 'And I, John,
saw the holy city the new Jerusalem coming down out of
heaven from God prepared as a bride adorned for her husband' (Apoc. xxi. 2). Una is the one, a living indivisible ✓
organism.

We must give Spenser credit for a certain consistency in
his treatment of his creations. The Red Cross Knight goes
through mental and moral changes; but Una does not, for
divine revealed truth cannot change. Far from Spenser, as
from everyone else in his time, was the idea that a proposition
could be true and not true, true then, but not true now, true
for *A* but not true for *B*. Spenser's logic still contained
a statement, called a primary law of thought, declaring that
something cannot both be and not be at the same time, and
that truth consists in the correspondence between the outward expression and that which really is, between Una as
visible Church and Una as divine revelation. Hence Una
can be seen more or less clearly, others may be mistaken
about her, or opposed to her; but none of this affects her in
the sense of being able to produce any change in her. Una is,

so to say, static, for another reason. Political, historical, scientific truth can, as related to humanity, be added to as far as humanity is concerned; Una, revealed truth, cannot. She is the 'truth once delivered to the saints' which can be progressively better understood, but not added to nor diminished. Hence Una moves through the poem producing effects, acting upon others, but not herself acted upon in any real sense, not, that is, having her own character modified. But here we should remark upon two episodes, one affecting her as she is Divine Revelation itself, the other as she is Church, the guardian of the deposit of faith. As Truth she is deceived by Archimago, as Church she is attacked by Sansloy. Duessa she never meets until Duessa is discovered, for truth and falsehood cannot co-exist. But Archimago represents false conduct, and it is not impossible that Truth should fall into bad hands, and be used for ill purposes. The first deception results in separating Truth and Holiness, as though faith without works were not vain, as St. James says; the second delivers her to lawlessness.

The attack of Sansloy against the person of Una is not really directed primarily against purity; it is not Cymochles but Lawless who is the aggressor. It is essentially an attack on truth in itself, a refusal to be bound by a law of belief, and, secondly, it is an attack on the Christian Church, a refusal to be bound by a religious discipline. Recent history supplied Spenser and his readers with enough examples to illustrate this point factually, but common experience, to say nothing of the disquisitions of psychologists, furnishes abundant examples of attacks on intellectual truth deriving from impatience of the moral restraints which belief in such truths would impose. As Maritain says (*Redeeming the Time*, p. 6), 'The burning inclination towards great sins constantly excites within us the inclination towards great errors.' The poet was not ignorant of what is now called 'wishful thinking', which may consist either in believing what one wishes to believe, or in disbelieving what it is inconvenient should be true. Unreasoning force, symbolized by the lion, which had been effective against the vulgar thief, Kirkrapine, is no protection from the traitor within. Una, in the story, is rescued by the satyrs who treat her gently and learn from her gladly.

Perhaps the innocent pagan satyrs represent that natural mythology, basically strangely similar all over the world, which
suggests that it is not in human power to choose and renounce
belief entirely at will, still less not to believe anything at all;
that, at the last resort, faith is always something given.
Spenser may, in accordance with what seems clearly a habit
of his thought, have intended to contrast the mad violence of
the sophisticated Sansloy, doing his best to corrupt revealed
Truth, and bend it to his own purposes, with that innocent,
because involuntary, paganism whose superstitions, however
fantastic, arise from inculpable ignorance, and who is ready
to accept the truth once it is known. That Spenser, who
knew not only something of classical mythology, but also
something, perhaps more, of the popular folk-lore of two
countries, had perceived that they corresponded to a universal human need to believe certain things, is very possible; and
when he shows Una teaching the satyrs, he may well have
meant to illustrate the pagan acceptance of that truth which
the apostate had rejected: 'Whom ignorantly ye worship,
him declare I unto you.'

Una's role, however, is mainly static in the sense that the
touchstone which magnetizes is static, for, as I have said, it
is not she who changes in character, but others who change
or are changed, in relation to her. She takes her part, of
course, in the action of the story. How is Fidelia related to
her, Fidelia, who, in the House of Coelia, instructs the Red
Cross Knight in heavenly truths? The distinction is clear
cut. Truth is not a virtue; but Faith is. Spenser clearly knew,
and by placing the three sisters in the House of Coelia
maintained, the distinction between the natural and the supernatural or theological virtues, those which are related directly
to God, as their end, and those which are related to man.
Fidelia represents the supernatural virtue whereby 'we believe
without doubting whatever God has revealed'. Fidelia holds
the chalice of the divine ordinances and the book:

> that was both sign and seald with blood
> Wherein dark things were writ hard to be understood

From that book 'That none could read except she did
them teach', she instructs the Red Cross Knight: 'Of God,

of peace, of justice, of free-will' and after this doctrinal
initiation, a knowledge according to faith, he undergoes an
ascetic training which follows the normal spiritual tradition:
repentance, penance, humility, patience, good works. These
lead on to further graces, so that, at last, he is admitted to
contemplative prayer, after which, as one would expect 'all
seems little and base which passes away with time'. Thus far
there is nothing which the author of the *Ancren Riwle*, or of
the *Cloud of Unknowing*, would not have known and approved.
Roffy and Algrind, indeed, were little likely to have led
Spenser far in the direction of reforming excesses, either
Lutheran or Calvinist.[1] Una herself is the truth, one, indivisible, but Fidelia is the virtue by which she is apprehended.
It is Una who brought the Red Cross Knight there, for
truth engenders faith, not faith, truth. Una's role at the
beginning, in the contest with Error, is similar; she remains
apparently passive, her hidden radiance does not shine out
to light up the darkness of Error's cave; it is the reflection
from the 'armour of a Christian man' which reveals the
monster, in accordance with the saying, 'He that liveth the
life shall know of the doctrine whether it be of God.'

This encounter, placed as the first incident in the story, is
a proof of the importance which Spenser attached, as did all
thinkers of his time, to right belief. As Una is not any truth,
historical, scientific, or other, but is revealed religious truth;
so Error is not any mistake; but is error in religious belief,
heresy. Spenser is laying down the prevalent principle of
many centuries when he insists that the soul seeking sanctity
must begin right by going, as Langland had already said, to
the Tower of Truth, and by adjuring and destroying error.
The intervention of Truth here, at the end of the conflict is
clear and emphatic: 'Strangle her, else she sure will strangle
thee.' Truth herself is indestructible. It is Sanctity that
Error may destroy.

To Spenser, as to any pious Elizabethan, the later poet's
dictum: 'He can't be wrong whose life is in the right',
would have seemed not only pernicious but absurd. The
whole career of the Red Cross Knight when separated from

---

[1] Respectively, the Bishop of Rochester, and Grindal, Archbishop of Canterbury, neither extremist, both mentioned thus in the *Shepherds Calender*.

Truth, makes clear that, though an honest mistake is not sinful, it does not lead to virtue, but to bitter temptation, and even to serious loss. Spenser's readers do not always recognize how practical his psychology is. The Red Cross Knight's position as to Una is clear enough. 'Truth is the touchstone.' She may seem static in the sense indicated, but only in her company can Holiness make any progress, or even stay as he was.

Book One, in which the Red Cross Knight is the protagonist, is in certain respects a contrast with the others, though not to the same degree with all.

In all the books except the first, the enemies met by the knights have an evident connexion both with the quest they are pursuing, and the virtue they represent. Such, for example, are the knights who fall in Guyon's way, and Mammon whose 'unsunned heaps' are intended to awaken the lust of possession 'for when this enters all other evils easily follow'. Such too is the giant of communism, or Radigund, tyranny, or Munera, all of whom Artegall encounters, or the enemies of Britomart. But the foes of the Red Cross Knight appear at first to be not a necessary part of his quest, but wanton crossings of it. For the machinations of Archimago and Duessa, their steady persistent enmity, are not inspired, apparently, by any exterior connexion with the dragon whom it is the knight's task to kill; nor do they ever appear as his allies. Cymochles is Acrasia's paramour, Paridell the enemy of all virgins; but what inspires Archimago and Duessa? It seems sheer hatred, sheer malignity, which urges them on. It is, of course, true that in the structure of the poem Archimago is the universal villain, just as Arthur is the universal hero; but it remains true that above all, he is the enemy of the Red Cross Knight.

It has escaped no critic that Book One is a general picture of the Christian combat; and that Spenser therein portrays the perfecting of the Christian soul as such, not the testing of individual natural virtues as in the other cases. In other words, this book narrates the making of a saint. Its hero is Holiness, and he will finally be proclaimed: 'St. George of merry England the sign of victory' ... Spenser must certainly have been thinking of Constantine's legendary vision before the battle *In hoc signo vinces*. By insisting as he does on the cross, Spenser has shown that, whatever he may owe incidentally to Aristotle, or Plato, or Seneca, his virtues are to be interpreted as Christian virtues, looking to a consummation very different from the this-world fruition of the *Nichomachean Ethics*. Indeed, the plan of twenty-four books which he outlines as developing his whole idea, might well seem to have been suggested by an ambition to show how Aristotle's antinomies could, in fact, be resolved.

The adventures of the Red Cross Knight have a double function, inasmuch as holiness may be regarded both in relation to the individual soul, and also as the salt of the earth, the leaven which will transform the lump. In the economy of the Church the saint, properly so-called, would seem to be he who is called to be holy not only for himself, but for others, 'Thou being converted, strengthen thy brethren.' The public mission of Holiness, to which Truth has called him, is the liberation of Christendom by the destruction of sin. This is a real freeing of the holy places; hence the story is rightly orientated as a crusade.

That kingdom of Una's parents, which once stretched from east to western shore, is surely the true undivided Christendom, and the dragon which ravages it is Sin, deliberate moral corruption in an inclusive sense, 'Evil, be thou my good', not the particular vices which it is the part of the other knights to correct. This is the real dragon of which Duessa's monster was the type. Against this corruption, holiness is the only remedy, and this Religious Truth, Una, has sought for: 'If ye know this, blessed are ye when ye do it.'

The poet conceives this Holiness in the traditional manner, as heroic faith, hope, and charity, centred in the crucified Christ. But it will also be seen that he exercises all the other virtues which the other knights singly represent. He is clad in the Pauline armour, the girdle of truth, the breastplate of righteousness, the feet shod with the preparation of the gospel of peace, the shield of faith, the helmet of salvation, the sword of the Spirit which is the Word of God. And on that breastplate and shield is scored the 'bloudie cross'; on his breast for love: 'the deare remembrance of his dying

Lord'; on his shield for hope: 'For soueraine hope which in his helpe he had.' The shield itself is the shield of faith, while he himself 'right faithful true he was in deede and word'. He thus exemplifies the supernatural virtues which are directly related to God as their end.

This distinctively religious and spirtual character is also specially illustrated in Canto X where, in the house of Dame Coelia, the Red Cross Knight is exercised in the active practice of these virtues, initiated into the ways of prayer and penance,[1] and thus led to the mountain top whence he sees the vision of the heavenly city, and is warned, after all great deeds done, to:

> Seeke this path, that I to thee presage,
> Which after all to heauen shall thee send:
> Then peaceably thy painful pilgrimage
> To yonder same Hierusalem do bend,
> Where is for thee ordained a blessed end. . .

Had Spenser ringing in his ears the lines we meet so often at the period:

> Hierusalem my happy home
> When shall I come to thee,
> When shall my sorrows have an end,
> Thy joys when shall I see?

Of the other virtues singled out by Spenser, The Red Cross Knight displays chastity, which is a sub-virtue to temperance, in his interview with the pseudo-Una, justice on the same occasion, temperance in the house of Lucifera, courtesy also there, but more especially in his dealings with the pseudo-Una and Fidessa-Duessa; friendship in his relations with Prince Arthur, and with Guyon in the second book. Nor are these the only occasions for these virtues, or the only virtues which he displays.

But, in spite of these, and of the supernatural armour in which he is clad, and by which he is well suited, as the introductory letter testifies, he is not yet perfect. He lacks in particular one virtue. It is Arthur who represents perfected holiness in Book One; the Red Cross Knight, like the other knights of Gloriana, is *in via*, holiness in the making, not yet

[1] cf. p. 104.

confirmed and secure. This is shown by his melancholy; he was of his cheer 'too solemn sad', and the pagan knight Sansjoy proves to be his most dangerous enemy save one. One may be temperate and not holy. The Evil One himself never errs as to temperance, as he says to St. Macarius in the desert, in an episode which is in the very spirit of Spenser's poem.[1] One may be just, and not holy. The Pharisee was doubtless perfectly correct when he vaunted the exact fulfilment of all claims upon him. One may also be pure and not holy; the nuns of Port Royal were said to be as pure as angels and as proud as devils. The virtue whereby St. Macarius overcame the demon was none of these; it was humility. To the virtues he possesses the Red Cross Knight must add perfect humility and this addition will cure his sadness.

Because the Red Cross Knight is thus insecure, he cannot yet fulfil his public mission; the apostle's first convert is himself. He must liberate his own soul before he can liberate Christendom. Hence, the series of adventures, initiated by Archimago and Duessa, though they seem to cut across the direct path of his quest, are really the means of his fulfilling it, and acquiring the one essential virtue in which he is at first deficient. The source of the apparently motiveless malignity which Archimago and Duessa display against him thus becomes clear. For Spenser could not have verified his reference to the armour of the Christian man without his eye falling on the verses immediately preceding: 'Put you on the armour of God that you may be able to stand against the deceits of the devil. For our wrestling is not against flesh and blood, but against principalities and powers, against the ruler of the world of this darkness, against the spirits of wickedness in the high places' (Eph. vi. 12). 'The rulers of the world of this darkness' there could not be a better designation for the powers of evil as Spenser conceived them. For in the bottommost slime of Spenser's abyss, there lurks 'great Gorgon'. If, as he himself says, Archimago is Hypocrisy, and Duessa Falsehood, behind them there looms a greater shadow, that of the Father of Lies: the apparently motiveless malignity which they display is the age-old hostility of evil and good, darkness and light, hell and heaven.

[1] Cf. H. Waddell, *The Desert Fathers*, Constable, 1936, reprint 1954, p. 17.

Book I

The structure of this book is thus seen to be integrally concerned with the special character of the protagonist, whose crusading figure is by far the best known of all Spenser's personages. Book One is also the most concentrated of all; it has none of the constellated figures which group themselves round the Knights of Friendship, Courtesy, Chastity. Even the single-minded Guyon treads a more devious path than the Red Cross Knight. He who must overcome Acrasia, may fairly go aside to visit Medina, bind Furor, defeat Pyrochles, defend Alma. But most of the Red Cross Knight's adventures happen because he is astray, and though he does actually gain by them in the end, they have delayed him, and the virtue that might have come to him sweetly and gently if he had remained all the time with Truth, is gained painfully and hardly, in prison and in penance.

Spenser is right, in so designing it. Not only are these adventures required to make the story a story, but also, his pilgrimage of a soul would lack reality if it did not pass the way of all souls but one, since the Fall: 'For God often suffers the proud to fall that they may know what they are', and in spite of the good convoy of Truth, most souls choose to learn by experience: 'Knowledge of good bought dear by knowing ill.'

If we follow the story a little way, we shall see how closely it pursues the realities of spiritual experience. Spenser, however, is entirely objective. He is as far as Shakespeare from the ego-centred tendency to indulge in public confession, and if to be romantic means to be suffused with the self-regarding sadness of a Coleridge, then we must say of this greatest of romancers that he was not romantic.

The story of the first book is, in a certain sense, an epitome of all the others. The virtues which are analysed in them are pre-supposed in the Red Cross Knight, and the quests they follow are all included in his primal contest: good against evil. It is in fact so necessary an introduction that the action of the other books could not proceed at all if this were lacking.

Truth and Holiness, then, are found together at the beginning pursuing their quest, and the first moment of real crisis for the Red Cross Knight comes when he is shown

Archimago's false enchantments. He and Una have both been deceived by Archimago, Hypocrisy, who has let them encounter him in the guise of a hermit walking along saying his rosary. Hermits have fascinated the imagination of story-tellers from Langland and Malory to Charles Kingsley whom no one will accuse of too much sympathy with the Old Religion, and there is a reason for this besides Gothic picturesqueness. The hermit is the image of the wholly dedicated life; of one whose passionate love of God is so over-mastering as to exclude all other permanent objects of attention. Total self-devotion can always compel, therefore this image exerts a perennial fascination even over those who admit little sympathy with the ideal it represents. The appearance of it will nearly always deceive, at least for the moment. Hypocrisy is an acted lie, but to be unsuspicious is a condition of nobility of character; so that virtue itself disposes the possessor to be more easily deceived at the beginning Cassius could not have deceived Cassius, or Iago Iago, but either can deceive a better man.

Up to this moment the Red Cross Knight has not really experienced temptation. He had been brought up in that country life, that pastoralism which stood, in the imagination of the time, for innocence and simplicity; (1. x. 66) he had taken the first step in independent personal virtue when he went to Gloriana's court, hoping to be a knight and follow her in honourable and laudable conduct. But the coming of Una marks a higher call. Her quest cannot be fulfilled unless her knight can wear the sacred armour she carries. This is the experience known as vocation, the call to devote oneself wholly to one heaven-chosen task. But this too comes rather easily. He is innocent, he is noble, aspiration to the highest comes, as it were, spontaneously, the armour suits him perfectly, and he sets out with Una. His first adventure confirms his confidence.

CAVE of ERROR

If the Red Cross Knight and Una had not entered the Wandering Wood and stayed longer than need be, they would not have found Error. But they have acted in good faith, and the point of this combat should be noted. Error does not attack Truth, for that would be useless; it tries to destroy Holiness: 'Be not deceived by vain philosophy', says the Apostle, by the teaching which strikes at the roots of virtue itself. The fight that follows is a sharp one but, fundamentally, it is a struggle with difficulty, not with temptation, Error is recognized throughout as hideous and hateful for, set beside Truth, her nature cannot be concealed. 'Truth is a touchstone.'

The next event is the meeting with Archimago, and this is the first real crisis, in which the dice seem loaded against the young crusader, since the trap is prepared by the hermit, the holy man, the man of prayer, the spiritual guide, who has abandoned the world, and who can have no interest to deceive. The psychology of Archimago's methods is interesting. He begins by dreams, false dreams which enter by the imagination, exciting and disturbing. When his victim awakes, troubled and ashamed, he presents the false image of Una tempting to wrong. In one sense, this temptation fails for Archimago, foolish with all his subtlety, apparently supposed that the Red Cross Knight would rejoice to find Una no better than himself. He did not reckon with the Christian hatred of sin, the Christian compassion for the sinner, or the chivalrous inability to deal roughly with a woman. But the magician has not wholly failed. Excited by his own emotions, shocked and startled by his interview with the supposed Una, the Red Cross Knight has not sinned, temptation is not sin, but he is agitated, the balance of his judgement is disturbed, there is nothing to check the beginner's tendency to violent solutions. Archimago proceeds to his next attempt, which essentially is an effort at bringing the primitive emotions of jealousy and revenge to reinforce a repetition of the original attack on Una. Again it fails in one sense, for an honest error of judgement is not sinful, and though perfect justice would have given Una a chance to clear herself, and perfect faith would have believed, even against the evidence of the senses, yet there is much more excuse for the Red Cross Knight than for Othello. He abandons Una; but under the influence of agitation and distress. In all this there is inexperience, folly, imperfection, mistaken judgement; but not sin.

Spenser narrated the whole of this episode with a detail and elaboration proportionate to its importance, using all

that contrasted imagery which is habitual to him. Archimago, like a sort of Faustus, invokes the powers of evil,
Hecate the night goddess, not Persephone, is 'Blacke Plutoes
grisly Dame', and calls out of 'deepe darknesse dred', heavy,
emphatic syllables which the alliteration insists on, sprights
'like little flyes', he had not forgotten his Bible, or Beelzebub
the Lord of Flies. The association with night suggests soft,
flapping, mothlike creatures. Then there follows the famous
description of the abode of Morpheus which is so often
quoted as an example of lulling verbal music. Yet the eternal
lullaby of the bee-like wind and the drizzling rain in that
dwelling under ocean and earth, is not really a sound of
peace, and Morpheus's behaviour is of one under a drug.
The dreams too are kept in 'prison dark', and are evil dreams.
A heavy unhealthy atmosphere broods over the whole description, a wet tropical warmth, well suited to the region whose
double gates of ivory and silver are, we learn from another
book (II. vii. 25), next to the gates of Hell:

> For nexte to death is Sleepe to be compard
> Therefore his house is unto his annext;
> Here Sleep, there Richesse and Helgate them both betwixt.

where the caesura in the last line throws the emphasis on
Helgate.

The second act shows false dream and false Una, made of
air, a creature like the witches' Florimell, combining against
the Red Cross Knight, the dream still pursuing him, even
when he has sent the lady gently away. He will not be so
scrupulous when Fidessa is his dame. There follows the third,
when Archimago in person, still seeming holy, and accepted
as such, displays what appears to be the falsehood and frailty
of Una, 'with feigned faithful haste'. This last blow is too
much, not for the knight's virtue, but for his reason: 'The
eye of reason was with rage yblent', and the lines with which
the poet describes the rest of his night: 'in torment great, and
bitter anguish of his guilty sight' and his hasty departure,
are strongly contrasted with those which tell of Una's
awakening from her peaceful sleep:

> Now when the rosy-fingred Morning faire,
> Weary of aged Tithon's saffron bed,

Had spread her purple robe through deawy aire,
And the high hils Titan discovered,
The royall virgin shook off drowsy-hed. . . (I. ii. 7)

One thing the Red Cross Knight learns in Orgoglio's dungeon is to trust Una. When he meets her again he never mentions the vile suspicion, or rather, assurance, which had driven him from her. In fact the dwarf, Natural Reason, had penetrated the deceit already.

The episode I have sketched is told at greater length than any, except that of the final battle, and rightly, for it serves the same purpose as the first act of a Shakespeare play, it creates the situation from which all the subsequent action arises, while also introducing the leading personages. Like those of the King in *Hamlet*, Archimago's fortunes rise on a mounting wave, until they reach the crest when the Red Cross Knight falls to Orgoglio and Una does not know where he is. Then his wave lips over, and falls, he sinks with it, and his enemy rises. In fact, his power is broken, his plots in later books are feeble and ineffectual when compared with his early efforts, and he is himself deceived by a Braggadocchio. The death of the dragon has broken the back of evil. Each knight must still win his own victory; but now that the dragon is dead, he can. Hence the first book, which seems to have so self-contained a story, is nevertheless organically connected with all that follows as an essential premiss. Unless sanctity has become possible, even natural virtue cannot be perfected.

Probably the detail in which the enchantments are told, had another reason too, one which may even have been the more prominent in Spenser's mind, the diffusion through the whole passage of the heavy, brooding atmosphere of Morpheus' cave, oppressive to reason, stimulating to emotion, the irrational atmosphere of the dreams which torment the knight. The dwarf, who later tells Una the whole story of Archimago's deceit, is silent now, and brings the knight his steed without protest.

Events follow a sequence which one would expect. At first the Red Cross Knight rushes away at random, trying by movement and change to escape from his agitated thoughts and feelings: 'Still flying from his thoughts and gealous feare.' Separated from Revealed Truth he is spiritually quite astray, and Reason does not, or cannot, help him or, rather, he cannot listen to Reason: 'Will was his guide, and griefe led him astray.' Yet he has not rejected Truth, he has abandoned one whom he now believes not to be Truth. Obviously, the first effect of such a shock would be to precipitate temptations against faith itself. For, if Una can be false, perhaps there is nothing true. Sansfoy is not to be confused with Error, already conquered, he is the opposite of the virtue of faith as already defined, and he is urged to the attack by Duessa, Falsehood:

> A goodly lady clad in scarlot red,
> Purfled with gold and pearle of rich assay.

'He that is not with me, is against me'; where truth is driven out, falsehood will creep in; there is no middle state, though the agnostic seeks one.

Spenser's more serious public would have no difficulty in recognizing the description of Duessa: 'the woman was clothed round about with purple and scarlet, and gilt with gold, and precious stones and pearls'—the Scarlet Woman of Babylon, the enemy of the faithful, represented on the historical plane, no doubt, by the Catholic Church.

The two knights struggle

> . . . as when two rams stird with ambitious pride
> Fight for the rule of the rich fleeced flock.

Spenser's fights are described elsewhere, but one may note in passing, how effective and varied his similes are, with unconventional comparisons drawn from evident personal observation: as here the two furious animals butting each other or, in Book Four

> two billows in the Irishe soundes,
> Forcibly driven with contrary tides

or, in Book Three, the six knights attacking one:

> Like dastard curres that hauing at a bay
> The salvage beast embost in wearie chace
> Dare not adventure on the stubborne pray.

This particular fight if sharp, is short: 'Curse on that Crosse (quoth then the Sarazin) That keepes thy body from the bitter fit.' Spenser, here recalling to us what he had already said:

> And on his brest a bloudie crosse he bore,
> The deare remembrance of his dying Lord . . .

suggests that, though the knight's judgement has been deluded, his heart is still pure, he is still in charity: *Ave crux, Spes unica*. Sansfoy falls, 'but two such victories would be worse than a defeat', True Faith has been abandoned, No Faith has been killed, False Faith remains. Yet, though the Red Cross Knight accepts Duessa-Fidessa, it is in honest simplicity, believing her true. A recent critic speaks of the Red Cross Knight's 'degeneration'. But temptation is not sinful, mistaken judgement is not sinful. He is foolish perhaps, and this folly has led him further astray; but neither is folly sinful, or few could be saved. Passion too helps to deceive him; but while there is no evil will, there is no sin and therefore, no degradation. Moreover, there still remains some deeper instinct which is true to Una; for the poet tells us that his 'seemly merth' is feigning; and when he escapes from Lucifera's castle his regret at leaving 'Fidessa' is not strong enough to make him risk anything for her sake. Not so is his care for Una.

In the spiritual life, pride is the most fatal sin. The Saviour told those given to spiritual pride, that the publicans and harlots should enter the kingdom of heaven before them. So when Archimago's minion has made good her hold on the Red Cross Knight, her first act is to lead him to Lucifera's castle.

HOUSE OF PRIDE

The poet's description of Lucifera's court is touched with the same humour that is perceptible in *Mother Hubberd's Tale*. Lucifera herself has the rudeness of the arrogant, and her attitude, raised on her lofty throne with a mirror in her hand in which to admire her own beauty, corresponds exactly enough with the usual definition of pride, 'the inordinate love of one's own excellence'. Around her are grouped courtiers, such as Bunyan would have placed in *Vanity Fair*:

> Her Lordes and Ladies all this while devise
> Themselves to setten forth to straunger's sight:

Some frounce their curled haire in courtly guise,
Some pranck their ruffes, and other trimly dight
Their gay attire: each other greater pride does spight (1. iv. 14.)

It is in such passages that it appears that Spenser had not read his Chaucer in vain. He has irony also, an irony that is often felt as a faint undertone to his verse, as when he describes Lucifera's drive in a 'coche' drawn by the Deadly Sins and driven by Satan through 'a foggy mist'. Evil to Spenser, always dims the light, and 'over dead sculs and bones of men whose lives had gone astray', adding: 'So forth they marchen in this goodly wise.'

Again the Red Cross Knight is not wholly deceived. He dislikes the Lady and her company, though Fidessa is the foremost among them. He has let himself be led into the proximate occasion of sin; but he has not consented to it, or taken part: 'Him selfe estraunging from their joyaunce vaine.'

In fact, worldly pride, showing itself in ostentation, the flaunting of position and wealth, especially if accompanied by arrogance, is not a very serious danger to one who, like Holiness, led by charity has deliberately renounced the world with all its pomps and vanities, and has been living consistently with that renunciation. Far more dangerous to him is the pagan knight Sansjoy, whom he meets at the castle. Self-regarding melancholy is an associate of pride, and a real menace to the spiritually minded. The poet rightly gives an important place to this combat with Sansjoy, the demon of Hamlet, the maggot of Malvolio. Melancholy is really the worst enemy of the Christian pilgrim, grave sin only excepted, and so clearly do the masters of the spiritual life recognize this, that habitual melancholy would be regarded as a serious obstacle to a religious vocation: 'In our calling', wrote Mary Ward, a religious foundress, Spenser's countrywoman and younger contemporary, 'a cheerful mind, a good understanding, and a great desire after virtue are necessary; but of all these a cheerful mind is the most so.' and again, 'Ours should take care to banish far from them all inordinate sadness', and, 'Be merry, we serve a good Master.' St. Francis de Sales, also Spenser's contemporary, and a famous director of souls, a founder and reformer of convents, says the same. Spenser is here, as so often, following the established tradition of asceticism. It was the myth of the Puritans that the inventor of laughter should admire long faces, Puritans who had forgotten that the blessing upon the mourner is that he should mourn no more.

The Red Cross Knight defeats Sansjoy, but he does not kill him: Spenser always distinguishes carefully between those things which can be stopped once and for all, and those things to which the temptation will always recur. Sansjoy is borne away and healed by the powers of evil whose friend he is, and Holiness, with the wounds of in-ordinate sadness still unhealed, as the poet is careful to point out, realizes the occasion to sin in Lucifera's castle, with the dwarf, Natural Reason's, help, and flees from it, only to encounter a more deadly snare.

Joined again by Fidessa-Duessa, whose falsity he has still not seen, the Red Cross Knight is persuaded that now he should take things a little easy. The psychology is that of experience. A certain reaction may follow a moral effort, and with it steals in a shade of self-complaceny. Something has been achieved, one deserves, one even needs, a little relaxa-tion, and one may safely allow it since one has shown what one is, others perhaps might still need to be more on their guard. The knight lays aside, only for a moment of course, the armour of a Christian man, and with it, it seems, the restraints he had always used towards Una. Naturally, it is at this moment that Orgoglio appears upon the scene. He is a giant of immense strength apparently, though in reality there is no substance in him, he is the son of earth and of wind (I. vii. 9), he is, in the expressive Biblical phrase, 'puffed up'. In fact he is spiritual pride, the pride of the pharisee who is not as other men are, and, in particular, not like that publican. The knight springs up to resist but he is unarmed, taken unawares, and still weakened by the combat with Sansjoy. And yet he is not wholly defeated; for this is the spiritual combat in which no one can be wholly defeated who does not will to be. But it is not his own strength that saves him:

> The Geaunt strooke as maynly merciless,
> That could have overthrowne a stony towre,

> And were not heauenly grace that did him bless
> He had beene poudred all, as thin as floure:

Still struggling, he is flung down by the wind of the blow, stunned, and thrown unconscious, therefore still unwilling, into a dungeon. Duessa saves him from death, little likely though that might appear for, obviously, the poet must save him both for the story's sake, and because Holiness can only be destroyed by mortal sin, and there is no mortal sin here because there is no free consent. All the same, there has been fault, a fault that keeps him prisoner and saps his strength. One of Spenser's more comprehending critics has hinted at accidie, sloth, not mere laziness, but a guilty neglect of known duty through the habit of yielding to self. But accidie is not, in actual experience, the characteristic temptation of the saint; and, according to Spenser's own words which immediately follow the lines just quoted, it was the wind of pride which felled the Red Cross Knight. What, then, has overcome him after so many victories? What is 'the wind of pride'? It is intense melancholy, discouragement, depression, caused by finding out that one is not so good as one hoped one was; a depression deriving from the root of pride; but not pride understood and consented to.

There is a book called *Saints are not Sad*, and this is the true title: saints are not surprised, horrified, or depressed when they fall into imperfection, because they know that they are dust, and have no power of themselves to help themselves. But the Red Cross Knight is as yet a saint only in the making and 'God sometimes lets the proud fall that they may know what they are'. It is in the dungeon of Orgoglio's castle that the Red Cross Knight will learn exactly how little he is worth by himself, and he will pine and be miserable until he is rescued by Truth and Humility.

In the meantime, the dwarf, faithful Reason, God-given Natural Reason, has neither been deceived nor imprisoned, he is free and in search of truth, and truth, when loyally sought for, is never far away. Moreover, Fidessa-Duessa has revealed herself, and even if the shock of this contributed much to the knight's distress, at least he is no longer deceived, nor will be again. The shock of meeting sin face to face may at times be salutary if thereby one learns the truth.

Spenser is as arbitrary in dealing with time as Shakespeare and, like Shakespeare, he takes for granted that the reader will have enough sense to assume that the intervals which the events following them imply have, in fact, passed. Indeed, the measure of his events is rather intensity than duration. Indications suggest that a time equivalent to about three months on this day's earth, has passed since Una and her knight were separated; but this humiliation will prove the occasion of ending the separation. For the moment it is the dwarf who holds the stage. The dwarf has never been described to us, and is not now. But even of the Red Cross Knight it was his armour that was pictured, not himself. It may seem strange; but it is the fact that this master of description describes his chief personages very little, and mentioning only what is essential to the story. Artegall's portrait is given in some detail, because it is Britomart's vision of him which is the occasion of her quest; but of Britomart herself we see only hasty torchlight glimpses of bright hair escaping from the helmet. Of Calidore we are only told that:

> he was full stout and tall,
> And well approved in batteilous affray,

probably because these are not quite the qualities one might attribute to the Knight of Courtesy. Guyon gets a little more:

> His carriage was full comely and upright,
> His countenance demure and temperate,
> But yet so stern and terrible in sight,
> That cheard his friends, and did his foes amate ...

This again is not pictorial, and is dictated by Spenser's wish to emphasize the more unexpected characteristics of his conception of temperance. It is the bad creatures that Spenser portrays in detail, Error, Mammon, Munera, Malegar, Duessa, and her dragon, the deadly sins in Lucifera's castle, the great dragon, the communist giant, Despair. All these are far more elaborately described than any of the good personages, except Arthur; perhaps because, at the last resort, these good personages are only the attributes of Arthur himself. But how powerfully Spenser suggests what he does

not describe. The exquisite Florimell, for example. She
passes in a flash of white and gold, and we see her in the
mirror of her effect on others:

> Oft did he wish that lady faire mote bee
> His Faery Queene, for whom he did complaine:
> Or that his Faery Queene were such as shee ...

Or again, even more strikingly: 'For none alive but joy'd in
Florimell.' The old witch cannot resist her, Satyrane is her
servant, even the despicable Paridell speaks of her with a
respect foreign to his nature; the gleam of her passing draws
after her both Arthur and Guyon, both vowed lovers of
Gloriana, and both masters of themselves. If the dwarf is not
described, he is in good company.

Why should he be a dwarf? In part, probably because
a dwarf is one of the usual 'properties', so to speak, of ladies
of romance; but also because of the proportion Spenser
allows between Natural Reason and Divine Truth. When he
is Una's servant he lags behind and is wearied; when he is
the only faithful companion of Holiness he is quick, clearsighted, trustworthy, well-judging. It was he who had discovered the deception of Lucifera's palace; he who had
secured his master's escape, and he now understands the
treachery of Duessa, and even, it seems, that of Archimago.
Left to his own devices he goes, straight as a hound on the
scent, to Una. But when his task has been achieved the dwarf
disappears out of the story which has no longer any place for
him. Spenser is too good a theologian to despise reason; but
the region he is now to treat of is out of reason's sphere, and
the poet gets rid of allegorical figures or symbols for which
he has no immediate use by the simple process of not
mentioning them. Thus the lamb, which, with its obvious
symbolism, completed the first impression of Una, but which
would embarrass the story afterwards, silently disappears.

Una, in the meantime, has had her own tribulations, some
of which have been alluded to in passing. Only a short time
can the lion, strength subdued by beauty and truth, protect
her. He is as faithful as the Salvage Man will be, later on,
to Serena; he is an effective guard against Kirkrapine and
the disguised Archimago is afraid of him; but he cannot save

Una from Lawless. That fact is reserved for the innocent rustic people, the fauns and satyrs, as though Spenser had known, or guessed, something of the Bushmen and the Pygmies, or at least of that true though limited belief which underlies the apparent idolatry of so many primitive peoples. Other superstitions there are, less innocent; these flee from the face of truth, the nymphs, dryads, and naiads, who 'enuie her in their malitious mind'.

And now Satyrane enters the story, one of Spenser's most attractive creations, passing by in one book after another, to do good deeds and get nothing by them. Only half-human, and the other half satyr blood, and brought up in the forest, he is yet a noble knight who keeps 'goodly company' with Revealed Truth, and learns her 'discipline of faith and veritie'. Yet Satyrane is Una's friend, not her follower; he frees her from the satyrs, and fights Sansloy for her sake but, as appears later, his heart is Florimell's, and she is not for him. In the allegory Satyrane seems one of the various figures by which Spenser represents Natural Virtue; not the cardinal virtues and their subordinated ones as contrasted with the theological virtues; but natural goodness itself, beautiful and noble but yet, in a fallen world not enough, and bound to be unfulfilled. It is after having left Satyrane fighting against Lawless for her sake (Lawless is her constant enemy) that Una encounters the dwarf, who reveals to her all that has passed. This is much; but this is not enough; Revealed Truth and Natural Reason both together, are unequal to breaking open the castle of Pride. Pride is in the will, and the intellect which can recognize it, cannot therefore overcome it, the inordinate love of one's own excellence with its reverse, the inordinate distress at one's own lack of excellence. Hence the necessity of Arthur, Arthur and his shield.

According to Spenser, Arthur represents the perfection of the virtue which is the subject of each book. His state, then, is Holiness but holiness in itself is no one virtue. What is here needed is the distinguishing virtue of the holy, the virtue contrary to pride, which is humility. Does it seem strange that the lordly Arthur, on his first appearance in the poem, with his golden-winged dragon and his gay multi-coloured crest, should be a type of humility?

> Upon the top of all his loftie crest,
> A bunch of haires discoloured diuersly,
> With sprinckled pearle, and gold full richly drest,
> Did shake, and seem'd to daunce for jollity,
> Like to an Almond tree ymounted hye
> On top of greene Selinis all alone,
> With blossoms braue bedecked daintily;
> Whose tender locks do tremble eueryone
> At euery little breath, that vnder heauen is blowne. (i. vii. 32)

Yet Humility, he clearly is. Orgoglio falls back into his original nothingness, dust and air, before him. Timias, here as elsewhere the sense of honour, is powerless before Duessa on her dragon, but Arthur defeats her easily enough; the castle of Pride opens before him, and Ignorance is found within. His shield is the immediate symbol of humility in action, that dreadful shield which he so seldom unveils deliberately, it is the shield of humility because it shows things as they are:

> No magic arts here of had any might,
> No bloudie wordes of bold Enchanter's call,
> But all that was not such as seemd in sight
> Before that shield did fade and suddeine fall:

When first Orgoglio, then the dragon, are paralysed by the radiance of the shield, accidentally unveiled, Duessa tries to rouse the giant to further conflict:

> But all in vaine: for he has read his end
> In that bright shield, and all their forces spend
> Themselves in vain: for since that glauncing sight
> He hath no powre to hurt, nor to defend,
> As where th'Almighties lightning hand does light
> It dimmes the dazed even, and daunts the senses quight. (i. viii. 21)

A brilliant conquering quality is this Humility that, knowing itself for nothing, becomes the champion of Truth, sweeping all before it, bright as the diamond which Spenser seems to take as its most appropriate symbol. The shield itself is of diamond: '. . . all of diamond perfect pure and cleene It framed was . . .' and Arthur's parting gift to the Red Cross Knight, which is surely humility also, since it heals any wound, is contained in a 'box of diamond sure'. Of diamond is the badge where Gloriana's face is carved, and that 'bright angels' towre' which dims the crystal brightness of Panthea in Cleopolis, was surely built of the 'terrible diamond'. It would be a natural choice, Medieval legend ascribed magical powers to the diamond; it was sovereign against both poison and insanity, both qualities appropriate to Spenser's use of it here.

The only inhabitant left in Orgoglio's castle is Ignaro his foster-father. It is clear from what follows that he is not only ignorant, but imbecile, a further comment on Spenser's conception of spiritual pride. The castle, though magnificently equipped, rather unexpectedly 'with bloud of guiltless babes and innocents defiled was' . . . where also the blood of martyrs was crying from the ground. The victims of Lucifera's castle are people whom the world would call famous: Scipio, Antiochus, Hannibal, Caesar, Pompey, Semiramis, Cleopatra, Nabuchodonosor, and so on. All these have followed the same course, traced out by the poet's psychology of ethics, pride, and riot leading to covetousness, then to anger and envy, then to ruin. The analysis is nearer to that of St. Ignatius Loyola than perhaps the poet would have appreciated. Lucifera's victims, then, have brought their doom upon themselves, like that

> Faire Sthenoboea, that her self did choke
> With wilfull cord, for wanting of her will.

Those of Orgoglio are not sinners but sufferers, the victims of the pride of others, not their own. The apocalyptic imagery borrowed for Duessa and her dragon in her capacity as the Scarlet Woman, may have led the poet's thought back to the original *non serviam*; so that he is, momentarily at least, identifying the figure of Orgoglio and 'he whom we call the devil or satan, the whole world's seducer', represented by Herod slaughterer of innocents, whose pride defied God, with, possibly, an historical allusion to the Marian persecution, or those of Philip II. But the vivid immediacy of the inspired seer of Patmos was not for Spenser. He passes on quickly to the necessities of the story, and the finding of the Red Cross Knight: 'A rueful spectacle of death and ghastly drere.'

Three months, we now learn, he has been sunk in that deep pit of black melancholy and deadly depression, the consequence of his weakness when, taken by surprise and unready, he fell beneath the blast of Orgoglio's club. Even when rescued, he is reluctant to speak of what had passed, and of his thus knowing what he was without his silver armour. Patience, Arthur tells both frankly enough, is his only cure, patience, and not going back on the past. Many a father confessor has said the same when one of 'the good' has had a similar experience.

Spenser shows himself a true artist in interpolating at this point the charming story of Arthur's fairy love which, for the poet is ever mindful of his dark conceit, is so told by Arthur as to show how he himself was humbled by learning that love was stronger than he.

When the two knights exchange parting gifts, the diamond box already mentioned, with its healing drops, and the illuminated testament—it is only the Red Cross Knight who stands so nearly on an equality with Prince Arthur as to do this—there follows a phrase which happily, even if almost accidentally, defines the differing status of the two:

Thus beene they parted, Arthur on his way
To seeke his loue, and th'other for to fight—

In Arthur the battle is already won, he fights as a guardian angel may, and it is not fanciful, in one so obviously influenced by the Scriptures as Spenser, to see an association between the name of Arthur's love, Gloriana, and that glory of which St. Paul so often speaks, 'the riches of the glory of his inheritance in the saints' (Eph. i. 18). How would the poet have managed the scene in which Arthur at length meets Gloriana, after a conflict more terrible than that of the Red Cross Knight and the dragon? Perhaps he had not yet visualized it in detail, he was only at the beginning of his work, there were to be ten or eleven more books before he would need it. Yet it seems evident that the Cleopolis that Arthur would finally reach, would be no this-world city. For if it had been the Cleopolis whence all the knights had come, Arthur's quest might soon have been over; but he is clearly destined to go about doing good, until all the other quests have been finished by his aid. Cleopolis on earth then, with its Queen Gloriana, is only a type and a foreshadowing of 'the Jerusalem which now is, and is a type of that Jerusalem which is above, which is our mother' (Gal. iv. 25, 26). Meanwhile this type, its representative on earth, will be like King Fisherman's Castle, like Carbonek, which recedes from him who would approach towards it. It is obvious, of course, that Arthur's function in the story requires that his personal achievement should be deferred, with that of all the others except Florimell and Marinell, until the last book. Spenser's suspended climaxes have not Ariosto's irrationality.

The Red Cross Knight's next adventure, after the parting with Arthur, forms one of the most justly famous passages of Spenserian poetry. It is the encounter with Despair. The scene is set with the same care as marks the description of Archimago's enchantments or Duessa's expedition with Night.

CAVE OF DESPAIR

Critics have said that Spenser was the first English poet who sought beauty as an end in itself, no usual quest at the present time, but some of his most famous descriptions are of things terrible or hideous, or, as in this case inexpressibly drab. There is nothing of dignity or grandeur in Spenser's conception of Despair. Here is no Ajax defying the lightning, no Faustus waiting for the clock to strike, no Satan awaking on the lake of fire:

> His griesie lockes, long growen and unbound,
> Disordred hung about his shoulders round,
> And hid his face; through which his hollow eyene
> Looked deadly dull, and stared as astound:
> His raw-bone cheekes through penurie and pine
> Were shronke into his iawes, as he did never dine. (i. ix. 35)

There is nothing heroic, nothing exciting in this picture, and the background fits it. Everything 'romantic' and picturesque has been subtracted from a scene which includes all the elements of romantic melancholy, cliffs, rocks, the shrieking owl, the wailing ghosts, the darksome cave. Somehow by his diction, including in that word both sound and sense, the poet has made of these things a scene as confined, mean, and incredibly depressing, as ever was a sixth-rate lodging where the torn wallpaper hangs from the decaying plaster, and tumbled, dirty, bedclothes encumber the unswept floor. Wordsworth attributes 'the moon's beauty' to Spenser, but long before Eliot, or the tribe of doleful moderns, he had seen the vision of squalid material ugliness; and he had known that it was not the truth. His psychology is correct. Despair is seldom tragic, dramatic, passionate, it comes, a blear-eyed idiot, when these things are over, not with thunderbolts and earthquakes, but with the last torn envelope too much.

This is the supreme temptation because it strikes deep into the roots of the knight's special quality, his devotion to God, 'and wonted fear of doing aught amiss', and there is the grain of truth in it which poisons so many lies:

> Why doest thou, O man of sin, desire
> To draw thy days forth to their last degree?
> Is not the measure of thy sinful hire
> High heeped up with huge iniquitie,
> Against the day of wrath to burden thee?
> Is not enough, that to this Ladie milde
> Thou falsed hath thy faith with perjurie,
> And sold thy selfe to serue Duessa vilde,
> With whom in all abuse thou hast thyself defilde?

It is all true, and he cannot deny it:

> Is not he just that all this doth behold
> From highest heauen and beares an equall eye?
> Shall he thy sins up in his knowledge fold
> And guiltie be of thy impietie,

'In whose sight the very heauens are not clean—'

> Is not his law, let every sinner die
> Die shall all flesh? What then must neede be donne
> Is it not better to do willinglie—,

The verse has taken a soft, dreamy, beguiling rhythm:

> Then linger, till the glasse be all out ronne?
> Death is the end of woes: die soone, O faeries sonne. (I. ix. 47)

Into this dim shadowy scene, and this hypnotic melody, breaks Una, a true woman, roused by the danger of one dear,

snatching the dagger 'enraged rife', with a reproach that cuts
short the drugging eloquence of Despair:

> Is this the battell, which thou vauntst to fight
> With that firemouthed Dragon horrible and bright.

Notice how the unexpected adjectives flash in that foggy
scene.

Stung in his self-respect as a man, the knight is roused
from his nightmare, and is able to listen as a Christian. Una
does not argue, does not excuse or explain away; that would
have been useless. She sweeps the whole thing aside with one
appeal:

> In heauenly mercies hast thou not a part?

All that Despair has urged may be true; but the mercy of
God is greater. The struggle is over, and it has been won in
the only way psychologically effective, by faith. Here again,
the knight has not sinned. He has been tempted but, in the
end, he did not yield. Yet it was not his own strength that
saved him, but Una's.

The whole of this episode is told in the detail, and with the
elaborate setting, and the full use of Spenser's genius for
appropriate verbal melody, which characterize the poet's
treatment of an incident which he regards as critical. The
whole scene makes a companion picture to that of Archimago's sorcery at the beginning for, structurally, it too marks
a major crisis, the turning-point in the knight's story, the
lowest point to which his fortunes will descend. Having
overcome this temptation, he will rise from now on until he
attains the height of Christian heroism required of him; and
on his reappearing in later books, he will be found confirmed
in his attainment, no longer wavering or insecure. Guyon's
palmer will recognize his superiority and its stability, when
Archimago's plot to make a quarrel between him and Guyon
has failed:

> Ioy may you have, and everlasting fame
> Of late most hard achievement by you donne,
> For which enrolled is your glorious name
> In heavenly registers aboue the Sunne,
> Where you a Saint with Saints your seate haue wonne. (II. i. 32)

'His be the praise that this atchievement wrought', answers the Red Cross Knight, thus illustrating that he had gained the one thing missing to him. The time for this is not yet but in the structure of his story the train of events has turned towards it.

Una now brings her knight to the House of Coelia, whose children are the supernatural virtues, Faith, Hope, Charity. There he is to be schooled, like a very hermit of the Thebaid, until he too shall have attained the height of contemplative prayer, and shall have seen such a vision as one of Spenser's contemporaries saw, which put out the light of the earth's glory as the sun puts out the moon. Thus prepared, he can face the dragon. One would imagine that Spenser had met a Dominican in Ireland, or during that famous visit to the north of England, for this is their teaching and *Contemplare aliam praedicare* is their motto.

Now the Red Cross Knight has conquered evil in himself, 'the lust of the flesh, and the lust of the eye, and the pride of life', and he can turn seriously to the evil in the world; he has gained the essential virtue of holiness which is humility.

The process of purification and spiritual training which the knight goes through in the house of Coelia, needs little discussion, both because the poet has made it perfectly clear, and because it is exactly what one would expect. Humility, Zeal, and Reverence mark the beginning; the next step is obedience, Fidelia, with her book of mysteries, follows, and her character has already been discussed. With her comes Speranza, a most necessary helper, especially at this stage.

The first effect of their ministrations is the realization of sinfulness, the condition, and the knight goes through that ancient discipline of contrition, penance, purpose of amendment, patience, the process called, for convenience, the Purgative Way.

Healed and humbled, the next stage belongs to Charissa, and Spenser's treatment of this virtue might need some comment.

Charissa's frank maternity has been a shock to some readers; she is presented to us as a sort of Christian Venus, a baroque picture full of cupids, and complete to the turtle doves. On the contrary the reader, perhaps subconsciously, was expecting something ecstatic, a development of the picture of Speranza, or something like Bernini's ballerina figure of the great St. Teresa. Yet the poet's imagery is not without reason, and the involuntary objection to it springs mainly from a change of social convention.

Today a woman may freely expose her person for professional, recreative, or aesthetic reasons, but she must conceal her functional activities. She may show that she is a woman; but she must not appear as a mother. That this is an artificial notion much art in many places exists to prove.

The poet is using this imagery to bring out more vividly the aspect of charity of which he is chiefly thinking. He is dwelling on charity as the second great commandment of the Law, like to the first, which is the same as that last one whereby the disciples were to recognize one another. 'By this shall all men know that you are My disciples if you have love for one another.'

Spenser is showing this love as the source of life, abundant, generous, bestowed first and most largely on the weakest and most helpless. It reproduces itself freely, since it is very true that love engenders love; it draws others to share in its beneficent activity; but that activity is maternal, not official; its bounty is given as we give to children, expecting nothing back; not by rule and measure, demanding a just return: 'To love one another; that from the first was the charge given to you (1 John iii. 11). Besides, just as the earthly, or natural Venus is seen by the poet as the generating power of nature which reduces the chaos of earth to order and form, so the heavenly, supernatural Venus is also life-giving, a source of ordered, beneficent activity, and, as usual with Spenser, there is Scripture for it: 'But whoso hath this world's good and seeth his brother have need, and shutteth up his compassion from him, how dwelleth the love of God in him?' (1 John iii. 17).

It is thus Charity who continues the knight's spiritual instruction 'in every good behest, Of love and righteousness and well to donne', for love is the fulfilling of the law. She appoints Mercy as a further guide, not only then but always, who would bring him to salvation in the end, and she too is an equally evangelic figure: 'Blessed are the merciful, for they shall obtain mercy', 'Judgement without mercy to him that hath not done mercy'.

This insistence on the deeds of charity, and the function of mercy, this emphasis on the seven brethren, the corporal works of mercy, traditional as it all is, throws light on the poet's attitude to one of the great religious controversies of his day. He is clearly versed in that Epistle of St. James which Luther called an epistle of straw; and by combining two of the works on the traditional list, that go naturally enough together, feeding the hungry and giving drink to the thirsty, he is able to bring in St. James's test of true religion: 'to visit the orphans and widows in their affliction. . .'. He also clearly remembers St. Matthew's parable where those are blessed who, having done it to His brethren, had done it to the Lord. Such was Spenser's attitude to the bitter controversy of faith and works. Yet good works were not the end of the road. Mercy leads the Red Cross Knight to the holy mountain. There she leaves him, and there he attains the saint's realization of what that is worth which passes away with time:

Till now, then said the knight, I weened well
That great Cleopolis where I haue beene,
In which that fairest Faerie Queene doth dwell,
The fairest city was that might be seene;
And that bright towre all built of Christall cleene,
Panthea, seemed the brightest thing that was;
But now by proofe all otherwise I deene
For this great city that doth far surpas,
And this bright angels towre quite dims that towre of glas. (1. x. 58)

Cleopolis and Panthea seem to stand here for the best that earth can offer. After all, they are the palace and city of Gloriana. It is a best, then, that is very good, the perfect earthly kingdom under the perfect earthly sovereign, Gloriana, Tanaquill, Mercilla, Elizabeth. But it is not the best there is: 'Our hearts are restless till they rest in Thee.'

When the Red Cross Knight descends the mountain he is no longer Una's pupil. He has learned what he is and to what he is destined, he has ended his preparation, he can proceed to the event.

Though Spenser is careful to save the character of Gloriana, 'heauenly borne', he seems in this place to identify her realm, or at least her capital city, with the natural world as it then appeared, that world of humanism already so absorbing, and to contrast it with the supernatural one, the Jerusalem which is above: 'So darke are earthly things compard to things divine.' The quest then proceeds. They enter the ravaged realm which Christendom now is.

Spenser is notoriously not over-realistic when he is describing single-handed combats, though perhaps he is not below some of the regular romancers of his time and earlier, but the first appearance of the 'huge feend' is dramatic. Una is just encouraging her knight, just warning him that the enemy is near, when the air fills with turmoil, the earth shakes, the evil thing they were looking for is already upon them. It is true to experience that the arrival of even a foreseen trouble always carries a shock of surprise.

The combat which now begins is not like the others. The Red Cross Knight is not now being tempted, the time for that is past, the interior battle has been won already. He, now the militant power of goodness in the world, is challenging the evil. If he were to fall now, it would not be as a sinner, but as a martyr. It is significant that whereas heretofore he has obeyed Una, now she obeys him, and, as she watches the fight, she fears for his life; but she does not fear for his soul. Here, as never in the other books, of which the ends are all rather indeterminate, Spenser is being universal, showing the total conflict in which the other knights each bear individual parts; Excess, Unchastity, Injustice, Contention, Calumny are all sins. But this dragon is Sin itself, 'the old dragon who is called Satan'.

There might seem to be an inconsistency; for in 1. xi. 7, the poet tells us that he will later narrate a greater battle than this ''twixt that great Faerie Queene and Paynim King'. Presumably, in the structure of the whole poem this would have been the culminating action of the twelfth book and Arthur's last adventure. Perhaps all the knights would then have been allowed to end their suspended stories, and the historical hint is clear. But, in the moral allegory, what battle could be greater than that of Holiness against Sin for the

liberation of Christendom? Possibly, in those lines the poet
was thinking only of the political contest in which for him the
struggle between good and evil was embodied, and was
hinting at some final, decisive, conflict between Elizabeth
and Philip II of which the Armada victory was a foreshadowing. But if not, he might have argued that the battle in which
all the forces of good in the world are finally arrayed to
defeat those of evil, would be, if not greater in essence,
greater in material scale and visible consequences than this
necessary preliminary single combat between the two forces
as they are in themselves, not as they are found embodied in
human society.

Una, after the active part she has taken in saving the
knight, and in training him in the spiritual life, now withdraws to a passive role; she does not even speak to encourage
him as she had done in earlier combats, she does not approach
him even when the fight ceases during the night and she
knows not whether he be dead or living. But Divine Revelation has done its part already; she has brought him to fight
the good fight and to keep the faith; beyond she cannot go.
'The devils also believe and tremble.'

Una remains above and apart. She would still be true, still
inviolate and inviolable, even if, *per impossibile*, Holiness
were to be finally defeated. Besides, there are ultimate
struggles in which everyone is alone.

And now comes the dragon. It is so huge as to cast a
shadow beneath its body like that of a mountain, puffed up
like a monstrous toad 'with wrath, and poyson and with
bloudy gore'. It is cased in sword-proof brass—strange if the
first-used metal had retained from primitive times the memory
of a magical hardness; his wings are large as sails, in those
days of swift galleys with huge sails; his long tail, that mark
of an evil dragon, recalls that which dragged down a third
part of the stars of heaven, and it is armed with stings like
those of the apocalyptic scorpions from the abyss; his mouth
sends forth smoke like that abyss itself, his glaring eyes are
deep set in pits of darkness. There is surely here a hint not
only of the apocalyptic dragon, but of those dragons' heads
which had symbolized hell in the earlier drama, still holding
its place, at least in the country, even to Spenser's day.

And now the struggle begins. In proportion, which Spenser is too wise to present directly to the eye, the knight is hardly bigger than a bee, or his spear than a bee's sting. That is, however, the right heroic proportion, and his readers knew their *Seven Champions of Christendom*. Besides, leaving the story again for the allegory, 'the weak things of the world hath God chosen to confound the strong'.

Is it enough to take the whole fight *en bloc* as symbolizing, in a general way, the combat of good and evil, or are we to assign a special interpretation to each phase of it? It would be possible; but though I do it, I think it likely that, though Spenser would not repudiate this interpretation, he may well have adverted to it only vaguely in the first place.

When the dragon realizes that its enemy is to be taken seriously, it swoops upon him and lifts horse and man high into the air in its claws:

> Long he them bore above the subject plaine,
> So farre as Eughen bow a shaft may send . . .

To be lifted up, to be above, this is again the attack of pride. But he who has seen the heavenly city is armed against even spiritual pride; the knight forces the dragon to put him back on earth, thrusts it under the outspread wing and inflicts the first wound it has ever known. Furious with pain, the dragon wraps its tail round horse and man, and the horse, without blame, throws his rider; outside help fails, however good and legitimate it may be. But the knight springs up, he is gaining strength and not losing it, and his next blow is so hard that the dragon dares not risk receiving another such. He brays and belches fire, fire that red-heats even the sacred armour of the Christian man, so that it burns its wearer, inflicting more suffering than the dragon could:

> Whom fyrie steele now burnt, that earst him armed.

In the fight between St. George and the dragon in the popular romance of the *Seven Champions of Christendom*, which Spenser is here following, sometimes rather closely, it is the venom flowing from the dragon's wound that consumes the armour, as Beowulf's sword was consumed by the witch's blood. It is a good touch, and the poet must have had a reason for making the change. The sacred armour is not consumed; it is not even injured; it only becomes extremely painful. But righteousness will suffer in this world; the attacks of evil can make life almost unbearable; and the danger is that the fighter may withdraw from the struggle and keep himself pure for himself apart. And now comes another change. In the original fight St. George was healed by an orange; Spenser substitutes the healing well, and adds, after the second day's fighting, a stream of balm which flows from the tree of life: the reader has not forgotten that we are in Eden.

WELL OF
LIFE

The fountain of healing, the water of life, would be no new invention whether Spenser got it from Irish mythology as I have suggested, or from the hundred other equally accessible sources from which he might have obtained it. His version, however, has caused some controversy. Critics have interpreted Spenser's insistence on the power of this 'springing well' to give life and to heal sin, and his subsequent expression 'baptized hands', to mean that this well stands for the Sacrament of Baptism. But is this possible? Spenser was not an Anabaptist, and he could not have supposed the Red Cross Knight able to wear the armour of a Christian man if he had not been baptized. Moreover, the instructions of Fidelia, that bearer of the serpent-entwined chalice which is still a sacramental symbol, and the rest of his training in the house of Coelia imply this. When he returns to Una, even before he meets Charissa, his conscience is 'cured' (I. x. 29). He is not now sinful but already holy. In this conflict he has not sinned, and is not sinning; he is simply suffering intensely as a result of his struggle with evil. It is not forgiveness he needs, it is strength. Therefore this is not the water of baptism but the water of grace, 'springing up to life eternal'. The same reasoning applies to the tree

TREE
of
LIFE

of life with its apples 'rosie red'. That tree grew before sin was, and it is not that fatal fruit that 'brought death into the world and all our woe': 'Great God it planted in that blessed sted'. It is not a remedy for sin, it represents the supernatural life which sin destroyed in men. This is why the dragon cannot approach it; he is dead already as far as that life is concerned:

> For nigh thereto the euer damned beast
> Durst not approach, for he was deadly made.

He is sin, and with sin came death.

But though the knight is refreshed and restored by grace, the living water St. John tells of, his blows are ineffectual for two days. Spenser has lengthened St. George's original combat, and to Una, watching from the hill, the issue seems uncertain. She cannot come to tend her champion, and she seems unaware of well and tree; she can only pray for him, an anxious yet a trusting woman. It is clear that the story as a story requires this; but there is also allegorical justification. The psychomachia which is the underlying theme of so much allegory is a struggle of the will, not of the intellect, and the graces the knight needs and receives are of strength and life, not of enlightenment.

The injuries the Red Cross Knight inflicts on the monster seem at first not to weaken it. But that very fact is really its destruction, for, though startled by the knight's recovery from his wounds, it dashes forward believing itself already victor:

> And in his first encounter, gaping wide,
> He thought attonce him to have swallowd quight,
> And rusht vpon him with outragious pride (i. xi. 53)

That pride is his downfall. The conflict with pride has been the theme of the Red Cross Knight's quest until now, and he has learnt how to deal with it: 'Fierce as hawke in flight' he attacks his enemy at the weak point his pride has disclosed, and the dragon is killed. Yet so terrible does it appear, even when dead, that neither knight nor lady can at first believe it really defeated: this is a very natural touch.

Courthope remarked that this is the best-described dragon and the worst fight in literature. It is true that the fight lacks one kind of realism, and also rapidity and suspense. Many a competent novelist could beat Spenser at that game, were it Reade and his leopard or Kingsley and his white bear. But Spenser can hardly be blamed for not doing what he did not try to do.

It is impossible that Spenser should not have known, when he devised his stanza, that it would not be suitable for

narrating violent action; and he had already shown in
Mother Hubberd's Tale, for example, that he was quite capable
of using a much quicker, more directly moving metre. He
also knew that much of the action in a chivalric romance or
romantic epic must necessarily be violent. If, in spite of all
this, he devised and used this stanza, he must have believed
that its deficiency in respect of action was of minor importance
when compared with other advantages. It is easy to see why.

The difficulty is greatest when it affects the narrative as
such. In this connexion one should remember that the rising
tension of excitement, of suspense, the sense of action and
movement to which Scott's metre so much contributes, is
not of vital importance in a fairy story, and in fact the popular
romances do not move in that manner. We know already
that the dragon will be killed, that the third time the disguised princess enters the prince's room she will be successful, that the wicked enchanter's heart, if it is not in the duck's
egg, will nevertheless be found in something else, that the
third brother will perform the impossible task. It was clear
beforehand to all the many readers of *The Seven Champions
of Christendom* that, whatever the odds, the Christians would
win in the end. The same convention applies to *Huon of
Bordeaux*, *Sir Ferumbras*, and any other of the romances
which, it appears, Spenser must have known, and also in his
Italian artistic models. If they had not known this, they
would not have read these books so eagerly. Taking pleasure
in watching the destruction of the weak is the refinement of
a later age. 'The Christians are right and the pagans are
wrong': that principle was clear, and no one doubted that
right would prevail. Even the tragic drama is evidence of
that. Whatever happened to the Red Cross Knight *en route*,
and his tale is as adventurous as any romance reader could
desire, there could be no doubt of the outcome of the conflict
which ended the immediate story even to the reader, if any
there were, who did not know the source Spenser was using in
the particular case.

But if the interest of such narratives is not in uncertainty as
to the end, it must be in the wonders that happen by the way,
in the telling, in the whole process of events. The how
matters more than the what.

Romances are not read as one reads a detective story, galloping through to see which solution is the right one, but taking pleasure in each separate incident for its own sake. This seems to be a principle of enjoyment at that period. Very few of the Elizabethan masterpieces depend much on the excitement of suspense and uncertainty, especially when the work is not tragic. We are not surprised that Portia saved Antonio, or Viola married Orsino; we always supposed they would; the interest is in how it comes about.

There is seldom place in Spenser for the excitement of the prize-fighter's ring. Not even Malory does his foining and tracing in that manner. Sometimes the struggle is more like a ritual, even a liturgical act, this being especially true of the combat which prompted this discussion. Spenser's other fights generally follow a similar pattern. The two knights hurtle together; one, if not both, is thrown so violently that he is in no hurry to get up again, a mild jest of which the poet never tires; a hand-to-hand conflict follows, rivers of blood flow, the issue appears uncertain. Then something, a wound or a cry, provokes the good knight to a supreme effort, and the victory is his. The present book offers several exceptions to this general design; but that is because some of the Red Cross Knight's principal contests are not with other knights, not with flesh and blood, but with 'spiritual wickedness in the high place'. And this brings us to the fact that, if prize-fighter realism is not required by the story, it is still less appropriate to the allegory.

Edmund Spenser knew a good deal more about real fighting than most poets. Indeed, of his own contemporaries few could have seen more of it than he who had accompanied Grey and Norreys, and had even acquired some reputation for skill in arms. The Spenserian myth dies hard. Because Wordsworth compared him with the moon, we think his head was always in the clouds. And yet he lived for twenty years in a country which was never at peace when armed force did not hold it so. It is, indeed, reasonably suggested that some experience with Irish kerns lay behind the description of the jacquerie that attacks the castle of Alma. If, then, he plays down the fighting in a poem where fighting was inevitable he had some reason for it besides the fairy-tale

convention of which I have spoken, and besides the evident
fact that he had no love for the theme.

Depth psychologists might be interested in examining the
imagery which springs to the poet's mind to illustrate combat. Though he seems concerned to give an impression of
violence and brute strength rather than skill, his imagery is
singularly impersonal. The good knight and his adversary
struggle as though not human. Bulls, boars, lions, a pouncing
hawk, eagles, two rams butting, a falcon swooping to death on
a heron's long bill, mastiffs, an eager hound, a butcher
throwing a bullock in the slaughter-house; these are frequent
comparisons. A second group concerns itself with elemental
forces, the contests of winds and waters. Thus Calidore's
fury swells like the mill-stream, Scudamour and Paridell
meet like

> two billows in the Irish soundes
> Forcibly driven with contrarie tydes.

Paridell has already rushed to the attack like a 'boistrius
wind', and he also enters the comparison of two fighters to
two warlike brigantines ramming each other. Alma's enemies
attack the departing knight like a waterflood bursting down
from the hills, and Triamond's conflict fluctuates like the
eddying water when the tide meets the current of the Shan-
non; those who fight about Florimell fight like the wind
against the sea; Arthur's assailants are like a storm that
passes from coast to coast in rain and hail; the communistic
giant, struck down by Talus, breaks up like a ship dashed to
pieces on the rocks.

Spenser does not reserve what might seem the more complimentary term for the virtues. Calidore, that cynosure of
grace and courtesy, it is who fells his enemy as a butcher
fells a bullock. Arthur certainly fights like a skilful mariner
contending with a storm, but he is also a ship taken aback,
and when assaulted by Pyrochles and Cymochles he is like
a bull between two mastiffs, or like a heron attacked by two
falcons; Diamond swoops like a vulture; the Red Cross
Knight, even after his fulfilment, resists six adversaries like
a savage beast brought to bay by the hounds.

Now it is quite evident that however vividly these comparisons may give the impression of contrary energies, they do not call up a picture of human conflict. In fact, it would seem as if Spenser were not trying to make us see these fights as human actions at all. Milton's commentators have pointed out how he uses similes to give not a physical but a moral impression. Satan is like Teneriffe or Atlas unremoved, he flies through chaos like a gryphon pursuing the Arimaspian, or like a fleet of merchant ships. Spenser is again the epic poet's forerunner. He, too, is not really dealing with physical facts; he is not trying to describe a fight between man and man, but 'the fell incensed points of mighty opposites'; the reader is to realize the clashing of those opposites like the collisions of elemental powers, but not like the mere assault and battery of angry men. Even in the fairy story the fights are hardly this, and in the allegory they are not material conflicts at all, but the strife of the struggling will to good against the powers of evil, which is no fencing match. These powers are not to be known by their exterior appearance. Orgoglio, even in defeat, falls majestically like a great tree, but at last is found to have been nothing but a windbag; and Paridell's similes are less complimentary than they might seem, because he is indeed as unstable and untrustworthy as wind and water. Water in fact seems not to have been one of Spenser's friends; sea and river seldom play a good part in his pageant.

If Spenser had described his fights with the vigour and realism of a Romany Rye fighting a Flaming Tinman, all that the story, considered as a real-life story, which it was never meant to be, might have gained, would have been lost by the allegory. Too much realism, the clashing and thumping of real bodies, stirring up the emotions of the football match or the boxing-ring, would have blotted out that true conflict which is the poet's real subject, the psychomachia which had lain for centuries at the core of allegorical narrative. One has only to think of Milton's war in heaven to understand the harm that misplaced material realism can do.[1]

That Spenser could nevertheless be realistic enough when he saw fit is proved by the delightful scene that follows the

---

[1] However, one must note that though they are used with a difference, similar comparisons are found in Malory and regularly in Homer, cf. *Iliad* throughout.

Red Cross Knight's victory, when all the simple people of
the neighbourhood, flocking out in that inexplicable way in
which crowds materialize where something has been going
on, come to admire the dragon's body, half afraid still that
it cannot be really dead, but taking a fearful pleasure in its
size and its claws:

> Some feard, and fled; some feard and well it fayned;
> One that would wiser seem than all the rest,
> Warnd him not touch, for yet perhaps remayned
> Some lingring life within his hollow brest,
> Or in his wombe might lurk some hidden nest
> Of many Dragonets, his fruitfull seed;
> Another said that in his eyes did rest
> Yet sparckling fire, and bad thereof take heed;
> Another said he saw him move his eyes indeed. (i. xii. 10)

Yesterday how terrible was his shadow passing over. Today
they would not have him an inch smaller.

There is but one more episode in Book One, though we
are not yet at the end of the knight's personal history. The
episode consists in an interruption of the rejoicings accom-
panying the wedding preparations in the now liberated palace
which represents Christendom released from the dominion of
sin. Evil has been defeated within those limits; but it has not
been destroyed altogether, and one last attempt is made by
Falsehood and Hypocrisy to separate Holiness and Truth,
this time by attacking Holiness. The scene is one which might
have suggested to Scott the appearing of the false herald in
Quentin Durward, as the disguised Archimago produces the
letter of Duessa-Fidessa. Humanity, without being fully
deceived, is rendered wary; Holiness no longer knows doubt
or fear. St. Paul points out in *Romans* that one effect of sin
is the dimming of the intelligence, and the Red Cross
Knight's spiritual victory is apparent in his serene discern-
ment of Duessa's new attempted fraud. Una too is now unveiled, so that shadows flee away, and the knight himself 'did
wonder much at her celestial sight'. He had walked by faith
until now. Archimago is unmasked and thrust into a dungeon.

And yet it is not the end of the story. Holiness and Truth
are united. Eden, the kingdom of Christendom, has been set
free; but there are lands beyond Eden; the heavenly city has

not yet descended upon earth. In fact, the real task of the
Virtues can only now begin and, without Holiness, could
not be concluded. He appears in later books in several
episodes in which he is chiefly associated with Guyon and
Britomart and, indirectly through Britomart, with Artegall,
and this sufficiently indicates his continued activity. Una
appears no more in the poem as we have it; her function
henceforward is rather to be than to do.

The association of the Red Cross Knight with the two
mentioned is not fortuitous; neither is the order of the six
books, or seven, if we justly assume that the Mutability
fragment was to have been an inset episode in the Book of
Constancy or Fortitude.

The bondage of sin being broken, the ideal of perfect
manhood, represented by Prince Arthur, can now be realized
step by step. The major struggle was that of the Red Cross
Knight, whose task was to wrench the perverted will of man,
deceived about himself and subject to pride, back to its
loving submission to God, his mind being at the same time
opened to the truth that comes from God. After that the
psychological struggle and training can begin; habits of
virtue can replace the caprices of perversion, and the microcosm of man be gradually restored to its original order. Then
all the various powers and qualities will work together in the
harmony for which they were designed, thus possessing that
final, rather mysteriously named virtue Magnificence, the
human being perfect in act. Now Spenser regards what he
calls Temperance, following the traditional list of major
virtues, primarily as the power of self-control, and some
degree of success in this must necessarily precede any serious
attempt at attaining any other virtue. Britomart's virtue is
Chastity, which, again according to the traditional system, is
a sub-virtue to temperance. In fact it is itself temperance,
applied to a particular case and, in its perfection, lifted to an
heroic level, the possibility of which had long been regarded,
and still is, as a special glory and triumph of the Christian
soul. There follows the book of Friendship. But only where
there is temperance and chastity can there be real friendship,
and this friendship was to be one of the distinguishing signs
of the Christian character. Tertullian, in an oft-quoted

passage, makes the pagan world itself regard this as the
criterion: 'See how these Christians love one another.' All
the same, there are larger problems of human relations,
especially in society, which friendship alone cannot solve,
and then it is the turn of Artegall, Knight of Justice. Not
till full justice has been done does Calidore become possible,
representing a courtesy more easily found in the works of
St. Francis de Sales than in books on etiquette; a higher and
more universal form of friendship, as chastity was a higher
power of temperance. Finally, after these might have come
Constancy or Fortitude, for 'He that endureth to the end, he
shall be saved'.

Structurally, the continued coming and going of the
personages after their own story is over serves to hold the
entire narrative together, so that the reader who goes straight
on, as readers were meant to do, feels the poem as a single
whole, each story weaving itself with no abrupt break into
the next; this is specially illustrated at the beginning of Book
Two.

Book One, after the discovery of Archimago's treachery,
proceeds to the marriage of Una and the Red Cross Knight.
The latter then departs, bound by his vow to Gloriana still
to serve humanity. Book Two begins with Archimago's
escape by magic from the prison in which he was placed
after his attempt to deceive the father of Una. He now seeks,
of course with the help of Duessa, to make a quarrel between
Sir Guyon and the Red Cross Knight. He fails for a note-
worthy reason. Guyon is deceived but, though he attacks the
Red Cross Knight, he cannot bring himself to strike the
shield which bears

> The sacred badge of my Redeemer's death.

Similarly, the Red Cross Knight will not direct his spear
against

> That faire image of that heauenly Mayd
> That decks and arms your shield with faire defence.

There can be no genuine conflict between Holiness and the
chief of the natural virtues: the one reverences the image of
perfect womanly virtue and beauty, human nature at its
highest, the other venerates the symbol of that redemption

which has given him and all his fellows richer content and a higher value. It is in this connexion that Guyon's companion speaks the words already quoted, recognizing the Red Cross Knight as a saint.

We next encounter the Red Cross Knight in Book Three. Arthur, Guyon, and Britomart, riding in the forest, are startled by the vision of Florimell's flight: 'The fairest dame alive': Britomart alone does not follow, and, going on her own way, comes upon one knight fighting six, the servants of the Lady of Delight. She hastens to help him.

If the six knights could not overcome the Red Cross Knight fighting singlehanded for his fidelity to Una, still less could they resist him when reinforced by Chastity in person. They enter the castle victorious; the night begins, and now it is the turn of Holiness to hurry to Britomart's aid. In the morning they leave the polluted place together—Spenser's heroes never travel at night whatever the crisis: 'The night cometh when no man can work'—and Holiness names for Chastity that Justice which she had sought without knowing. They then part, and he goes on 'to seeke adventures', passing thus out of Britomart's story, having for the second time insisted on the value of natural qualities. And here he passes out of the whole story as we have it; though no doubt he would have appeared again in that last book at which the account of his crucial battle hints, in which all the stories would have been ended, and Arthur, the perfect man, would have been united to Gloriana the perfect woman.

The Red Cross Knight is the favourite among all Spenser's heroes. His figure is known to many who would not recognize any of the other protagonists. There is more than one reason for this popularity, one being that sanctity really is more attractive than morality. In many ways his story is the most satisfactory, considered simply as a story, and it has the most satisfactory provisional conclusion. He may remain an errant knight; but that is overshadowed by the fact that he does kill the dragon, the dragon which is a much more impressive adversary than Acrasia or the Blatant Beast, and he does marry Una. None of the other books works up to such a climax. Doubtless the identification with St. George, and his appearance of a faithful crusader, as to which, popular legends were current, helped this, though no one ever actually calls him by that name. Nor are any of the other heroines, even Britomart, so charming and so human in her inviolacy as Una.

The pattern of Book One is very clear: it follows two lines at first parallel, then divergent, then convergent, and lastly parallel again. There is never any real delay. For, though the Red Cross Knight is put out of action for a time when imprisoned by Orgoglio, this does not hold up the story. On the contrary, it enables Una to rejoin him, and it gives an effective entrance for Prince Arthur. The longest pause is that in the house of Coelia, and this is justifiable in the story, and essential in the allegory.

Besides this relatively simple pattern, Book One has all the other elements of a good fairy-tale; a quest, a princess, an enchanter, a witch, a giant, a dragon, two dragons in fact, to say nothing of the dwarf, the good grotesques, the pagan knights, the friendly lion, the enchanted trees. None of the other books is so rich in these elements. Moreover, Spenser has been positively lavish with incident: those who have a vague idea of his narrative as a dreamy, dragging thing, where nothing much happens under the shadow of mighty trees, have certainly not counted up all the alarums and excursions which are crowded into so short a space. But still, that impression of dreaminess must have been created by something. There is enough action in Book One of the *Faerie Queene*, or in any of the other books, to furnish forth each a romance for Sir Walter Scott. Yet Scott is a proverb for vivid rapidity and Spenser for dreamy slowness. The contrast derives from the contrasting purposes of the two poets, and the consequently contrasting means they adopted. Scott, who is emulating the realistic action of the ballads, moves his verse emphatically, with strong accents quickly recurring in short lines, the rhymes being in strong relief:

> The stubborn spearmen still made good,
> Their dark impenetrable wood

Even his metaphors are photographic. The sound of Scott's verse brings the vigorous action of his figures near to our eyes. But Spenser's sound deliberately veils his action, moving it to a distance, so that it seems slower than it is. Some readers are so much lulled by the rise and fall of his waves that they are hardly aware of what is going on beyond a passing of shining figures in chequered light and shade. Yet in Book One there are certain scenes which are as fully revealed as any scenes could be, in darkness or in light.

Among these are the Cave of Error, a Rembrandtesque scene, illuminated only by a faint glow from the knight's armour which just allows the dim figure of Una to be seen on one side, with the shifting coils of the writhing monster in the background. Una under the tree makes a vivid contrast with this, sunlight replacing gloom, the tawny lion with his proud submission instead of the strangling serpent. Then there are the sepia tones of the place where Despair has his dwelling, his own wretched rags; the flashing glimpse of the heavenly city, the people crowding round the dead dragon.

Some of the famous passages of Spenserian verbal music are also found in this book: the often quoted description of the abode of Sleep and the still more beguiling melody of the speech of Despair, to name only two examples. Hence if the modern method of testing by sampling could ever justifiably be applied to a poet, the student who limited himself to Book One of *The Faerie Queene*, could gain from it a true though an incomplete impression of the poem.

But such readers recall the ancient story: how a giantess, having obtained the right to choose a husband from among the gods of Asgard, was obliged to make her choice while seeing only their feet. She chose the whitest and most graceful, thinking thereby to marry Balder the Beautiful. But they were the feet of Niord, god of winds, and stormy was her life thereafter.

IV

TEMPERANCE

'Nor is the sin of luxury to be charged to beautiful and fascinating bodies but to the soul which perversely loves sensual pleasures by neglecting that temperance which makes us cleave to things possessing the higher beauty of the spirit and the incorruption of immortality' (St. Augustine, *De Civitate Deo*, xxi. 7, 8).

Sir Guyon, knight of Temperance, has suffered very much from the modern association of the word temperance with the habit of refraining from the use of alcoholic liquors. Even those who realize as they read that that question does not enter still retain a vague impression that he must be a colourless, negative figure, concerned with a colourless, negative virtue. Actually, as shown by Spenser, Guyon is the most fiery and quick-tempered of all the knights, as he evinces more than once. It is not a negative sign either, that alone of all the six he is seen without a lady. The casual reader vaguely supposes that Sir Guyon is too cold to be shown as a lover. But the truth is the contrary. Guyon is a more faithful, more romantic, in a certain sense more unreasonable lover than any of them; for he loves where he knows it is in vain, one who could never be for him even if she were not destined for another. Guyon's troubadour devotion to Gloriana,

My life, my liege, my soueraine, my deare, (ii. ix. 4)

is enough by itself to disprove the superficial interpretation of his virtue, and to make us search more deeply into Spenser's conception of it.

Professor Tillyard points out that whereas the action of the first book moves on the plane of grace, that of the others develops on the plane of nature. The truth in this must not be exaggerated. Nature and grace are not mutually exclusive, and it is evident that Spenser does not think them so. All the knights of virtue equally belong to the Order of Maydenhede which is itself a grace-conception, and the Red Cross Knight reappears in later books commending the natural virtues and taking part in their adventures. Moreover Sansloy, Una's enemy, appears again in Book Two as the lover of Perissa.

There is no difficulty in the difference of levels between Book One and the others when one remembers that Spenser was a Christian moralist for whom grace perfects nature. He is not thinking of the natural virtues to which pagans may attain with the help of reason and a good natural disposition; but of those which a Christian should possess, rooted in, and permeated by, the spirit of Christianity. In the hierarchy of Christian virtues the Red Cross Knight represents the super-natural group; Faith, Hope, Charity, of which we see a special aspect in the House of Coelia: these are the virtues which have God for their object. In this sequence there next follow the virtues exercised among men, and, first of these, the four cardinal virtues, so called because all the others can be in some way subsumed under one or other of them. These cardinal virtues are Temperance, Fortitude, Justice, Pru-dence. Three of these Spenser chose, supposing that the Mutability cantos really represent an episode inset into the adventures of the knight of Constancy or Fortitude. Pru-dence he apparently omitted. It is obviously a virtue re-calcitrant to knightly adventure, and, in so far as it is necessary to demonstrate it, Guyon's palmer can cover the part, or Glauce. The three remaining places are taken by Chastity, which, in the traditional scheme is a sub-virtue to Temperance, Friendship or Concord, and Courtesy; all three fitting into the extended treatment of love which begins with Britomart's adventures, and is an integral part of the poet's plan.

Temperance, then, is the virtue as conceived by one who knew what Aristotle thought of extremes, and who knew also what place temperance holds in the Christian scheme. In neither is it a virtue of refraining; it is one of balance and control. Acrasia, Guyon's enemy, is not pleasure, indulgence, luxury, simply as such but in excess; the etymology of the name suggests as much. Indeed, whatever disadvantage it may be to Sir Guyon as a romantic hero, to be pitted against a woman not even a hideous giantess like Argante, Acrasia gives the poet the occasion to set forth his inherited doctrine about pleasure and its use, a doctrine which affects our understanding of much medieval literature. That excess, having to be given a concrete form, is made corporeal in a figure representing inordinate sensual pleasure, is a mere matter of logic and psychology; the knight whose combat is principally with the faculties of anger and desire, must in his crowning adventure defeat the enemy where he is strongest, and the poet judged the temptation to be strongest not in the more obvious, grosser, contests with Pyrochles or Cymochles, or in the Caves of Mammon, but in the Bower of Bliss. In the individual case he might be mistaken; but the historian will hardly deny how frequently this has been found the weakness of the strong.

The expression used above, 'inordinate sensual pleasure', contains a word which is a key to Guyon's character, and also illustrates the harmony which Christian moral theology recognizes between the natural and the supernatural virtues. The perfect man, the perfect Christian, must possess both; hence in this book Arthur will appear as ideal Temperance, and the work of this virtue, properly understood, is the normal sequel to that of Holiness. The Red Cross Knight had struck against sin at the root which is pride, 'How art thou fallen O Lucifer, son of the morning.' Sin in itself, the definition is traditional, is, precisely, inordinateness something which is contrary to, rebellious to, the rule of right reason. Some desire, some passion, has escaped either the power of reason to recognize it, or of will to control it. This possibility arises from the disorder in human nature itself, it would be several centuries before any poet would reckon without original sin. Hence it would be useless for Cambell and Triamond to vow eternal friendship, or for Artegall to seek justice, or Calidore courtesy, if they had not that elementary control which makes a man master of himself and his actions. This ability to act as virtue requires because all the natural powers and qualities are held in due subjection; so that they all work harmoniously together, and none assumes an irrational domination, is that virtue of exquisite balance which ancient Greek educational theory aimed at, and which Aristotle summarized in his doctrine of the mean. It comprehends more than seeing, knowing, and yet refraining; it involves acting positively, exactly as the occasion requires, no more and no less, and includes therefore, courage, exquisite powers of judgement, and complete self-mastery. Temperance, as Spenser develops his conception, is that good order of our nature which it possessed before original sin disturbed it, and which, even assuming the grace of God, only resolute will can now restore or maintain. This interior integrity is what must be tested and perfected in Sir Guyon. Where it does not exist at least in some degree, Britomart rides in vain. It was St. George's task to rectify the will by the conquest of pride; it is Sir Guyon's to make the sovereignty of the purified will effective by controlling anger and desire. The proof of this will be found in the course of his adventures.

Has Spenser's choice of a name for him any special significance? In his usage, a chief knight who is seen as a human character as well as a quality, should have a name which is appropriate but not abstract, not an obvious label. The Red Cross Knight's name, little as it is used, is evidently suitable; he is to be associated with England, and his story is based on the popular one of St. George and the Dragon. His soubriquet is still more suitable; both historical and moral motives combine to approve the choice, we can neither forget that he is the patron of England, or that he stands for the Christian soul. Guyon's case is different; there was nothing which presented itself so inevitably, no name that he could borrow from his Italian models since moderation, however understood, was never conspicuous among them.

It has been suggested that the name was taken from Gwynn ap Nudd, once a Welsh deity, but by Spenser's time, transformed into a fairy lord in an underground kingdom such as King Orfeo found, though also appearing as the Wild Huntsman.[1] Guyon, being one of the few knights who is really an elf and not a human changeling, or half-human, or human altogether, as the Red Cross Knight, Britomart, Artegall, Arthur, Triamond, are, might appropriately be given a real fairy name, and a Welsh one too, if the theory that, in the historical allegory, the fairies represent the Welsh is correct. Spenser clearly has a certain knowledge of Arthurian localities in Wales. But, on the other hand, the legends associated with Gwynn do not give him a character

---

[1] G. I. Elton, *Origins of English History*, chap. x, p. 243.

consonant with the one Guyon is to bear. Spenser would probably be justified in supposing that most of his readers would not advert to this. Perhaps, however, this was in fact one of the things that provoked Gabriel Harvey to say that, in the *Faerie Queene*, Spenser had let 'Hobgoblin run away with the Garland from Apollo' (Gabriel Harvey letters).

There is another possible source. The romance of *Sir Ferumbras* contains, in the person of Guy of Burgundy, a very suitable prototype for the Knight of Temperance. He is 'wys and god, a dozty knight, and hardy ynow', he is the 'gode Gy', or the 'kynde knizt' and, courageous as he is, his counsels tend to modify the wild recklessness which characterizes most of the other personages. Moreover, his name often appears in the form Gyoun. That Spenser was a reader of popular romances is sufficiently evident. The matter, though it has some interest, is not of great importance even if it be left undecided. There seems no special reason why the poet should not have known both names, and had his choice confirmed by finding it suitable on either count.[1]

Critics who are seeking evidence that Spenser worked over his text at least twice, do not fail to note that there is an inconsistency in the statements about Sir Guyon's quest. According to the Raleigh letter, the palmer appears before Gloriana bearing the infant with the bloodstained hands, and demanding justice on Acrasia, a witch who has murdered the child's parents; the adventure being then assigned to Sir Guyon. But, in the actual text of Book Two, Sir Guyon and the palmer have wandered far together, 'Through many hard assayes which did betide' (ii. i. 35), before they come on the dead and dying parents and the bloodstained child, while, explaining his quest to Medina, Guyon says the palmer came to Cleopolis to crave redress in general for the crimes of a wicked fay.

If Spenser discovered, while actually writing, that the story escaped a little from the first design, refusing to work itself out quite as intended, he would certainly not be the first or the last writer to have had that experience. Shakespeare sometimes communicated so much vitality to a minor character that he had to kill him to get him out of the way

---

[1] The name appears in other romances as well.

of the protagonist; and sometimes his story rebels against him and he has to do violence to it in order to reach his pre-determined conclusion. But why did Spenser never trouble to bring the Raleigh letter into harmony with the poem as actually written? There is a difficulty like that of Guyon about the beginning of Florimell's story, where she leaves court to seek the wounded Marinell, who in fact is not wounded until some time after. It is possible that the Raleigh letter represents the narrative in the form it had when Harvey complained so bitterly of its popular character, Spenser simply adding what was necessary to an old summary which he did not remember precisely, and which he was reluctant to re-read, as authors frequently are. It is less incredible that, perhaps in the press of other work or away from his papers, he threw into his letter to Raleigh his original rough notes of the story unverified, than that he should have written that passage after the poem had been composed in its present form.

Where no certain conclusion can be reached it is waste of time to pursue such a discussion long; it must be enough to note the problem, to advance a reasonable hypothesis, to admit that it is only an hypothesis, and can in the nature of things never be anything more, unless documents should turn up that there is no reason to hope for, and then to turn to something more important.

Sir Guyon's story opens, 'thrusting into the middest', like the Red Cross Knight's. We are shown him riding 'underneath a shady hill' accompanied by his palmer and there meeting Archimago who has escaped by magic from the King of Eden's prison, and who has added revenge to his usual quest of evil: 'For to all good he enimy was still.'

Structurally, this episode is a link connecting the action of the two books, and bringing Archimago and Duessa back upon the scene. It is also a link in the allegory, Holiness makes his bow as it were, and resigns the stage to Temper-ance, leader in the new phase of the conflict, when the battle is turned against the rebels within. Guyon too begins by being deceived by Archimago and Duessa but, first proof that a false contrast is produced if the natural and super-natural virtues are regarded as opposed, Guyon, though deceived, and though in his zeal he has outrun his palmer,

Reason, cannot bring himself to strike the cross on his opponent's shield, and Holiness though attacked, cannot in his turn bring himself to deface the image of human perfection which Sir Guyon bears as arms. In fact, it is enough that the two should meet; Guyon at once realizes his mistake. Holiness, spirituality at its most intense and elevated, and Virtue in its primary sense of moral strength, can never be hostile, nor fail to recognize each other even when some mischance has set them on apparently opposite sides. There follows the palmer's arrival and his eulogy, thus ending the brief separation which Archimago's momentary success had brought about. The paths of Sanctity and Virtue are not then so different. The poet has made it very clear that his Temperance is no mere philosophic restraint, whether stoic or Epicurean, but is the militant virtue St. Paul describes: an abandoning of the ways of darkness, a putting on the armour of light, a 'pressing towards the mark', a training to take part in a race run for an imperishable crown.

At this point one may ask what exactly is the role of the palmer whom I called Reason above, who is the accuser of Acrasia, and Guyon's guide and adviser, performing, that is, the function which belonged to Una in Book One. It is a part which never appears again, Glauce and Talus are companions without authority, Cambell and Triamond are equal, Calidore pursues his quest alone. The structure of the story in the form Spenser ultimately adopted, does not need the palmer except to bring the message to the court of Gloriana. Indeed, it rather taxes Spenser's ingenuity at times to get rid of him when he is in the way and to bring him back when he is wanted. One immediate problem is that of movement. Symbolism as well as custom requires that the knight should be on horseback; and no one who remembers Plato's allegoric use of the black and white horses, will quarrel with the prominence the poet gives to Brigadore who may in a like manner symbolize the bodily nature Guyon must direct. The palmer both for his own character as a pilgrim, and in his function of restraint on Guyon's impetuosity, is properly on foot. But this situation is too awkward to be maintained; the knight cannot be presented to the eye for long riding at the pace of an old man's walk, and having to

gallop away from him whenever an adventure begins, even
a commendable one. Thus Spenser ingeniously takes advantage of the Ruddymane episode to let Braggadochio, who
haunts this book, steal the horse and put the knight and his
mentor on equal terms. Perhaps it was with his secret smile
that the poet made the composed, dignified, Guyon tramp
along on foot carrying his things.

Supernatural revealed truth alone can guide sanctity, itself
supernatural, aright; but the power which should rule and
guide human passion and impulse is human reason. Conscience is no special faculty; it is right judgement applied to
moral questions. It is obviously moral judgement which enables a man to keep a just measure in conduct, as it is unreasoned impulse which leads to faults against temperance
or just measure. Hence the palmer, the true pilgrim or hermit
that Archimago pretended to be, is in himself Reason, under
the aspect of Right Judgement, charged with guiding the
knight, in fact rather impetuous, to the overcoming of
Excess in the concrete form of unbridled luxury and sensual
pleasure. Here it is well to notice that the common, so to say,
cheap embodiments of excess, have no part in the story of
Sir Guyon. Spenser certainly describes Gluttony: 'Deformed
creature on a filthy swine', with fat swollen face and long thin
neck, whose greed includes drunkenness:

> Still as he rode he somewhat still did eat,
> And in his hand did beare a bouzing can,
> Of which he supt so oft, that on his seat,
> His drunken corse he scarce upholden can. . . .

But he is part of a procession which passes before the eyes of
the Red Cross Knight without affecting him. Spenser would
not have erred as Milton did, when he gave 'Command these
stone to become bread' so coarsely materialistic a paraphrase.

Guyon then, and the palmer, that figure traditionally con-
secrated by having visited the Holy Places and seen the land
which saw the Christ, Reason not simply Aristotelian, or
Platonic, but baptized, having parted from St. George, are
drawn into the tragedy of Amavia and Mordant, Guyon's
first actual contact with the doings of his enemy Acrasia.
The episode has all the greater present interest because there

have since been so many prose versions of the story so many proofs of the disaster of denying that Guyon's virtue is a virtue at all, in modern times when the consequences of un-bridled passion are often appallingly evident.

In Mordant, Spenser pictures one who is led into infidelity by sheer inability to control his natural passions, though he still loves and even prefers, Amavia his wife. He is strong, so Guyon comments, against everyone but himself. And Amavia with courage to act and magnanimity to forgive, has not strength to endure. Had she been born in the present age of enlightenment, she would have shut the window, turned on the gas, and allowed her child to share the same destruction. Existing before progress had reached this point, she only stabbed herself, leaving the infant to live if it could.

Spenser insists so much on the bloodstained hands of the child, stains that water from the fountain of purity will not remove, that they must have had some special meaning for him. Amavia and Mordant are in a sense more sinned against than sinning. He was led away and finally poisoned by Acrasia, she overcome 'Of anguish rather than of crime.' But that will not save the child. They have left him an evil heritage; the consequences of their unruled passions. Spenser had seen too much of the world not to know that it is the child who expiates such faults of the parents, both by the situation in which they leave him, and by the heredity they have given him. Guyon and the palmer moralizing on the event, remark that temperance with its golden square could have measured a mean between these extremes of abandon-ment to pleasure and to grief, and the knight does his best for the child by leaving him in the care of Medina, the golden mean. In her charge he passes out of the story.

The Castle of Medina is on a rock adjoining the sea, the symbolism of this would seem evident, the rock of will in the middle the waves of contrary passion (but how often Spenser, usually credited with nothing but forests, brings in the sea). The castle is nevertheless shaken by internal conflict, Too-much against Too-little, and both against the Mean. Huddi-bras, the champion of Elissa, Samuel Butler noted that name and that knight: 'More huge in strength than wise in works he was', soon quarrels with Sansloy, Una's old enemy, now lover of Perissa, Too-much. Guyon, trying to separate them suffers the usual fate of those who interfere in a quarrel, and is attacked by both; but he saves himself like a tall ship riding over two contrary waves. Medina pacifies them finally, but the banquet of reconciliation which followed must have been an uncomfortable entertainment, Elissa sulked, Perissa was extremely silly, Huddibras glared at Sansloy, Medina kept the peace by sheer moral force; the whole scene is life-like. Doubtless it was in part to create a diversion that she asked Guyon for his story, and elicited one of those out-bursts about Gloriana in which the knight of Temperance outdoes all the other members of the Order of Maydenhede. Apart from Arthur, he is the only one whose heart is wholly given to his sovereign in whom

> the richesse of all heauenly grace
> In chief degree are heaped up on hye.

There follows the story of Amavia and Mordant, told in such a way—strange gift for a conventional Temperance—as to hold that incongruous auditory enchained, as though Ulysses had been speaking in the house of Alcinous.

Why should it be in the story of Temperance that Brag-gadochio enters the romance by stealing Sir Guyon's horse? Thereafter he is rather conspicuous as a minor character, especially as he is also involved in the strange story of Florimell.

Braggadochio having picked up the squire Trompart on the way, passes himself off as a great knight, even deceiving Archimago whose druidic powers of illusion might have better warned him against another deceiver; but Archimago is not what he was since he lost his first contest.

Certainly the boaster is a stock character in most of the sources Spenser had before him, classical or Italian; the poet might well have looked upon him as inevitable, and he is the right companion later for the crew of light-minded com-panions, Paridell, Blandamour, and the rest. Boastfulness on analysis is a fault of excess. It arises, no doubt, from vanity not from pride, but in itself it transgresses the measure of reason and truth as much as of good feeling. But Brag-gadochio, though he may properly first appear in Guyon's book, is no temptation to Guyon, any more than Lucifera was to the Red Cross Knight. Guyon can be tempted to rage, passion, discord, ambition, wealth, luxury, but not to showing off. Though they come so near, the two never meet until Braggadochio has been discredited by Artegall. It may be over-subtilizing, but perhaps in the removal of Guyon's horse the poet is hinting that his virtue cannot be achieved without the practice of a certain bodily hardness and labour.

Another important background character brought first upon the scene in this very connexion, is Belphoebe, that beautiful extreme, the representative of virginity. She is, moreover, described with a fullness and elaboration not quite in proportion with the importance of her intervention at that moment, especially as she then passes off again, and does not appear further in Guyon's narrative. One may divine particular reasons in this case. Belphoebe is one of the special types of Elizabeth I, and her first coming on the scene must therefore have a certain dignity and amplitude; it must be marked as an occasion. This book, too, would have been left without any such type if she had not appeared in it, and Guyon whose only love is Gloriana, destined for another, is fairly matched as the virgin knight, by the virgin huntress, even were purity not also a sub-virtue to temperance. However, it is also part of Spenser's complex structural plan to dovetail the books by weaving the stories across from one to the other, and by bringing in in advance personages whose narrative is to follow. This in itself would sufficiently account for Belphoebe's passing, a terror both to Boaster and to Liar. Thus also, the fountain of chastity which cannot be soiled by guilty blood, leads into the theme later to be more fully developed in connexion with Britomart. Indeed, many things indicate that, careless and inconsistent as Spenser was at times about points of detail, the general course of the whole story was before him from the beginning. In Book II. ix. 6, there is a mention of Sophy as being, with Artegall, Gloriana's most trusted knight, Wisdom and Justice, just the pair we should expect, and this implies that the poet had his complete list of knights before him, though in fact he never reached the point where Sophy was to enter.

From the point of view of the story, the Braggadochio-

Belphoebe episode gives Guyon time to leave the Castle of Medina far behind on his way through the world of illusion which is faerie land. There is a broad hint that the next encounter, the curious one with Furor and Occasion, is not meant to be visualized as happening materially, but rather as taking place in that world within which the knight will penetrate still more deeply when he reaches the Castle of Alma. The palmer, we are told, instructed him when tempted by strong passion or weak fleshliness and then, without any other introduction, 'He saw from farre, or seemed for to see' Phedon dragged by Furor and followed by Occasion, Rage, and Provocation together.

An audience which made no difficulty about the mingling of abstract quality, type, and individual in the pre-Shakespearian drama, and which, even later, could accept such figures as Rumour with a hundred tongues, need not object to the figure of Occasion in itself. Nevertheless, the whole scene is so grotesque with its padlocked tongues and iron chains, and Spenser is usually so careful about what he presents to the eye, that it seems probable that he intended this to be received emblematically not realistically. Temperance, say the moralists, is concerned with 'The concupiscible and irascible faculties', Spenser, is simply saying metaphorically that fury, irrational rage, cannot be controlled while in the heat of provocation, and even afterwards, must be mastered by sheer force; it is a tumult of the feelings and cannot be reasoned with. Guyon himself is shown as inclined to sudden gusts of anger so the lesson was not uncalled for, nor was the figure of Phedon, so abandoned to emotion as to seem to have no longer any being apart from these; for he and his mainly imaginary troubles vanish like smoke at the approach of Atin and Pyrochles. At this point Spenser is demonstrating various aspects of discord operating in private and in public affairs. No doubt Queen Elizabeth's claim to excel in justice and temperance (letter to Leycester printed 1586) meaning by the latter, apparently, a combination of moderation and prudence in political action, was not absent from the poet's mind when he made Pyrochles so prominent an enemy of Guyon, though he must in fact have been in the foreground in any case, since he, Quarrelsomeness, Choler, with his

brother Cymochles, Bodily Passion, sons of Acrates and
Despight, represent the twin faculties which it is Guyon's
business to dominate. Atin stands for the process, sometimes
called 'Looking for Trouble', which ministers matter for the
quarrelsome to quarrel, by finding, or creating, the injuries
which have to be avenged. Spenser had seen enough, both in
Ireland and in England, to find in public life as well as in
private, the illustration of his theme. The author of *Allegory
and Courtesy*[1] remarks that: 'In the *Faerie Queene* there are no
accidental wounds. He only who is vulnerable is wounded.'
Guyon, whose effort is to keep or restore peace, not to avenge
a personal attack, masters Pyrochles without receiving any
injury, his coolness easily giving him the advantage over his
turbulent foe. Yet both Furor and Pyrochles are only
momentarily restrained by Temperance. Spenser is again
distinguishing between the faults which can really be eradica-
ted, as when humility not only defeats but destroys spiritual
pride and its false semblance of being something great, and
those which arise from qualities misused but so inherent, in
human nature that they can never be more than restrained
while the time of trial lasts. Guyon in particular is not a
hunter of wild beasts, but a lion-tamer, and every time he
enters their cage he will do so at his peril.

Any one excitement in human nature easily leads to another; the bodily excitement which accompanies conflict,
even righteous, opens the door to other bodily passions;
anger and sensuality prove themselves companions. Agitation, as Spenser himself says, is the real enemy of Temperance for it arouses all the others.

The description of Cymochles as Atin finds him, gives
occasion to discuss an interesting subject, interesting especially from the perplexity it seems to cause. What is the place
of pleasure in the traditional morality? Is it authoritatively
condemned as wrong in itself? Some of the medieval allegorists might seem to imply this. Yet in so far as they were
orthodox theologians, they would hardly have intended to be
so interpreted, for they were obviously not Manicheans or
Albigensians, heretics attributing evil to the body as such and
condemning marriage. The doctrine I have referred to as

[1] Dr. Chang, *Allegory and Courtesy*, Edinburgh University Press, 1955, p. 184.

essential for understanding Guyon's virtue, applies here also, namely that sin lies in inordinateness. To be abandoned to physical pleasure of whatever kind is sinful because inordinate in itself, contrary to the structure and harmony of a nature whose supreme quality is reason, and in its object, that is, the end of the action has become the gratification of the passion, whereas this passion and the pleasure resulting from its gratification are only means. The discussion has usually been confused by being referred too exclusively to love. It is true enough that, even in lawful marriage, sin could arise in the case of any partner of it who was governed by the impulse he shares with the brute, and treated his partner as a utility for procuring pleasure. If the argument be transferred to a field without so many literary and poetic associations, not haunted by the shades of Helen, Tristram and Iseult, Lancelot, Guinevere, Abelard, Aucassin, and Nicolette, and the whole flock of Petrarchan lovers, the matter becomes clearer.

The eater, the drinker, the drugtaker whose passionate addiction to his chosen pleasure makes him sacrifice every other consideration to his dinner or his bottle, is obviously misusing what was intended for another purpose, and the misuse is wrong. He who would condone it most, would still not admire it. Such a one is also degrading himself, since reason has been subjected to an impulse from a lower level, and his human dignity has been lost. The victims of Circe, Acrasia, Comus, may be pitiable; but they are not heroic. Milton had understood this, as he shows in *Paradise Lost* where the first effect of eating the apple is an uprush of animal passion on which no light of romance is shed.

That this is also Spenser's view is clear from his whole treatment of the theme in connexion with Cymochles, Acrasia, the Bower of Bliss, and the Gardens of Adonis. It is also the reason why Scudamour cannot achieve his adventure, or Amoret, virtuous as she is, free herself from the power of Busyrane.

In the present case Atin hastens to find Cymochles to avenge his brother. Cymochles is a famous knight and the lover of Acrasia. We should expect sensual passion and luxurious excess to be associated. But Cymochles, though

found at the Bower of Bliss—more easily reached than later
by Guyon—is not found in Acrasia's arms but flowing:

> . . . in pleasures and vaine pleasing toyes,
> Mingled among loose ladies and lascivious boyes.

Amid a company of girls he takes his pleasure by awakening
and enjoying desire for its own sake without any act, as
though a drinker should pass his time gazing at a bottle of
his favourite vintage, or an eater smelling a cookshop. The
titillation itself is his degraded aim.

There follows the curious incident when first Cymochles,
and then Guyon, is led away by Phaedria, idle Mirth, who
resolutely refuses to have anything to do with either Atin or
the Palmer. Phaedria too is a servant of Acrasia, but a comparatively innocent one. Her idle pleasure-seeking life is un-
becoming to a knight; but she does not mean harm, though
harm will surely come of her; for even 'just having a good
time' ends by debasing and corrupting those who have not
better business. Guyon enters the trap innocently enough;
he lingers, however, too long, and though escaping serious
fault, Cymochles is able to wound him. Yet though not
overcome he is not victor. Spenser knew well enough that
that is a conflict not to be won outright. In the same way
Pyrochles could not really be killed by Furor, though he
might learn by bitter experience what it means to burn with
fury. It is at this unlikely moment when Pyrochles, on fire
within, tries to drown himself, anger is self-destructive, that
Atin in his affection for his frantic master becomes for
a moment a human and appealing figure. Here, too, Spenser's
pattern begins to reveal itself. Archimago who, deceived by
Braggadochio, had flown off on the wings of the north wind,
the witch's wind, to steal him prince Arthur's sword, is now
on his way back and passing by this Idle Lake, the meeting
point of all evils Spenser seems to hint, is able to rescue
Pyrochles and relieve his torments.

Special interest attaches to the visit of Guyon to the underworld which now follows. Mammon, whose kingdom this
part of the underworld is, is not a character of classical mythology at all, even in name or appearance, and is not simply
a money-god. Even if the Gospel passage (Luke xi. 9) had

not suggested the name, Spenser certainly could not have used it without remembering those allusions and realizing that, in that context, the word stands not only for literal money but for the putting of worldly values first. Mammon in the Gospel is not only money but the alternative to God, the other claimant to an exclusive service. That this is really Spenser's idea is proved not only by the name but by Mammon's temptations, which include much more than a mere offer of money. Indeed, he himself claims that larger character: 'God of the world and worldlings I me call', though he is of course the money-god as well. Perhaps the greatest danger of the Guyon type endowed with enough self-control to escape obvious wrongdoing is respectable worldliness.

Another interest resides in the poet's conception of the person of Mammon. He does not belong to classical mythology nor, in spite of his first appearance, like that of the traditional miser, does he represent Avarice. Avarice is not the form in which money could tempt Guyon. Mammon is not conceived as a god but as a goblin, a being like the knockers or mine-fairies of Cornwall, equally generous in disposing of their wealth, or like Fafnir, or any other of the metal-working dwarfs of northern legend: that curious tradition—tradition is social memory—of the time when metal was a wonder and the power to work it magic. His portrait and dwelling, far from human habitation, are painted with Rembrandtesque power:

> At last he came unto a gloomy glade,
> Covered with boughes and shrubs from heauen's light,
>   [darkness, always a warning sign in Spenser]
> Whereas he sitting found in salvage shade
> An uncouth, salvage and uncivile wight,
> Of griesly hew, and foule ill-favoured sight;
> His face with smoke was tand, and eyes were bleard,
>   [Vulcan rather than Pluto]
> His head and beard with soot were ill bedight,
> His cole black hands did seeme to have beene sear'd
>
> In smith's fire-spitting forge, and nayles like clawes appeard.
> His yron coate all ouergrowne with rust,
> Was underneath enveloped with gold,
> Whose glistering glosse darkned with filthy dust,
> Well yet appeared to have beene of old

A worke of rich entayle, and curious mould,
Wouen with antickes and wild Imagery:
And in his lap a masse of coyne he told,
And turned vpsidedowne, to feede his eye
And couetous desire with his huge threasury. (II. vii. 3–4)

Round him lie heaps of gold, some still in the ore, some cast
into bars or plates, much coined and stamped with 'The
antique shapes of kings and kesars straunge and rare'.
Again, what is the reason of this special episode? Certainly
the poet might wish to conform to classic convention sufficiently to make one of his heroes visit the underworld, and
Guyon, besides being the one who most resembles the pious
Aeneas, is really the only one who could appropriately do so.
But Spenser is not so much the slave of the conventional
idea of the epic as to do this were there no other reason.
Structurally the incident runs curiously parallel with the Red
Cross Knight's imprisonment in the Castle of Orgoglio. It
happens when Guyon has been separated from the Palmer,
as St. George was from Una, when he has been wounded by
Cymochles on the Idle Island, as St. George by Sansjoy at
Lucifera's castle, his sojourn in the underworld may be compared with the actual imprisonment, and the effect on both
is a prostrating weakness, though Guyon's is transient. Both
are saved by the arrival of Prince Arthur. But the Red Cross
Knight, overtaken by Duessa, is surprised by Orgoglio without his armour in a moment of sinful weakness, whereas
Mammon has apparently not sought this meeting and is even
alarmed by it. However, though he disguises his enmity, he
is quick to take advantage of the chance. Guyon, too, has
his moment of weakness though the whole incident is less
crucial than the corresponding one in Book One. Deprived
of the guidance of Right Reason, having given a moment's
advantage to Cymochles, his animal nature, he has sought
adventure in vain:

And evermore himselfe with comfort feedes,
Of his owne vertues, and prayse-worthy deedes.

Spenser was a Christian and knew his Bible; he had just represented Pride as the greatest enemy of Holiness; even if
his sense of the becoming had not warned him of the effect of

these lines on the reader, he could not have supposed that
Guyon's doing this, not being a Pagan philosopher but
a Christian Virtue, was other than a defect, the defect of
self-complacency. But this secret satisfaction that, after all,
one is something, is exactly what would lay a soul open to
temptations of worldliness; since it would seem but right and
reasonable that these virtues and achievements should be
recognized and rewarded. Hence the appearance of Mammon. On the other hand, Guyon really is virtuous, and the
god's first vulgar offer of whole heaps of money does not attract
him; he retorts with a diatribe against wealth, and the luxury
which exacts wealth, that Milton certainly did not forget:

> Then gan a cursed hand the quiet wombe
> Of his great Grandmother with steele to wound,
> And the hid treasures in her sacred tombe,
> With sacriledge to dig.

Both the speech of Comus to the Lady in praise of luxury,
and the acts of Mammon in hell: 'the least erected spirit of
all that fell', admit the parallel.

Mammon's second attempt is better advised. Guyon is not
vowed to poverty; it is not the part of Temperance to refuse
to use at all, but to use well, and when Mammon, instead of
offering a vulgar surplusage, suggests in a reasonable tone
that Guyon may take what he thinks proper in view of
changed times in which it is impossible to live with the
ancient simplicity, Guyon only objects that he cannot use
what City people call 'dirty money'. Mammon undertakes
to prove it honest by showing whence it came, and the underworld journey begins. The god's own appearance, and the
darkness and filth of his surroundings while they prompt
Guyon's evident suspicion, also suggest the poet's feeling that
money getting and keeping is necessarily an unclean pursuit.

The downward way is like that of many a fairy-tale,
though no fairy-tale would own the dismal road where they
then arrive which leads to the door of Hell: the guardians of
that road are enumerated in lines of the same melancholy
music of which Spenser had already shown his mastery in
the speech of Despair:

> And ouer them sad Horrour with grim hew,
> Did alwayes sore, beating his yron wings:

And after him Owles and Night-rauens flew
The hateful messengers of heauey things
Of death and dolour telling sad tidings;
Whiles sad Celeno sitting on a clift
A song of bale and bitter sorrow sings,
That hart of flint asunder could have rift:
Which hauing ended, after him she flyeth swift. (II. vii. 23)

The door of Richesse next to the great gate of hell with the house of Sleep on the farther side, is guarded by self-consuming Care, but behind it lurks a nameless fiend who haunts Guyon, following him silently as long as he remains in Mammon's dwelling, a figure of Coleridgean suggestion. The knight will be his prey if he should yield to covetousness, lust, or even to sleep. Sleep might seem innocent enough; but to sleep in someone's house is an act of trust and friendship which would be treachery here; moreover, the sentinel on duty must not sleep. Thus they come to the treasury which Mammon calls 'the worldes blis'; a darksome cave where, Spenser has not forgotten, the riches lie which moth and rust can corrupt.

We are told that Temperance is led through these vaults that he may 'see and know and yet refrain'. There is truth in this; but it does not explain the prolonging of the experience. Riches in four different forms are offered to Guyon by the money-god, and refused, always for the same reason; not that they are bad, but that he does not want them: 'All that I need I haue.' This is the first stage, the temptation to be dazzled by great wealth so as to desire it for itself, wishing for the superfluous because it is superfluous, thus making riches from a good servant into a bad master. Guyon rejects this, as many men do who prefer learning, or art, or adventure, or some other thing to the chance of making 'big money'. There is no great virtue in this, for this is no great temptation. They enter next through a golden gate on the second stage, the temptation to prefer worldly values, to desire and to set first the goods this world can offer. Here sits Philotime enthroned, 'the fairest wight that wonneth under skye', her father Mammon calls her, the love of 'honour, renown, and a great name among men'. But Guyon has given his heart to a lovelier lady than Philotime, to

Gloriana, true and eternal honour, the treasure above which moth and rust cannot corrupt. Spenser is wise to note that even Temperance is not temperate for itself but because of a greater love. Mammon leads him on a third time to the Garden of Proserpine. By it runs the river of Cocytus, full of damned souls (it would seem that Mammon's door is another way into Hell in the end), but in it stands a tree of golden apples, Proserpina's fatal tree in Claudian's poem,[1] bearing Atalanta's apple, that which Paris judged to Aphrodite, which was transplanted to the Hesperides. Spenser must have known too what other apple that tree would suggest:

> Whose mortal taste
> Brought death into the world and all our woe.

But what special temptation does this tree represent? Those in the black river near it, were lost by unbridled desire; the evil implicit in the golden apples is pride. Guyon has already refused riches as such and worldly honour, but there remains a more deadly temptation a touch of which was in the self-complacency which engendered this whole experience; the temptation to find his riches in himself by seeking his own will and desire. Christian temperance is not the Epicurean restraint that pleasure may be more perfect; it is a detachment which can use earthly goods, but will not cling to them, nor even allow desire for something good to go beyond the bound; for all these things are secondary. So ends the triple temptation; Mammon has failed. Spenser has added a silver stool under the apple-tree; if Guyon relaxes there he will lose the fruits of his victory, but he does not. No sooner does the knight reach upper air than he collapses. It is good folklore that the intrusion of a living being into the underworld should be subject to condition, and all know that one should not eat the bread of the fairies. Guyon has stayed the three-day limit of time in the underworld without food or sleep, and by his resistance has escaped both the goblin and the demon; therefore it does not surprise us, in the story, that he should now faint. But that the Knight of Temperance should break down after successfully exercising his virtue, and should

---

[1] Claudian, *The Rape of Proserpine*, bk. ii, l. 290. Latin and English texts are accessible in the Loeb Classical Library series, ed. M. Plattnauer, vol. ii, p. 293.

then receive the ministrations of an angel which not even Sanctity was granted, seems to require some explanation.

Though Guyon emerges successfully from the trial, it was his own self-complacency which exposed him to it. It was another weakness, curiosity, in these conditions wrong (cf. ii. vii. 24) which induced him to follow Mammon's lead and dally with the evil thing; thus offered it was evil, though indifferent in itself. Moreover, and this I suspect was more active in Spenser's mind, an atmosphere impregnated with the love of money and worldly good really is dangerous to higher aspirations. There was probably never an adventurer turned dictator who was not an idealist of some sort at the beginning; and Guyon's virtue is specially open to this type of weakness, since worldliness can so easily put on the garb of reason. Spenser had visited the court where Philotime was honoured, and we know from his satiric poetry what he thought of it:

> Where each one seeks with malice and with strife,
> To thrust downe other into foule disgrace
> Himselfe to raise: and he doth soonest rise
> That best can handle his deceitful wit,
> In subtil shifts, and finest sleights devise . . . (C.C.C.H.A.)

Guyon has been breathing poison all this time; it is no wonder if the return to purer air overcomes him. Helpless and alone, if ever a Christian champion needed heavenly aid this one needed it then. There follows one of the most beautiful passages in the poem, the famous guardian angel stanzas:

> And is there care in heaven? and is there love
> In heavenly spirits to these creatures bace
> That may compassion of their euils moue?
> There is . . .

> How oft do they their silver bouers leave,
> To come to succour vs that succour want?
> How oft do they with golden pinions cleave
> The flitting skyes like flying pursuiuant,
> Against foule feends to aide vs militant? (ii. viii. 1 and 2)

It might seem strange that the severe Guyon, who is, if any are, the faultless among the knights, and whose very virtue might seem somewhat less attractive than some impulsive, lovable, weakness, should, at the moment when his enfeebled spright is overcome, be guarded by a being, 'of wondrous beauty and of freshest years', gentle as 'Cupid on the Idaean hill' when he plays with his mother. But there is more than one good reason for this apparently special favour. Guyon is not so strong as he looks, he has just proved it, he needs help, and he is a lonely figure solitary among the others, his lady a distant dream, his guide a weak old man now absent, even his horse stolen. Self-mastery is an essential virtue, the ground and firm foundation of all the others. But it is a lonely one, fated to be surpassed, the guardian of the purgative way, perhaps not destined, at least in this form, to go beyond it. Moreover it is subject somehow to that vague distaste which most people feel for the Elder Brother in the Parable of the Prodigal Son. It has not even the comfort of being self-sufficing: it is not of himself that man can rule himself, yet, 'Greater is he that ruleth his spirit than he that taketh a city.'

The angel, then, comes to the one who needs him most, and incidentally forms a useful link in the narrative situation by enabling the palmer to find his master, or pupil, again without being dependent on a chance coincidence. It is of course at this moment, when Guyon is exhausted, that Pyrochles and Cymochles reappear, with Archimago, as usual, lurking in the background.

Spenser never suggests that Guyon's little interlude in the company of Phaedria was in itself a very serious matter. Indeed, we incline to think better of Guyon for that unbending. Nevertheless, like other things trivial almost innocent, it led to issues greater than itself. On that Idle strand he met Cymochles, fought him, and was slightly wounded (felt the first impulse, a weakness, but not a sin) and on that same strand Archimago encountered both brothers and set them on his track. Now, in his physical weakness and unawareness, they assail him and succeed in seizing away his shield before they are interrupted by the sudden appearance of Arthur, perfect Temperance (the protests of Reason were not heard by Passion). Arthur's appearances at the moment of need require no special explanation. It is his function so to appear. He is the good and perfect gift which comes down from the Father of Light at the providential moment, the grace of the occasion, but always taking the form of the virtue immediately concerned.

It was at a very similar crisis that prince Arthur came to the rescue of the Red Cross Knight, led in that case by Una and the dwarf. He, the Red Cross Knight, was also in a state of collapse, spiritually speaking, owing to his long imprisonment by Orgoglio in deep despondency. He too was unable to help or heal himself, as Guyon is, to whom the House of Mammon, though he entered it freely, perhaps because he entered it freely, was as perilous as the Castle of Pride was to the Red Cross Knight. Una's part is here performed by the angel; while the Palmer corresponds to the dwarf. The difference of size may be understood symbolically, natural reason is dwarfed by divine revelation and sanctity; there is little in them if they do not overgo that; but temperance needs a guide and the Palmer is not unaided natural reason only; his title and his black robe alike indicate that he is that reason as enlightened and elevated by religious faith. Like the historical palmer, he has come from the holy places.

Guyon's deliverance is not achieved without blood. He has lost his shield, he is no longer protected by that virgin's face, the symbol of the treasure in heaven, Cymochles, Sensual Passion, holds it, and for a time, by this pretence of possessing something higher, he saves himself; for Arthur will not risk destroying the good and lovely with the bad. He may even fairly doubt whether what is so protected is bad at all. Both passions have a stolen aid; for Pyrochles has Arthur's sword Mortdure (it is not yet the time of Excalibur) which Archimago stole. But it does not avail him, for it will not wound its rightful master. Arthur then is untouched by Choler, the irascible passion, but a wound from Cymochles makes him aware who and what it is which has masked itself behind the shield where Gloriana's face is painted. Spenser's heroes, the most faultless, are generally wounded at least once in every serious fight. They are all vulnerable at some point. Allegorically that is called for; no real temptation can be repelled without some suffering, and the first impulse, or even a longer rebellion of the lower nature, is sufficiently

well symbolized by a wound; there is no sin where there is
no yielding. But also, reasoning as a story-teller, the poet
understood that an ever invulnerable hero is not 'simpatico'
as having what seems an unfair advantage. Arthur's wound,
however, in this case reveals the truth to him, and in itself,
is 'turned to favour and to prettiness' 'red as a rose'. It is an
experience which warns without corrupting. Then the Palmer
passes Guyon's sword to the Prince who, fully armed and
aware (at the beginning of all assaults of the passions there
must always be an element of surprise), rages like a lion
'which hath long time sought His robbed whelpes' and like
a 'Salvage Bull whom two fierce mastives bayt'. Spenser has
a quite oriental sense of the power and majesty of the bull,
and his perfect Temperance is no bloodless, curatic figure
but a focal point of concentrated energy, akin to that Galahad
whose strength was as the strength of ten because his heart
was pure. Arthur's character of perfect Temperance is well
illustrated by stanzas 47 and 48 of this eighth canto, where
his coolness and self-command are contrasted with the frantic
fury of Pyrochles. Just as once he slew Orgoglio and Duessa's
dragon, so now he slays both brothers, Choler and Lust.
For him and in him, but not by his own strength, Guyon's
enemies are vanquished, and he awakes 'Life having maistered
her senceless foe'. He had erred, but by bad judgement
rather than bad will, he had not deliberately abandoned the
Palmer, and his error was a passing one, there was no
deliberate or habitual yielding. Therefore his weakness is
passing also; he is again himself and his sword and shield
are restored.

The parallel with Book One can be pursued still further.
As the Red Cross Knight after his rescue and encounter with
Despair is led to the House of Coelia to be fully healed, re-
stored, and elevated, so now Guyon, still accompanied by
Arthur, finds himself before the Castle of Alma, the true
home of Temperance.

But here too there must be an encounter first. The
dwelling of Alma is no peaceful house but a castle besieged.
It is in fact, that sieged city of Mansoul which Bunyan was
later to write of. But it is not at this moment assaulted after
Bunyan's manner, but by a rabble rout which seems like

a clairvoyant vision of the attack that would end in the burning of Kilcolman:

> Some with unwieldy clubs, some with long speares,
> Some rusty knives, some staues in fire warmd.
> Stern was their look, like wild amazed steares,
> Staring with hollow eyes, and stiffe upstanding heares. (II. ix. 13)

There is little need to ask Lord Grey's secretary where he had
seen such warriors. These besiege the castle of the human
soul, and these attack the approaching knights as they have
attacked and slain many others.

And yet they are idle shadows: 'For though they bodies
seeme, yet substance from them fades.' And they are dispersed by the two knights like a swarm of gnats driven off
by the North wind. Few poets have noticed insects as
Spenser does. This victory is not final; but in the meantime,
the siege is raised, and the two knights enter the castle.

This castle of Alma's seems to present a difficulty to
writers on Spenser, a difficulty greater to writers than to
readers perhaps.

The critic, unlike the happy public of the fairy story and
romance, is taken aback by the complete simplicity with
which the poet is prepared to allegorize the human body,
working out the correspondence of its parts with those of
a house in a detail which some have found quite unblushing.
They feel that Spenser with his admitted passion for beauty,
and when composing a moral, even a religious poem, ought
to have been too polite to admit any reference to bodily
operations. The poet might retort that he had good authority
for asserting that it is not these things which defile a man; or
he might assume indignation on his side, and remind his
critics of the rebuke given to Peter: 'What I have cleansed
that call not thou common or unclean.'

To this argument the critic might rejoin that what is
theologically and morally acceptable is not necessarily a
proper subject for poetry. But Spenser was an Elizabethan,
and he might counter this by demanding blankly why not.
The tabus about the body vary with place and time, and the
Elizabethan drama would suggest that theirs were not as
ours. These are not ideas which are controlled by reason. In

some times and places it may be incorrect to mention the foot or the elbow;[1] but there is no difficulty about the digestive area, which elsewhere must always have its euphemism though elbow or foot need no disguise. In a somewhat similar manner they pierce the ear for ornament in some places, and in others, the nose. Originally there may have been a practical reason for those social customs; sometimes it is clear that there is. But if they rest on any underlying idea that a bodily organ functioning normally, is in some way disgraceful, that is the Manichean heresy. But Spenser was a Christian, and he felt no shame of the body from which no part had been excepted, when God declared his creation good. Indeed, there is every indication that he felt a childlike delight in the working out of his analogy. It must be noted, however, that Spenser is considering the human body as it would have been if man had never fallen, when there would have been no disorder or lack of balance in the development or operation of any part or function. This being so, the poet could regard the digestive process, chosen as an example as being one of the passages most disliked, with complete objectivity. He sees nothing to object to in the process as such; it is not wrong, therefore it is not shameful, and in the ideal state assumed there is nothing that could displease the senses or even be perceived by them. Coming at the end of the conceit to a point where the senses would enter, he gives us a fleeting image of gates and passages. There is, nevertheless, one thing which he does not mention at all. It would not have been appropriate; he could not make the ideal castle of Alma, universalized as it must be, either masculine or feminine.

In itself this entry of Guyon into the inner kingdom is well conceived, the metaphor may be pushed to the extreme of conceit, but the idea is just and serious. This is the composite human being with its body and soul and all its qualities and parts, moral and material, all ruled by Alma, the soul, without rebellion or resistance. Just as the Red Cross Knight was shown in the vision of the heavenly city, that which was the end of his warfare, so Guyon sees the end to which his own labour tends; for here is the human being as it should be, exercising with effortless ease that self-mastery which it is

[1] In Italy, for example.

Guyon's task to impose. But what then are the ghostlike
assailants whom prince Arthur and he had to disperse? On
both the occasions when these nightmare figures appear,
Spenser is at pains to insist at once on their strength and
their unreality. Maleger, their leader, is a macabre figure of
corruption and decay insubstantial as a dream, yet strong
enough to give a fall to Arthur himself; and though they
never enter Alma's castle, neither can she drive them away,
while they have destroyed many would-be helpers. Yet
Temperance defeats them at their first assault easily.

In actual fact there are two groups of assailants, those wild
disorderly kernes who are dispersed like a swarm of gnats at
eventide by the two knights together, and those who, after
Guyon's departure, are attacked in sortie by Prince Arthur
alone. These form a real army and are conducting regular
siege operations but, apparently, they have no more real
substance than the others who 'though they bodies seem, yet
substance from them fades', for when their captain, himself
spectral, is defeated, they disappear.

This second, regular, army is divided into twelve parts; of
these Spenser names five and their subdivisions: they are the
temptations to sin which may come by what Bunyan will call
Eye Gate, Ear Gate, &c.; such things as lawless lusts,
corrupt envies, slander, ill counsel, flattery, foolish delights,
luxury, and so forth. The poet does not name the other seven
divisions, but he says they conduct the main frontal attack.
There are various Pauline lists which the poet may have had
in mind; but the context is better satisfied by the list of
seven sins in the twelfth chapter of St. Matthew's Gospel:
'Evil thoughts, murders, adulteries, fornications, thefts, false
testimonies, blasphemies. These are the things that defile
a man.' There is much in this chapter that might well have
been in Spenser's mind when he described the Castle of Alma.

Against all these Arthur issues forth, and is attacked by all
at once. But Arthur, perfect in self-mastery, mounted on the
fierce Spumador, the good horse of Plato's vision, disperses
and tramples down the

> . . . raskall flockes:
> Which fled asunder, and him fell before
> As withered leaves drop from their dried stockes.

They are not the real enemy. That is Maleger, attended by
two hags, Impotence and Impatience 'armed with raging
flame'. And who is Maleger, that ghastly figure like 'a ghost
whose graveclothes are unbounded', 'cold and drery as a
Snake', crowned with a dead man's skull, Adam's, and yet
sketched from the Irish kerne as Spenser described him in
the 'View'? To call him original sin, as has been done, is
rather an over-simplification, and it is, moreover, not within
the scope of Temperance to defeat Original Sin. But one of
the immediate consequences of original sin has already
entered the discussion and it is the real enemy of Guyon, and
of Arthur in his present phase. It is what is technically
known as concupiscence, the wound or disorder left in
human nature by original sin, which makes it prone to evil
desires, and gives temptation a strength it could never have
had if the perfect harmony of original justice had remained.
Maleger's tiger is then unruly passion, swift as the wind,
outrunning reason, and the incurable wounds of his arrows
are the injuries we do ourselves when Maleger gets his way.
But there is more to it. 'By sin came death', and this explains
Maleger's own diseased, decaying person, and his attendants
Impotence and Impatience. The inward, psychological, disorder is truly and forcibly symbolized by the sick outward
body, and this too is consistent with Spenser's general attitude
towards evil things. Weakness and impatience are the usual
companions of sickness as every invalid knows, and even on
the moral plane, natural weakness, though dangerous, is less
so than the still more natural impatience with ourselves for
being what we are and other people for being what they are.
St. Francis de Sales, Spenser's contemporary, warns his
penitents against the intolerant bitterness in doing even what
is right in itself, which poisons so much reform, and so many
reformers. Spenser had seen enough of this in the religious
and political controversies of his own day. It is Weakness
that gives Maleger back his arrows, and that traps Arthur
into the clutch of Impatience, his most dangerous conflict in
the whole poem, and little experience is needed to prove how
right Spenser's psychology is here and in the next event. For
Timias the squire intervenes with more success than when
he was last mentioned in his attempt to help Arthur before

the Castle of Orgoglio. Many a man has been saved, when too much carried away for reason or conscience to be heard, by the instinctive recoil from infringing the understood code of his kind. Burke was mourning for something more substantial than an unbought grace of life, when he mourned the decay of honour, that inborn, unreasoned, holding to the man's side against the beast's which seems to lose its grip when there is no religion to assure that man really is more than beast.

Timias, therefore, saves Arthur, attacked and borne down by the two hags and Maleger, functioning as bodily sickness, together; but the essential combat with Maleger, the wound in our nature, Maleger-Concupiscence, must still be fought out by Arthur alone. Here Spenser makes brilliant use of the fable of Briareus whose strength is renewed by contact with the earth. Maleger, strong as a nightmare and with as little being, for he is evil, cannot die as long as he touches the earth. His life is in the body of this death, in the clay of our flesh. At last the prince understands this, and 'scruzing' out his life in the air, throws him into a pond. Possibly he is here thinking of baptism, but since Maleger represents the consequences of original sin rather than original sin itself, it would seem more appropriate if the pond stood for 'the fountains of the Saviour' in a more general sense: 'Who shall deliver me from the body of this death?' exclaims St. Paul (Rom. vii. 24, 25) and answers his own question 'The grace of God in Christ Jesus our Lord.' 'The body of this death' Maleger is an illustration which Blake might have painted, of these words.

Thus Arthur has performed for Guyon the same service as for the Red Cross Knight, though not in the same circumstances. By killing Orgoglio he freed the prisoner and thus made it possible for him, after further purification, to kill the dragon who drew his strength from pride. By killing Maleger, the enemy within, Arthur has made possible Guyon's relatively easy final conquest of Acrasia. Considering him simply as a story-teller, Spenser had another strong reason for this long and elaborately described conflict. As a romantic hero, Guyon is labouring under a great disadvantage by having to attack a woman, though she be Circe, Calypso,

Comus, all in one. He certainly cannot have with her such a combat as Spenser's readers would be expecting as the climax of the book. Artegall may attack Radigund for she is versed in fighting, and armed with sword and shield. Moreover, there was classical precedent. Acrasia's weapons are those of Salome the dancing girl. Besides, she is already defeated by Guyon's successful penetration of all her defences. The final scene instead of being a heroic struggle, is an episode like the taking of Ares and Aphrodite by Hephaistos as Ulysses heard it sung at the court of Alcinous. Psychologically, this is correct. Excess, specially in pleasure, is not normally conquered and self-mastery attained, by a single terrific effort, but by a long-continued series of lesser struggles. Guyon has been fighting Acrasia from the first moment he heard of her, and this encounter is only the final phase of the conflict. It would be interesting to know if St. Augustine's vivid account of a similar contest in the 'Confessions' had contributed to Spenser's thought on this subject; but in actual fact, the experience of living is all the source he would need.

All this is true; but all this is not tragic, dramatic, or in any way romantic or thrilling. Hence the narrative necessity of Arthur's combat with Maleger. But why not let Guyon kill Maleger? Partly, in all probability, because he cannot, any more than he can kill, destroy, Acrasia or Furor. It is only Arthur, the perfect man whose nature has its original integrity, who can eliminate not restrain. But also it is not Spenser's plan. Arthur is the real though hidden victor of both first and second books. He is not a genie coming out of a bottle at the right moment to rescue the hero, and then going back to it till the next occasion. He is himself the real hero of the whole poem, as opposed to the secondary protagonists of the various books, and, especially in the first two books, which narrate the restoration of the human soul to its right relation to God, and its right relation to its own complex being, he must play a vital part. In the later books his appearances may seem less crucial; but that is because the main battle has been already won.

To complete this discussion, I have been anticipating, and therefore summarize the narrative. Arthur has a big fight with a dangerous antagonist because Guyon cannot have a real bodily conflict with Acrasia, and yet, in a knightly narrative, a fight there must be. Allegorically, Maleger must be overcome, and Arthur only has strength to do it. In the meantime the two knights have remained in Alma's castle, where they are about to ascend to the rooms of her councillors, Imagination, Practical Wisdom, and Memory. In terms of time these faculties are referred to the future, the present and the past.

Like all the Renaissance scholars, Spenser had an immense respect for memory. As an index to intelligence it took the place now occupied by speed and slickness. This was natural at a time when the ability to remember the contents of books not immediately available, was of such great practical value. Hence the leading position given to Eumnestes. But surely some recollection of college libraries lurks behind Spenser's loving description of the apartment of Memory, its books and its tenant, the scholar aged yet still alert and still working, an anticipation of Browning's Grammarian, a portrait meant for the same period:

> That chamber seemed ruinous and old,
> And therefore was remoued farre behind,
> Yet were the wals, that did the same vphold,
> Right firme and strong, though somewhat they declind;
> And therein sate an old oldman halfe blind,
> And all decrepit in his feeble corse,
> Yet liuely vigour rested in his mind,
> And recompensed him with a better scorse:
> Weak body well is chang'd for minds redoubled forse.
>
> This man of infinite remembrance was,
> And things foregone through many ages held,
> Which he recorded still as they did pass
> Ne suffred them to perish through long eld,
> As all things else, the which this world doth weld,
> But laid them vp in his immortall scrine,
> Where they for euer incorrupted dweld:
> The warres he well remembered of King Nine,
> Of old Assaracus, and Inachus divine. (ii. ix. 55, 56)

The power of Spenser's melody is singularly felt in these

simple lines where no imagery reinforces the picture he none the less evokes.

Arthur the man, and Guyon the elf, each find the history of their own people in the charge of Eumnestes, and the tenth canto is devoted to narrating what they read. I have discussed the sources of Spenser's historical summary elsewhere, and the reader who is interested will find in Greenlaw's book on Spenser's historical allegory, the thesis that, in that allegory, the elves are the Welsh, and Guyon's book represents Welsh-Tudor history culminating in Queen Elizabeth, whereas Arthur's English chronicle can obviously not go beyond himself (it is completed by Merlin in Bk. III). However this may be, the reading itself has a part to play in the immediate context. (An interesting further analysis from another point of view is to be found in Rathborne's *Meaning of Spenser's Fairyland*, but its discussion is not relevant to the present purpose.)

It seems part of Spenser's usual technique that the protagonists of a story should, after their first great crises, be detained, set aside, as it were temporarily, from the main current of events, and made to follow a sort of educative process, after which they are near the culmination of their quest. The Red Cross Knight, who approaches the borders of Eden so soon after leaving the House of Coelia, is the most obvious illustration, but by no means the only one. Calidore's stay amid the Arcadian simplicities of Meliboeus' hut; Artegall's imprisonment in the Castle of Radigund, Britomart's painful inactivity while waiting for news of him, are all examples of that longer or shorter pause before the culminating effort which Spenser imposes on all his knights. Even Marinell and Florimell undergo something equivalent before being united.

On seeing the histories of their own countries, both knights are seized with the desire to read them, and both read with such absorption that they forget time and place. Arthur's chronicle, together with other tales that may still interest a later reader, gives at some length relatively, the story of Lear, with the happy ending which Shakespeare rejected, and breaks off abruptly at Uther Pendragon. It elicits from Arthur an outburst of patriotic feeling, as

though he whose figure stands in the poem as a sort of embodiment of that country to which a virgin queen was wedded,
had attained a new consciousness of himself; for as yet he
did not know his origin. No doubt this reading would have
led on to that last book in which, as one cannot doubt,
Spenser meant to show Arthur defeating the enemy hinted
at in Book One, and gaining both his kingdom and his
bride.

Guyon's case is a little different; for the history he reads is
that of Gloriana's house not his own, and one purpose of the
perusal was, probably, to detain him longer in that House of
Alma where he can breathe in the pure atmosphere of the
inward kingdom rightly ruled. But still, the reading is in
keeping with his own destiny when we consider the special
relation in which he stands to Gloriana. He has visited
the House of Medina, he is now in the House of Alma,
herself as

> Faire as faire mote euer bee,
> And in the flowre now of her freshest age,
> Yet full of grace and goodly modestee
> That euen heauen rejoyced her sweete face to see. (II. ix. 18)

In that house he has played, as usage required, the courtly
game with Shamefastness, too of 'louely face' and robed in
symbolic blue. But none of these are for him, or he for any
of them, and before he attempts the last stage of his quest,
and confronts the illusion of Acrasia's beauty, he is reminded
of the ideal far above him, the treasure in heaven, the perfection for whose sake he has pursued the path of his difficult
virtue. 'Everyone that striveth for the mastery refraineth
himself from all things: and they indeed that they may receive
a corruptible crown: but we an incorruptible' (1 Cor. ix. 25).
To serve Gloriana with complete self-abnegation is Guyon's
choice, and he is now reminded who and what she is whom
he thus serves. 'Fairer and nobler liueth none this howre....'

That this reading is felt as the climax of the preparation is
shown by the fact that the next morning, without any more
hesitation or doubt as to direction, knight and palmer set off
straight down to the river bank where Alma has appointed
a 'Ferriman' to row them direct to their destination; for
Acrasia's abode like Phaedria's or Circe's, or Calypso's, is

on an island. Since the quality required to get Guyon to his journey's end is will, it seems safe to assume that the Ferriman represents this, for which indeed, the figure of a rower is a very good symbol.

It is probably not a coincidence that water must be crossed to reach both Phaedria and Acrasia. In spite of the number of similes which Spenser draws from ships, waves, the wind at sea, he seems no great lover of river or ocean. In the present reference, the waters which Guyon has to traverse, though it does not appear that Atin or Cymochles did, may symbolize instability in general and, more especially, what makes human beings unstable, that is, excess of feeling, uncontrolled imagination, nervous excitability, all hostile to the virtue that Guyon represents.

A peculiarity appears here in the second book. Guyon in approaching the end of his trial, seems to recede a little, and the foremost place is taken by the palmer with the staff which only now proves to be 'vertuous'. The Red Cross Knight dominates in the last scenes, but Guyon still needs explanations, guidance, even admonition, and the last act of all is not performed without help. Temperance is the servant of Reason; but Holiness was the master.

The boat proceeds, day and night, across the sea waters that Spenser knew so well and trusted so little. It again illuminates his conception of Christian self-mastery that it is Guyon, of all the knights, who ventures on those wild wastes in nothing better than a rowing boat. They pass, with another adaptation of Scylla and Charybdis, between the Gulf of Greediness and the Rock of Reproach. It is not greed in the usual sense, but the overweening desire of this world's goods which yet are always escaping. To those who are lost here, there is not left even the poor consolation of returning as ghosts 'that often creep Back to the world bad livers to torment' (there is something singularly horrible about the idea of a creeping ghost), and thus at least see again what they loved so foolishly, though others possess it; they are swept down to darkness for ever. On the other side is a rock, or rather a rocky island, like the legendary loadstone island, with threatening cliffs above, and the wreck of ships below, the ships of the prodigal sons who never returned to their fathers. Yelling birds, flesh-eaters, perch there, waiting to swoop. It would be interesting to know if Spenser had really seen the high cliffs such as there are on more northern islands, where seabirds congregate in thousands, or whether his imagination built up the scene from some slighter hint.

They see next the wandering islands on one of which Phaedria from Idle Lake is seated, with her little skiff floating beside her, ready to distract and dissipate wherever she should be admitted. The islands are beautiful to look at, but capricious and unsure, useless fancies, vain expectations, velleities.

Whether or not the poet had seen such bird-thronged cliffs as there are at Lofoden, he had certainly noticed the checked, discoloured, water under which a quicksand lies. Its name, Unthriftyhead, shows its nature well enough, 'The expense of spirit in a waste of shame' Shakespeare was even then calling it. There, too, is the whirlpool with 'circled waters rapt with whirling spray', apt figure of the ruin of such lives sucked down and down.

And now all three are frightened, as the Ancient Mariner will be some centuries later, at the spectacle of the sea moving without wind, the frightening tremor of the imagination stirred from below. It brings no phantom ship, but all the nightmare monsters that have ever been seen or imagined in ocean depths: 'Most vgly shapes and horrible aspects', vain fears such as St. Augustine tells of, showing, incidentally, how much Spenser knew about nixies and kelpies and all the folklore of dangerous waters.[1] Had Shakespeare this passage in mind when he makes Alonzo, bereaved, exclaim:

> . . . Mine heir
> Of Milan and of Naples, what strange fish
> Has made his meal of thee?

Terrible as they are, they are illusions, and the palmer dispels them with that 'vertuous staff' which is so like a druid's wand.

The next encounter shows more subtlety. Guyon, of all the knights, is the quickest to compassion, and this quality is to be used to beguile him into yielding to soft emotion and

[1] Cf. however, Conrad Gesner, *Nomenclator aquatilium Animantium*, 1560.

weakening sentiment. But again the palmer exposes the
'womanish fine forgery'. Then comes that Sirens' song which
even Ulysses dared not listen to, and to which Spenser adds
a consort of enchanted viols and recorders:

> With that the rolling sea resounding soft,
> In his big base them fitly answered,
> And on the rocks the waues breaking aloft,
> A solemne Meane vnto them measured,
> The whiles sweet Zephirus lowd whisteled
> His treble, a straunge kind of harmony . . . (ii. xii. 33)

That, as Milton has it, Guyon should see, and know, and yet
abstain, is of the very essence of his virtue which is the
exquisite balance between the too little and the too much,
that makes peace between the warring elements in the world
and in man. But the sirens' temptation is one that all flesh
is heir to, especially the flesh of those who seek to advance in
virtue and the spiritual life, the temptation that now it is
enough, one may repose, enough has been gained:

> O turn thy rudder hitherward a while
> Here may thy storm-bet vessel safely ride:
> This is the port of rest from troublous toyle,
> The world's sweet In, from paine and wearisome turmoyle.
>
> (ii. xii. 32)

It is not by chance that the sirens' bewitching song should
almost be an echo of that of Despair:

> Is not short paine well borne that brings long ease,
> And layes the soul to sleep in quiet grave?
> Sleepe after toyle, port after stormie seas
> Ease after warre, death after life does greatly please. (i. ix. 40)

'That strain again, it had a dying fall.' No wonder if Guyon's
first motion was to listen only for a moment to the melody.
But Reason quickly intervenes, and the knight sails on un-
harmed; for the first motion, which no one can control, is not
sinful. Spenser always distinguishes these things with great
precision.

There follows darkness and the flight of ill-omened birds,
a sudden reaction of irrational fear and doubt, to be ignored,
not fought with, and then light and the island itself; the
voyage is over. Atin, seeking Cymochles, had come a shorter

way, but Acrasia knew him no enemy. These mirage defences, perceptible only to the hostile, suggest a certain resemblance with those curious Chinese allegorical illusions of which Dr. Chang has told us.[1]

The landing itself, however, recalls like the sirens, the landings of Ulysses and the islands both of Calypso and of Circe. Like him they are greeted by the howlings of wild beasts; they have reached to brutish passion undisguised. Here the poet takes occasion to tell us of the divine quality reposing in the palmer's staff. The strength of natural reason alone, though sovereign against illusion, is not enough when irrational bodily passion is aroused: 'Not by logic has it pleased the Lord to save His people', said St. Ambrose. The palmer, Christian Reason, is reason aided by grace. Temperance, though first for Spenser in the order of natural virtues, is not natural in the humanistic sense which would make man and his qualities self-sufficient. No one receives such obvious actual graces as Guyon; the angel is for him, and for him is the staff impregnated with spiritual strength which subdues the beasts, as it could subdue even 'the Furyes when they most doe rage'.

Spenser's conception of the garden the two now enter must be understood in relation to that of the Temple of Venus and the Garden of Adonis; and these are inspired by that idea of the relations of nature, art, and earth, which has been already discussed. The poet has been blamed for lavishing the full power of his genius on making this Bower of Bliss as alluring as possible. But the whole point of Guyon's trial is that he cannot have it out with a giant or a dragon, but is always under attack like Alma's castle, and has as his worst enemy, the rebel nature within. It is not in the last brief episode in Canto XII that he overcomes Acrasia; but by the thousand nameless contests fought by the way. When he reaches the witch herself he is already victor; for that reason he takes her helpless in her sleep. Little merit were there in that victory if an easy conflict had preceded against a facile enemy. Guyon's can be no fugitive and cloistered virtue; it must be proof against all that Spenser can marshal

---

[1] Cf. Dr. Chang, *Allegory and Courtesy in Spenser*, pp. 23 et seq. Edinburgh University Press, 1955.

against it, reinforced by Tasso and Ariosto as allies, for some
of this description, notably the episode of the maidens in
the fountain, is actual translation from the Italian, and the
Gardens of Alcina and Armida are obvious parallels. Real
good and real beauty, but perverted from the proper end, this
is the secret, and the malice, of the Bower of Bliss. Yet
Spenser has not left the reader without due warning; the
outer gate is watched, not guarded, by a significant figure,
there, but falsely, called Genius:

> He of this Garden had the gouernall,
> And Pleasures porter was devized to bee,
> Holding a staffe in hand for more formalitee—

a sort of counter-figure to the palmer. He has several notable
characteristics, 'semblaunce pleasing *more than naturall*', but
yet unfit, in his womanish drapery, 'for speedy pace or manly
exercize'. But, though with an aspect 'That trauellers to him
seemd to entize', and with an emblematic bowl of wine, he is
not really the true Genius:

> Not that celestial powre to whom the care
> Of life and generation of all
> That liues pertaines in charge particulare . . . ,

but

> The foe of life, that good enuyes to all,
> That secretly doth us procure to fall
> Through guilefull semblaunts which he makes us see.
>
> (II. xii. 47)

Again Spenser's favourite contrast between the false and the
true, being and not-being, false life which can reproduce
nothing but barren imitation, art in the bad sense which
Spenser gives it, contrasted with the true sentinel of that
garden of generation where the mighty energies of real life
truly directed, are working. Spenser's symbol is justified; the
garden of sensual indulgence is really entered by a false ideal
of life and art and, in spite of its lovely appearance, 'more
sweet and holesome than the pleasant hill of Rhodope', it is
sterile and full of things which seem to be what they are not:
a gate which is not a gate, wreathed in a vine where artificial
gold grapes are mixed with the real ones, watched by a
figure of Excesse already coarser and more degenerate than

that of false Genius. Guyon, who has passed through the
outer purlieus wondering at the beauty around him but not,
so to speak, taking it to himself: 'Bridling his will and
maistering his might', passes Excess with indifference and
enters the inner garden:

> There the most daintie Paradise on ground,
> Itselfe doth offer to his sober eye
> In which all pleasures plenteously abound,
> And none does others' happinesse enuye:
> The painted flowres, the trees vpshooting hye,
> The dales of shade, the hilles for breathing space,
> The trembling groues, the Christall running by:
> And that, which all faire workes doth most aggrace,
> That art which all that wrought appeared in no place. (ii. xii. 58)

If Spenser had been speaking of that first paradise of innocence which Milton describes for us, he could hardly have
spoken otherwise, but, as he proceeds with the description,
we see again how the false is mingled with the true, perver-
ting it. There is here no alliance between art and nature such
as he describes in connexion with the Temple of Venus, but
a rivalry and confusion of function, so that the ivy which
overspreads the famous fountain, is really of gold, coloured
green, alive only with the horrible energy of corruption.

Guyon cannot pass that fountain and its maidens without
the natural physical reaction the absence of which would
remove all merit from his resistance; but he does pass it,
though not without the palmer's warning him to guard his
eyes better. And now music again, one of the most charming
of Spenser's evocations of the part-singing and playing which
was so much the characteristic social pleasure of his time. But
these are Lydian airs, sweet and enervating, banished therefore from Plato's republic, and with the *carpe diem* motif which
is so often heard as an undertone to Renaissance luxury. This
is the last appeal to armoured knight and black-robed palmer,
figures both from another philosophy, and it is made in vain.

The danger now is not that the enemy may conquer; but
that she may escape. Spenser is here facing a difficulty inherent in his subject. Acrasia, in the abstract, is Self-indul-
gence, but, in the concrete, she is a beautiful woman, taken
by surprise, unprotected. Somewhat the same situation had

arisen in Book One. But Duessa had come actively to Orgoglio's aid riding her dragon, we know her treacherous intervention with Night, and her hideous reality has been described by Fradubio, and is again revealed when her power fails her. This may pass, but the reader could not see two armed men rushing upon Acrasia unaware and admire them. The poet evades the difficulty by using another device from those adventures of Ulysses which seem to have been so much in his mind while he has been telling Guyon's story. Acrasia and her companion are taken in a net as Hephaistos seizes Aphrodite, and a few lines suffice for the whole struggle, which the poet is too wise to dwell upon. There follows a destruction of the beauties of that beautiful place which might seem sheer vandalism if we did not recall the falsehood and perversion that corrupted it. This has been only the beauty of a drugged dream or a mirage. Death was inherent to it, as its own inhabitants know.

However, the last act of Guyon is not one of destruction; for the end to which temperance is directed is not negative, but positive good. Its triumph means the restoration of Acrasia's victims to the human level. But here Spenser's thought goes farther than Homer's fairy-tale. These enchanted men had assumed forms which symbolized their own moral debasement. They do not welcome their forcible reformation, they resist it: 'Let Gryll be Gryll and have his hoggish mind.' Thus the book ends on a note of sadness which makes us turn to another's wisdom: 'Take from no one what he loves unless thou art prepared to give him something that he loves still better.'

This is the end of Book Two, but not of Guyon's story; there is no more rest for him than for any other of Gloriana's 'Knights of Maydenhede'; virtue may be perfected, but the world is not ended. Book Three shows him rejoining Arthur in Alma's castle, sending Acrasia under guard to Cleopolis, and himself seeking further adventure in the company of the prince. But the next adventure narrated at length, is the puzzling encounter of Guyon and Britomart, in which Guyon is defeated. Temperance defeated by Chastity; it requires some explanation.

From the point of view of the story, it certainly provides

a dramatic entrance for Britomart, who thus begins the book devoted to her, while Guyon's chagrin, the palmer's arguing, and Arthur's tactful handling of the situation form another illustration of Spenser's humorous observation. But how does this fit the allegory? When beginning Book Two in very much the same way, by an encounter between the protagonist of Book One and the new hero, Spenser had carefully, and by a touching device, avoided any real conflict, concerned as he is to show grace as the crown of nature, not its enemy. But Guyon is most signally and unequivocally defeated by Britomart's enchanted spear.

One must first consider that though technically in ethics chastity may be considered as only a sub-virtue, or department, of temperance, it had in fact long established a special position. In part, this was traditional. However much the laws of chastity might have been disregarded in the medieval cult of courtly love, there is no doubt of the contemporaneous respect for chastity as such, stemming at least in part, from devotion to the Blessed Virgin, and nourished by appreciation of the ideal expressed in monastery, convent, and celibate priesthood. Many a legend and story, not least in Chaucer, glorified the cult of chastity, and this cult had certainly suffered no eclipse in the court of the Virgin Queen. It is brought significantly forward in the drama of the period. How often Shakespeare's plots involve chastity, accused or attacked, in wife, or maiden.

Yet, granted that chastity had, for various reasons, attained this high, independent, position in popular esteem, is it not going a little far to make it actually defeat temperance? The reason may probably be found in the fact that Spenser, guided by the Epistle to the Galatians (v. 22), where chastity is named as a fruit of the Spirit, is thinking of it as a supernatural grace, infused from above. In the recipient it may indeed be made possible by Guyon's efforts; but it surpasses his unaided attainment. Britomart is that chastity of which Milton will say that, should it be in need, 'heaven itself would stoop to her', as indeed it did, and sat on the point of her enchanted spear. That supernatural chastity exercised a sort of miraculous power over wild tempers and wild beasts was a common belief, illustrated by many stories, a regular

characteristic of heroines of romance, and not without contemporary evidence to confirm it. Britomart is Spenser's one
unconquerable figure. Arthur himself once needed the help
of his squire for, in fine, he is a man, subject to sickness and
death if to nothing else; but Britomart, though refusing no
friendship, needs no human help. It is usual in Spenser to
suggest in the preceding books the virtue which is to be the
motif of a later one: the three, Guyon, Britomart, Arthur,
now vow eternal friendship and mutual aid, 'and with that
golden chaine of concorde tyde', they go on together. Concord is the virtue next to be illustrated, but doubtless Spenser
also wished to insist that temperance and chastity, though
the one be got by labour, and the other given by grace, can
have no lasting quarrel. There follows one of Spenser's most
beautiful invocations, recalling that ancient and too visionary
time when right, not interest, was the cause of war:

> O goodly vsage of those antique times,
> In which the sword was seruant vnto right:
> When not for malice or contentious crimes,
> But all for praise and proof of manly might,
> The martiall brood accustomed to fight:
> Then honour was the meed of victorie
> And yet the vanquished had no despight
> Let later age that noble vse envie
> Vile rancour to avoide and cruel surquedrie. (III. i. 13)

Spenser, a civil servant in the Ireland of the first Elizabeth,
might well say so.

The next event begins a curious and in some ways enigmatic story, which will occupy a fair proportion of this and the
two following books, and though Spenser may have learned
from his Italian master to weave stories together into a rich
and complex whole, that art cannot be the only reason.

The *Faerie Queene* is among other things, a *roman à clef*,
and it may be that Spenser's first readers saw a meaning in
the love story of Marinell and Florimell which is lost to us.
But the factual or historical aspect of Spenser's allegory was
never his main interest, and this story, particularly with its
marked insistence on Florimell's surpassing beauty and
lovableness, must also have had another significance for him.
Guyon, who is present at this beginning of the tale, passes off

the stage in pursuit of Florimell, and only reappears at the
happy ending in Book Five, when he also regains the horse
Brigadore that he had lost at the outset of his own adventure,
the poet making gentle fun at the same time of those two
serious-minded persons, Guyon and Artegall.

In view of this surely deliberate association with Guyon,
and to avoid returning over the same ground in successive
chapters, it seems well to discuss the whole story of Florimell
and Marinell at this point; in the hope of determining exactly
who these two are, why Florimell, in particular, is so important, and why this story alone can be concluded. I discuss
elsewhere certain historical interpretations.

It must first of all be noted that the principal theme of this
and the following book is love, love in its human aspect, the
direct love of God having been dealt with in Book One, this
being inseparable from sanctity. Florimell, then, whose story
takes up as much place as Britomart's own, represents some
quality closely related to chaste love, but also capable of
mimicry by the witch's sham. Chastity in a general sense is
represented by Britomart herself, chaste married love is seen
in Amoret and Scudamore, chaste friendship in Arthur, and
also in the two sets of noble friends Cambell and Triamond,
Canacee and Cambina, chaste lovers are Aemylia and Amyas,
courtly love is seen chaste in Timias, chastity in chosen
virginity in Belphoebe; while their contraries, parodies, and
enemies are seen in Blandamour, Paridell, Hellenore, Malecasta, and many more. There is no place for Florimell here
though she can love, be loved, and is finally wedded. Her
'beauty's wonderment' surpasses that of all the other fairest
ladies, even Amoret, even Gloriana:

> A fairer wight did neuer sunne behold
> And on a palfrey rides more white than snow,
> Yet she herselfe is whiter manifold:
> The surest signe whereby ye may her know
> Is that she is the fairest wight alive I trowe. (III. v. 5)

Like a magnet this beauty draws after it Gloriana's true
lovers Guyon and Arthur. Even the false lovers admire and
respect her; Satyrane, Una's defender and friend, has given
his heart to her; the witch cannot be harsh to her, the witch's
brutish son is sick with love of her, and though she is usually

seen defending her honour, they are brutelike men, monsters, or inhuman beings such as Proteus, who distress her, no one with any tincture of civility, or even natural humanity: 'For all the world rejoiced in Florimell.' Yet her story alone is finished, as though she would have no part in that final climax when virtue and right were to triumph, and all the quests be ended. Moreover, Marinell, her husband, half a sea-creature, is himself mysterious, neither knight errant like Satyrane, nor following Gloriana's commands like the others, the knights of Maydenhead. Her name, too, suggests something lovely as a flower, sweet as honey, exquisite indeed, and chaste as Belphoebe herself (the famous girdle, the test of chastity, is hers), but somehow touching and fragile as even Amoret and Serena are not. She shows herself trustful and unthinking of evil, or human opinion, yet resolute both in flight and defence when evil is thrust upon her. When she is attacked by the 'fosters', and in her flight draws Arthur and Guyon after her—once panic-stricken, she flies beyond reason. She has been hastening without a thought of self to the help of Marinell whom she believes wounded or slain. He is, in fact, about to fall under Britomart's spear. When she takes refuge in the witch's hut the witch is struck with terror at the sight of her; but afterwards thinks to adore her for her beauty: 'T'adore thing so diuine as beauty were but right'; the lumpish 'laesie' son is equally awestruck at first, and neither the one nor the other understands what it is which is so beautiful. For the moment both 'wicked woman' and 'wicked sonne' are tamed as Una's lion had been. But brutalized human beings are more brutish than animals, and the Chorle who cannot feel love itself, feels love's desire. Even so he is restrained by a power beyond himself:

> Yet had he not the hart or hardiment
> As vnto her to vtter his desire . . .

So much of human still remained in him. But when she goes away passion embodies itself in the hideous monster which pursues her. She takes refuge on the sea, a dangerous expedient with Spenser, is rescued from a fisherman by Proteus and by him imprisoned in ocean depths till she will yield to him.

Having regard to the whole theme of Spenser at this point, and also to the other parts he has apportioned, there seems but one quality which corresponds to all the requirements. Florimell represents innocence in that first freshness which, though not altogether ignorant, is as yet untouched even by temptation in the opposite sense. Such innocence even a Paridell respects, and to Guyon and Arthur, being what they are, she is a vision of surpassing beauty, a glimpse, like Michelangelo's Adam, of what man was before the Fall. Britomart as an allegorical figure, may well perceive that such a quality, so protected, has no need of aid from her, and as a human character, by a very natural touch, thinks that the having drawn away both her companions ought to be enough without her following as well (Spenser hints at Archimago's machinations here). Yet Britomart enters Florimell's story more effectively than either Guyon or Arthur, for it is she who gives Marinell the deadly wound of which Florimell has, apparently, heard a prophetic rumour—unless that too had been part of Archimago's game.

Marinell is altogether a more puzzling figure than Florimell. As a mythical figure, the child of a sea-nymph, he recalls with his territory of the Rich Strand, the Irish god of headlands, and also all the folklore and ballad legendry about the marrying of neckans with human beings. But to interpret the whole story as solely a nature myth, like that where the Fomorian from the sea wedded the child of the divine race on earth, would not be in Spenser's manner, nor in the manner of his time, in spite of the episode of the marriage of Thames and Medway which is associated with Marinell's adventures. In addition, it would not explain Florimell's special character, nor Spenser's insistence that Marinell's humanity dominates his sea-nature. He lives by the sea, he can live under it, its riches are tributary to him; but the earth is his home, and when he marries Florimell his sea-character seems to sink into abeyance, and to leave him wholly an earthly knight. Perhaps by that time he has lost his allegorical character and is only a figure in the story since, though the poem is a continued dark conceit illustrated from time to time by historical parallels, there are moments when the story is only a story. Perhaps Spenser is only using such legends as those alluded to above, as far as they serve his purpose, since Florimell was to have a lover, and tournaments on her account formed part of the structure of the romance. But there seems allegorical intention at least in the first part of Marinell's story, when we consider the general theme of love and chastity which Spenser is working out in these books. For who can marry Innocence? No one surely, who has been touched by the world as it is. She is not for Satyrane, but for Marinell.

At the beginning Marinell who, warned by his mother, rejects the love of women, even the exquisite Florimell's, and keeps apart from human society, is not really manifesting a virtue. Belphoebe is virgin through deliberate choice of what she holds the higher state; Marinell is simply afraid to experience love. It is Britomart, Chastity, who strikes him down, and it is in consequence of that wound that Marinell, wandering undersea during his recovery, finds the prison of Florimell. Now healed by the wound of chastity of his timid coldness, and ignorant, negative, innocence, he learns what pure love may be. Knowing this, he is no longer a solitary defending his sterile gold on the sea strand; but becomes a noble knight, and takes part with others in the usages of chivalry.

But the story of Florimell and Marinell is rendered more complex by the addition of two other characters. The first is Satyrane who might in many respects seem a fitter choice for Florimell than the son of Cymoent, for, though Satyrane too is but half-human, his other half-nature is of earth, not of the withdrawing sea. But perhaps because of this very suitability, which excludes the element of healing and reconciliation, Satyrane like Guyon is destined to love faithfully, but in vain. Yet Satyrane is prominent in the story; it is he who finds the girdle, the test of chastity; he who binds with it the monster of jealous passion, he who, after other adventures in which he is always the defender of right, holds the tournament for the prize of the girdle which, of all the ladies present, Amoret alone can wear. The half-satyr nature in him, as in the satyr rescuers of Una, seems to have been mingled of the gentler elements of the forest, the strength and courage that his father taught him, freedom, simplicity, frankness, the innocence of civilized sins, which Arcadian surroundings connoted to that age. His dual nature is, in fact, harmonious as Marinell's is not, and though he loves Florimell, he does not need her for completeness.

The second figure is that of the false Florimell, the witch's snow image, whose character offers further proof that the true Florimell stands for innocence. For whereas the true Florimell has the courage of trustfulness proper to one who thinks no evil, the false Florimell goes boldly to anyone because she does not care what happens, and has neither love nor fidelity nor anything real to give. However, she prefers Braggadochio, for like will to like, and he too is a sham. The two Florimells are contrasted as innocence with shamelessness, but 'truth is a touchstone', and when they meet at last, false Florimell disappears like the snow wreath she is.

Perhaps it is not too fanciful to suggest that the allegory may carry a double burden, and that Spenser, who introduces himself and his own bride in Book Six, was in the two Florimells contrasting the convention of courtly, Petrarchan love with genuine human affection. Then false Florimell stands to true, as Idea and all the other insubstantial objects of the sonnet sequences, stand to her for whom the Amoretti were written. Here may be one reason why this story only is ended; the contrast with the sterile emotion of fashionable love poetry required that the genuine lovers should reach the normal conclusion of happy marriage. In this way Spenser's study of human love is completed by a sketch which bears out what he says more explicitly in *Colin Clout's Come Home Again*:

> And is loue then (said Corylas) once knowne
> In Court, and his sweet lore professed there?
> I weened sure he was our God alone:
> And only woond in fields and forests here.
> Not so (quoth he) loue most aboundeth there,
> For all the walls and windows there are writ
> All full of loue, and loue, and loue my deare,
> And all their talk and study is of it.
> Ne any there doth braue or valiant seeme,
> Vnless that some gay Mistresse badge he beares:

Ne anyone himself doth ought esteeme,
Vnless he swim in loue vp to the eares.
But they of loue and of this sacred lore,
(As it should be) all otherwise deuise,
Then we poore shepheardes are accustomed here,
And him do serue and sue all otherwise . . .

Of that 'otherwise' snow-Florimell and her passing amours
is the symbol.

The story of Florimell and Marinell serves as one means towards the structural development and unity of the three books
where love is specially treated. Florimell's first appearance
affords an exit for Sir Guyon, and an occasion for Britomart's
being left free to pursue her own quest. Satyrane's tournament, at which the girdle of chastity, and then false Florimell
herself, are the prizes, creates a situation which launches
other adventures, and lastly Marinell's tournament in Book
Five in honour of his wedding, when Braggadochio is unmasked, and false Florimell unmade, serves as a secondary
climax in which the problems and actions set in motion in
the third and fourth books reach a solution and leave the
field clear for Artegall.

Among those who make their last appearance at that
tournament is Sir Guyon. His deeds are not described—
doubtless they were valiant—but when Braggadochio is unmasked, Guyon recognizes his horse, his Brigadore, which
the false knight had stolen from him at the beginning of
Book Two. His eager claiming of his steed, and Brigadore's
own refusal to let anyone else handle him, are charmingly
told. Still more revealing of Spenser's secret irony is the
little following scene when Guyon, whose passionate seizing
of his own right has just been checked by Artegall's prudent
counsels, checks Artegall in his turn when the Knight of
Justice too is touched upon the raw:

Much was the knight incensed with his lewd word,
To haue reuenged that his villiny:
And thrise did lay his hand vpon his sword,
To haue him slaine; or dearely doen aby,
But Guyon did his choler pacify . . .

The meeting of Justice and Temperance is that of Greek and
Greek.

Thus Guyon regains his horse, symbol of the physical constituent of man with its energies and desires, by Temperance alone to be moderated and guided. Having regained it he passes silently from the scene. Not even the palmer accompanies him now, and when the whole story is to be ended with Gloriana's final triumph and the fruition of all the other knights, it will still be Guyon's lot to rejoice for others, not for himself. Christian self-mastery and Hellenic balance, temperance is a lonely virtue even though, as Sir Lancelot could not, it can walk upright across the sword-blade bridge.

V

CHASTITY, LOVE, AND CONCORD

IN this chapter is comprehended that part of the poem where Britomart is a principal figure; that is to say, Books Three and Four, with a part of Book Five; in this section the main theme throughout is chastity in love.

Britomart in one aspect of her dual personality may seem a little hard and repellant with her unprovoked attacks, and her enchanted spear. But in her other aspect she makes, together with Una and Florimell, the third of the three graces of Spenser's mythology. Even Pastorella has less human appeal than this warrior princess who, out of her armour, is so vulnerable.

The first part of her story is one of the most charming pieces of Spenser's fairy-tale narrative, in which, however, the protagonists are as human as the Imogens, Mirandas, Perditas, who owe so much to them. Temperance and Chastity, despite their outward severity, are the two most romantic of the poet's personages, except Arthur himself, whom Britomart resembles in more than the striking similarity of their private quests, the one for the woman he has seen in a dream, the other for the man she has seen in a mirror. Not only does Britomart never need Arthur's help for herself; but she is also equally a saviour and helper in her own sphere of action; in fact in her own book she is chiefly shown in that capacity. Chastity is a source of strength to its possessor.

Yet it would be a pity to insist too much on the allegory at the beginning of Book Three; it is better to leave it its own enchanted atmosphere of magic and romance; a Malory king and castle, with a lovely daughter and a magic mirror, like that of Virgil in the *Gesta Romanorum*, in which is seen Artegall wearing the armour of Achilles. Then follows the visit to the white magician's cave; but this, like Glauce's charm, is not Malory, but sheer folklore. Merlin's prophetic visions here form a parallel to the chronicles read in Book Two which they continue. Certainly a compliment to Queen

Elizabeth I was being worked in, and Spenser was establishing a claim to be the Virgil of England, with the Tudor sovereign for his Augustus (Britomart's descendants are traced as far as 'a royall virgin's raine'). Nevertheless, this second and third canto, culminating in the romantic departure to seek the reality of the vision which she has seen, as Arthur saw Gloriana, or Angus the swan-maiden, must chiefly stand as an example of Spenser's art simply as a narrative poet.

In keeping with his usual method, Spenser begins the adventures of Britomart in the middle, and the story I have alluded to is introduced by way of explanation in the second and third cantos of the book. This explanation is called for both to account for Britomart, and also to set out the theme of chastity in love which will occupy the poet until the focus shifts to justice in Book Five. In all this section Spenser will follow a system which he has already used more simply in the tale of Guyon's adventures. The Knight of Temperance not only falls in with tempters and qualities hostile to his own, he also encounters Medina and Alma, both manifesting aspects or functions of the virtue of which he is himself the major example. In the same way, but much more elaborately, Britomart encounters not only the various enemies of her virtue, but also those who display it in special aspects. She herself represents chastity in its more general and universal sense, and since this virtue is most usually exercised in the relations of ordinary life, Britomart's career, as completed by Merlin's vision, shows her as girl, wife, and mother. But as these later functions fall outside the action of the poem, they must also be illustrated within the poem itself by other personages. Moreover, the struggle towards perfect chastity is not seen in Britomart who has received it as a gift, which she must all the same fight to defend, since she has this treasure in an earthen vessel. That struggle forms part of the tale of Amoret and Scudamour, chaste wife and chaste husband, while in Florimell we see the girl as yet unaware in her innocence. Aemyllia illustrates another aspect of this theme, while the mother is shown from one point of view in the figure of Venus Genetrix, the foster-mother of Amoret, this idea being more fully exposed in the descrip-

tion of the Garden of Adonis. Other aspects of motherhood
are seen in Cymoent, mother of Marinell, in Agape and her
three sons, and also in the delightful passing picture of the
mother of Satyrane. The chastity of deliberately preferred
virginity is represented by Belphoebe, twin-sister of Amoret
but fostered by Diana. She has already appeared in Book
Two as a terror to the coarse and vulgar Braggadochio and
his treacherous servant who both, though uncomprehending,
felt

> ... how awful Goodness is, and saw
> Virtue in her form how lovely—

It is clear that, in the conditions both of his time and of
his story, Spenser could not represent virginity otherwise
than by the classical figure of the virgin-huntress. But it is no
part of his conception that Belphoebe should be supposed
merely cold, unloving, or solitary. She is, in fact, actively
beneficent, a helper of the unfortunate, a healer of wounds,
ready with the love of friendship if her friends will accept the
limitation she imposes. She who in a certain sense loves all;
but gives herself to none, is another reality contradictory to
the counterfeit, snow-made Florimell who loves, and can
love, no one; but who gives herself to all as a barren gift
without fruition. Evidently also, though all the chaste and
beautiful women of the poem may at moments stand for
Queen Elizabeth, yet, as long as Gloriana herself cannot
enter the scene, Belphoebe will be her best image, as indeed,
is made clear in the Timias episode which hints at the
Queen's vexation when Raleigh married.

But the alternatives of marriage and virginity do not exhaust
the possibilities of chaste love, Spenser's real subject. Of his
lofty conception of marriage more will be said later in connexion with Amoret; but Spenser, who had been Sidney's
friend and Raleigh's, who had risked much in his fidelity to
Leicester and to Grey, can certainly not conceive of love as
existing only in that relationship. Therefore, throughout
Books Three and Four, he glorifies the love of friendship
which he seems to identify with that virtue of *concordia* to
which the Romans erected a temple.

In treating of the love of friendship, Spenser was taking

up again a medieval, even a classical, theme, as he is taking up and transcending the still more popular theme of courtly love. He is too sane to go to the extremes portrayed in such a tale as that of Amis and Amile, for example; but he takes trouble to show pure and unshaken friendship subsisting in every imaginable human relationship; that between equals of the same sex, as Britomart and Amoret, Cambell and Triamond, that of opposite sexes, as Britomart and Scudamour, or Arthur with Amoret and Aemyllia. The friendship where love has made the equality which it did not find, is seen between Britomart and Glauce, and between Arthur and Timias, while perhaps the most original of all Spenser's variations in friendship is shown in the affectionate loyalty of the Salvage Man to Serena, and in his instant response to the attraction of Arthur's high character. Indeed, this motif worked out at such length by Spenser, receives another series of brilliant illustrations in the Sixth Book where Calidore, the chivalrous lover of Pastorella, is everybody's friend, even his rival's, and is also the one to whom Spenser concedes the supreme award of friendship by showing him in a vision the bride of Colin Clout.

Why then should the poet start with a heroine standing for chastity, if his real subject is human love in all its manifestations? Why should his treatment of love begin at just this point of his whole story, and why should the union of Justice and Chastity be an indispensable theme in it?

Logically it would be appropriate that the treatment of chastity should follow that of temperance, since chastity is in fact one aspect or department of the larger virtue, though, taking it here as the fruit of the Spirit, Spenser counts it higher in dignity. Moreover, what has already passed in connexion with Acrasia is a necessary preliminary to any treatment of chastity or love, especially of love in marriage. The shame of Cymochles, of Acrasia, of the foolish Verdante, and indeed of all Guyon's special enemies and tempters, had lain in treating the means as the end and, in the case of most of them, using for mere indulgence the pleasure which had been intended to promote the proper purpose of marriage. This, with the ancillary infidelity, had been the ruin of Mordant at the very beginning of the story. Even the sin to which

Mammon tempted was not simply the desire of money, money being indifferent, neither good or evil of itself, but the desire of money as an end independently of its use.

All this doctrine underlies Spenser's thought in Book Three, and is specially necessary to the understanding of the principal story, that in which Britomart interrupts her own quest to come to the aid of Scudamour in the rescue of Amoret. It applies also to the elaborate inset narration of the birth and bringing up of the twin sisters Belphoebe and Amoret, the virgin and the chaste wife; while the Garden of Adonis is deliberately set in contrast with that of the Bower of Bliss.[1] Since Britomart's first exploit, the overthrowing of Marinell, has been already discussed, it is possible to proceed at once to this part of the subject.

Chrysogone, mother of the twins, was of faerie descent, but her daughters are born without a human or an elfin father, and even without the mother's knowledge of the sun's intervention. As Belphoebe was to be identified with Elizabeth I, this was a prudent precaution on the poet's part, and it had enough classical precedent not to appear too forced. If Professor Greenlaw is right that in the historical allegory the elves stand for the Welsh, this would explain the insistence on Chrysogone's faerie descent.

And now the poet explains the formation of these two exponents of the two principal aspects of chastity. Belphoebe is adopted by Diana 'To be vpbrought in perfect maydenhed', Amoret by Venus 'to be vpbrought in goodly womanhed' in the Garden of Adonis. In Spenser's mythology Venus represents the source whereat life is generated and form imposed on chaos. He describes her heavenly dwelling as:

> The house of goodly forms and faire aspects,
> Whence all the world derives the glorious
> Features of beautie, and all shapes select,
> With which high God his workmanship hath deckt. (III. vi. 12)

He had spoken similarly in another poem published in 1596, though, by his own account, composed earlier, where he addresses her as:

> . . . great Goddess, queen of Beauty,

[1] *F.Q.* III. vi.

> Mother of Love, and of all world's delight
> Without whose soverayne grace and kindly dewty,
> Nothing on earth seems fayre to fleshly sight . . .
>
> *(Hymn to Beauty)*

She is the custodian—Spenser was also a Platonist—of the Idea of Beauty, whence all that is beautiful is derived: 'That wondrous Paterne whereso'er it be', and from her it flows upon earth in all that is good and fair. The instrument of this is the Garden of Adonis:

> . . . a joyous Paradize,
> Where most she wonnes when she on earth doth dwel,
> So faire a place as nature can devise . . . (IV. vi. 29)

It is surrounded by two walls, of gold and of iron, and through its two gates passes out and in the unending stream of life in living forms, new and renewed. Here watches Genius, the true Genius of whom Acrasia's guardian was a base counterfeit,

> Not that celestiall powre, to whom the care
> Of life and generation of all
> That liues pertains in charge particulare . . . (II. xii. 47)

but the foe of life. Spenser is full of the love and admiration of life, and all the processes by which it is generated or preserved are precious to him, while all that frustrates it is hateful; this powerful conviction underlies his contrast of the two gardens, one of frustration, and the other of fruition; and the two passions, one false and barren, the other pure and fecund, of which he began the illustration with the tale of Florimell.

The true Genius, then, of the Garden of Adonis, gives to each being its right material form and since here all beauty and harmony reign, all know their own place and take it of themselves. Here the trees bear both fruit and flower at the same time, not by a dead and sterile imitation, but by superabundance of life. Within, 'in the middest of that Paradise', is the abode of Adonis himself, 'Father of all formes', 'eterne in mutabilities'. Spenser seems to envisage here a fruitful union or marriage between Venus, source of earthly love and human beauty, and Adonis, the principle of material life, ever changing its outward appearance or passing from one to

another, but never lost or destroyed. But Spenser is careful
to tell us that all this is still of earth, earth at its most beautiful and fertile, but still earth, subject to Time.

> ... who with his scyth addrest,
> Does mow the flowring herbes and goodly things.

Here lives also the grown-up Cupid, faithful to Psyche,
mother of Pleasure. Spenser is no puritan suspicious of
pleasure in itself. In her right context she is beautiful and
innocent, pleasing to gods and men, and with her is Amoret
to be brought up. Here, in the highest perfection of their
nature, are all the things which had been perverted and misused in the Bower of Bliss.

Scudamour's account of the Temple of Venus in Book
Four, x, should be compared with this of the Garden of
Adonis. And let it trouble no reader if, in Book Three, vi.
52, Venus is said to have brought Amoret to 'Faery Court'

> to be th'ensample of true love alone,
> And lodestarre of all chaste affectione;

and that it is further told that, sought by many, she chose Sir
Scudamour; whereas in Scudamour's own story in Book
Four, he won her by force of arms at the Temple of Venus.
For the Temple of Venus, like the Garden of Adonis, or the
House of Alma, or the Castle in the *Roman de la Rose*, is not
to be thought of as a clumsy structure of lumpish clay crudely
and coarsely anchored to one piece of ground. When Scudamour overcame his many rivals in Gloriana's court in Cleopolis, he also struck down the twenty knights who attacked
him outside the Temple of Venus. In actual fact, the whole
action of all six books and all the land of faerie with its
forests, castles, and sea-shores, exist in Arthur's soul, and
there only. It is within him that the drama of transformation
of the struggling actual into the triumphant ideal, is really
taking place. Like Hamlet, he can count himself the lord of
infinite space; but his dreams are good. The events of the
narrative are identical whether expressed in moral or
material terms.

Scudamour, then, obtained the shield of love which carried
with it the claim to Amoret, by striking down these twenty
knights, the sentinels of the bridge that leads to the fortified

entrance of the island where Venus's temple stands. Was
Spenser, perhaps, thinking of the bridge to the strange land
of Gorres which Lancelot had to cross in the *Chevalier à la
Charette* of Chretien de Troyes? However that may be, the
fortress itself is such a one as Guillaume de Lorris might
have described. At its door stand Doubt and Delay. The
second gate, of 'Good desert', is guarded by Danger, also a
familiar figure to readers of the *Roman de la Rose*. He, a
terror to others, yields with all his attendant evils to the enchanted shield of love, and the knight passes on to another
garden which outdoes in rare device the Bower of Bliss itself
but, significant fact to Spenser, 'All which by nature made,
did nature self amaze'. At the door of the temple proper
stands Concord—Book Four treats of friendship—whose
sons are Love and Hate; Hate the elder, Love the stronger.
The same idea, which the poet had got from the Greeks, that
the ordered universe arises from chaos through the power of
warring energies sovereignly harmonized by love, appears
in the *Hymn of Love*, a further guide to the understanding of
Spenser's thought at this time:

> Ayre hated earth, and water hated fyre,
> Till Love relented their rebellious yre.

It is Concord, mother also of Peace and Friendship, who
finally admits the knight to the Temple where he sees the
veiled image of the goddess, the serpent twined about her
feet, a very ancient symbol. But, and here we are back in the
Garden of Adonis, this is Venus Genetrix, mother of all
living:

> She syre and mother is herselfe alone,
> Begets and eke conceives, ne needeth other none. (IV. x. 41)

From her flows all the vital energy which makes

> The waters play and pleasant lands appeare,
> And heauens laugh and all the world shew ioyous cheare. (IV. x. 44)

The 'daedale' earth—Shelley would adopt that adjective—the
herds, the saluage beasts, 'all the world', drew from her the
creative force which makes life reproduce life, and she thus
becomes an earthly anti-type of Charissa who had taught the
Red Cross Knight in the House of Coelia.

Beside the altar of Venus stands the group of qualities which make Amoret what she is, the pearl of Gloriana's court, Womanhood, Shamefastness, this Temple of Venus stands very near the Castle of Alma, Cheerfulness:

> Whose eyes like twinkling stars in euening cleare
> Were deckt with smyles . . .

Modesty, Curtesie.

> Soft Silence and submisse Obedience
> Both gifts of God, not gotten but from thence,
> Both girlonds of his Saints against their foes offence. (IV. X. 51)

Spenser is always conscious of the fact that his gods and goddesses are not of divine right but are powers of nature, subject to 'high God'. In the midst of these is Amoret, happy in her maiden state, reluctant to leave it, yet conquered in her turn by the sight of the shield on which Cupid and his arrows are blazoned, and following him from the castle 'with sweet, reluctant, amorous delay'. Here, clearly, is no inconsistency, but only Scudamour narrating in allegorical terms his courtship of Amoret. It is double allegory certainly, for what is assumed as historical by Scudamour is allegory as well to us. And now Britomart enters the story.

When Scudamour was leading his bride from the castle or, to put it in factual terms, when the marriage ceremonies at Gloriana's court were over, and the marriage feast was ending, the blood of all being heated with wine, a masque was brought in, such as Spenser's first readers will have seen themselves on like occasions. Under cover of it Amoret is carried off by the enchanter Busyrane and imprisoned in a castle surrounded by flames which Scudamour cannot pass through. Amoret moreover is wounded, and that same fatal masque is repeated daily. Britomart, called to help, passes the flames without difficulty, and even in the hand-to-hand encounter with the magician she receives only the slightest wound, though indeed they are few that succeed even so far against her. But only the enchanter with reversed charms can undo what he has done (the poet of *Comus* remembered that), and when all that castle of illusory pain and pleasure has vanished, Spenser, by a significant change in his original ending, has removed Scudamour, so that the reunion of loyal wife and loyal husband is deferred through further perils and proofs, and the climax of the story is suspended like that of the others, till the end of the poem.

Probably the changed ending has a very simple explanation, and does not reflect any real change in Spenser's mind. He published the first three books by themselves in 1590; he could not know how long it would be before the next instalment could be ready (if his hopes of promotion had been realized, a very long interval might have elapsed), he could not leave the third book broken off abruptly, with neither Scudamour's adventure nor Britomart's concluded. He wrote, then, the famous description of the meeting of Amoret and Scudamour, and for this, when the fourth book followed, he substituted the three verses which leave the story open, since, when Amoret appears with Britomart, Glauce and Scudamour are gone. Doubtless when the meeting finally came about, Spenser intended to make good use of the rapturous lines he now set aside.

Neither his system of linking the books, nor his practice of deferring the ends of his principal adventures, would have allowed him to leave so strong and definite a conclusion standing to check the flow of his story when once Book Four was ready to follow. Besides this, the friendship of Britomart with Amoret, and then with Scudamour, is one of the features of Book Four, and the poet must therefore exercise his ingenuity in keeping Amoret and Scudamour apart. Both, good as they are, have still something to learn from Chastity. But their original separation presents a different problem, in treating which Spenser completes the moral doctrine which is implied throughout Book Two.

Scudamour is a good knight who has honourably won the love of Amoret. They have been duly married; what evil enchanter can come between them, kindling flames which Scudamour's courage cannot avail against, and inflicting wounds which Amoret's loyalty cannot heal? And Britomart, though she can pass unscathed through the flames and vanquish the enchanter, cannot herself free Amoret from his spells.

That the flames are those of unruly passion is fairly obvious. Why they should burn so furiously for Scudamour is not, at first, so clear. Spenser is concerned to show the part

played by chastity in lawful marriage; it is for Britomart that
the flames sink. Chastity he says, in effect, is not merely the
virtue by which both parties are faithful to their bond. It is
indeed that virtue, as he will show in the powerful episode of
Malbecco and Hellenore, and as he has shown already in the
picture of Florimell faithful to her future husband. Here he
is thinking of chaste relations between the married pair. But
he does not mean by this that they should abstain. As in
treating of earthly beauty Spenser had laid down that the
physical was the least important element in it, so, even in
earthly love, the physical, which lawfully enters, cannot lawfully predominate. Thus, in the *Hymne of Love*, he writes,
after describing love as the principle of order among the
warring elements, and as the creative urgency which impels
living things to mate:

> But man, that breathes a more immortall mind
> Not for lust's sake but for eternity,
> Seeks to enlarge his lasting progenie.
> For hauing yet in his deducted spright
> Some sparks remaining of that heauenly fyre,
> He is enlumind with that goodly light,
> Vnto like goodly semblant to aspyre: . . .
> . . . For loue is Lord of truth and loialtie,
> Lifting himself out of the lowly dust.
>
> On golden plumes vp to the purest skie,
> Above the reach of loathly sinfull lust . . .
> Such is the powre of that sweet passion,
> That it all sordid baseness doth expell,
> And the refyned mynd doth newly fashion
> Vnto a fairer forme . . . (*Hymne to Love*)

An Amoret and a Scudamour cannot, even in wedlock, mate
like a Hellenore and a Paridell, as though that passing
pleasure were their primary motive.

The author of the *Epithalamion* and of the verses which
were the first conclusion of Book Three, was no Manichee,
nor unaware either of the strength of the physical component
of marriage, or of the due place to be given to it. Nevertheless, says Spenser, there is a virtue which has for function the —
'moderating of the concupiscible faculty', and which teaches
both sexes to love at the human level, as those do who are

'enlumind with that goodly light', and not as beasts do who go down into the clay. That 'moderating' is the office of chastity. It is Scudamour's own unguardedness which has kindled the flames he cannot pass, and Amoret has her own trouble symbolized by the pierced, bleeding, heart, significant in Spenser as elsewhere, of unsatisfied desire. She cannot meet Scudamour in 'the marriage of true minds' if she come to him loving like Cleopatra; she must come as Miranda to Ferdinand, not, Spenser's constant teaching, treating pleasure as an end in itself. Amoret, the pure and perfect wife, will stray from Britomart and be rescued by Arthur, and Scudamour travel long in the company of Britomart, before Spenser allows them the pure yet impassioned meeting which he foreshadowed in the first ending of the third book.

Medieval romance had made a false distinction between the lover and the husband. The cult of the great lady had suggested that strong or passionate love, such as is still called romantic, must be sought outside marriage, the wife's part being that of Griselda. Already in the *Legend of Good Women*, Chaucer, by bringing in Alcestis, had suggested another possibility. Spenser, followed by Shakespeare, and in despite of the writers of fashionable sonnet sequences, throws over the whole idea of 'courtly love', save as a fashion in manners, and transfers 'the glory and the dream' to the image of the wife. Nothing will be more striking in Shakespeare's love stories than his resolute defence of the marriage bond.

It appears then, why Spenser treats of love after, but in connexion with, his treatment of Temperance, and side by side with his treatment of Chastity, whose own story, moreover, is a love story. Love which is not chaste is not, for Spenser, love at all. Chastity without the knowledge of love is no true virtue but merely a state, such as Marinell had been in before the wound given by Chastity had occasioned his learning love. Thus, in the *Hymn in honour of Beautie* Spenser had written, addressing:

> . . . ye faire Dames, the world's deare ornaments—

> Loath that foul blot, that hellish fierbrand,
> Disloyall lust, faire beauties foulest blame,
> That base affection that your eares would bland,

> Commend to you by loues abused name;
> But is indeed the bondslave if defame,
> Which will the garland of your glorie marre
> And quench the light of your bright shyning starre.
>
> But gentle Loue that loyall is and trew,
> Will more illumine your resplendent ray,
> And add more brightnesse to your goodly hew,
> From light of his pure fire which by like way
> Kindled of yours, your likenesse doth display,
> . . . For Loue is a celestiall harmonie
> Of likely harts composd of starres concent
> Which joyne together in sweete sympathie
> To work each others ioy and true content, . . .

As for the Blandinas, Hellenores, Paridells, Blandamours, Sir Guyon's palmer has the last word: 'Let Gryll be Gryll and have his hoggish mind.'

Book Three differs in several respects from the others. In it Arthur is displaced from his usual office of deliverer, and his part is taken by Britomart, to whom the help she hardly needs is given by the Red Cross Knight. Wherever she appears, in this and the two succeeding books, Britomart is as invincible as Arthur whose faithful sword and powerful shield are not more deadly than her enchanted spear. Indeed, Britomart is seldom seen in the posture of defence; the negative aspect of chastity, its resistance to attack, is sufficiently shown in Amoret, Florimell, Aemyllia. Britomart's is a militant virtue, an energy of purity which even when assaulted, defends itself by attack, and if meeting evil, is more often the assailant.

A biography of the period[1] tells us of an Elizabethan lady, some thirty years younger than Spenser, who passing on a journey near a house of ill fame and hearing a violent quarrel going on within, immediately entered it; the power of her presence and her words being such that she not only made peace among those unfortunate women, but led them to repent and abandon that kind of life for the future. When that happened Spenser was dead; but such, in the terms of real life, were the deeds of Britomart.

[1] 'The Life of Mary Ward', unpublished manuscript in the possession of the Inst. B.M.V., Rome.

Yet Britomart is no Amazon. Beneath the armour of the Saxon Queen there beats a very tender heart. No one in the whole course of the poem is more tender and, in a certain sense, more helpless in love than the invincible Britomart. This appears in the scene between her and Glauce in the second canto, where the old woman coaxes out the story of her love for the shadow seen in the magic mirror and tries to comfort her. It is vividly displayed again after she has met Artegall, and he is leaving her to pursue his quest:

> And by the way she sundry purpose found
> Of this or that the time for to delay,
> And of the perils whereto he was bound,
> The fear wherof seemd much her to affray.
> But all she did was but to weare out day.
> Full oftentimes she leave of him did take;
> And eft again devised somewhat to say,
> Which she forgot, whereby excuse to make:
> So loth she was his companie for to forsake. (IV. vi. 45)

Juliet too knows such reluctant farewells. In Book Five, also, when no news comes of him,

> One whyle she blam'd herselfe; another whyle
> She him condemned as trustlesse and untrew
> And then her griefe with errors to beguyle,
> She fayned to counte the time again anew.

This is followed by the description of her reception of the bad news of Artegall's imprisonment by Radigund, and anyone who doubts the flesh and blood reality that Spenser can give to his personages, would be well advised to read this passage (v. vi. 9–18).

Besides his dramatic sense of the requirements of the story, Spenser may also have had in mind to bring out clearly that the virtue of chastity as he conceives it is full of warmth and even of passion. He no more envisages true chastity existing without love, than true love without chastity.

There was a third question to be answered; what is the secret affinity which draws Britomart to Artegall rather than to any of the other virtues? A more superficial moralist than Spenser might have paired her with Guyon, who would thereby have lost the moth's desire for the star which vivifies

his virtue; or perhaps with one of the knights in the Fourth
Book, or possibly with Calidore. But Spenser had perceived
that, apart from the other reason given, of Guyon's resulting
loss, a union between him and Britomart would have been as
useless as inappropriate. For perfect temperance includes
chastity, and Guyon, victorious over Acrasia and the rest, no
more needs Britomart than she him. But, also, as chastity
arises from temperance of which it is one function, there
would seem to be something unnatural in its returning there
whence it first drew its being. The representatives of friendship or concord, in the fourth book, must indeed be chaste.
Spenser will point out in it that all the false and feeble
friends are men of light character; but concord as such
brings no fulfilment to chastity. Justice, however, is, according to the stock definition, that virtue which gives what is
due to all. But chastity does exactly this in all that relates to
the complex of feeling and desire which is summarized in
the word 'heart'. But if chastity functions like justice in what
relates to bodily and affective good, justice regulates all goods
of any other kind. Each is therefore the complement of
the other: justice is the chastity of the soul, and in marriage
each has an obligation in justice to give what is due to the
other.

Is there any special significance in the fact that when Britomart first encounters Artegall they are, each being unknown
to the other, on opposite sides in a tournament (Satyrane's
for the girdle of Florimell) and that Artegall, hitherto the
victor, falls, as Guyon did, to Britomart's enchanted spear?
Artegall, moreover, is a bad loser and this leads to a much
more serious combat in which, swords being the weapons,
Artegall has the advantage. Britomart's sex and beauty are
revealed before harm is done, and when Artegall too lifts his
visor, they see each other truly for the first time, and seeing,
love.

Artegall's anger, though it misbecomes him as a knight,
is proper to him as a virtue. Justice ought to prevail; when it
does not, something is amiss. There is but one virtue to
which justice can yield, and that virtue is charity. But love is
the whole explanation of Britomart's knighthood; it was not
chastity alone which fought, but love also, and when Artegall

knows Britomart for what she is, his anger goes and he too becomes a lover. But all the same there is a blemish in the narrative here. Artegall's resentment at losing the prize to an unknown may become him allegorically; but it certainly looks ugly in the story. Yet those who admit the tantrums of Homeric great men might accept this also. After all, Artegall wears the armour of Achilles.

This problem has some connexion with that of the minor role played by Arthur in Britomart's books. Here there is a practical difficulty. Britomart with the symbolic spear in hand is, and must be, invincible. But so too is Arthur. These two neither need help from the other as friend, nor could either defeat the other if they were foes. They must therefore be kept apart unless the occasion is peaceful, and this Spenser contrives; the two meet as friends, ride peacefully on together, and are plausibly separated by the vision of Florimell. That Britomart should be thus invincible, and so leave Arthur no part to play in her own personal story, is bound up in the very nature of her virtue and of Spenser's conception of it, to say nothing of the cult of chastity and Britomart's association with Queen Elizabeth.

I have explained Guyon's defeat by Britomart by the suggestion that since chastity is mentioned as one of the fruits of the Spirit in those Epistles of St. Paul which it is clear Spenser studied, the poet regarded it, an infused grace, not an acquired habit, as higher in dignity than temperance and stronger also, and that he symbolized this 'grace-character' by the enchanted spear. Her next combat after Guyon's in the story is with Marinell, not a very arduous one. Marinell falls because his innocence or virgin state is no dedicated condition like Belphoebe's, but mere natural slowness and timorousness, not virtue at all. It is here, however, that Spenser tells us that Britomart is one of the special objects of Archimago's hatred, and that he had arranged to lure her companions away so that she might be alone. We are not to forget him, nor that his evil power may lie behind apparently chance happenings. But Archimago never dares face Britomart in the light.

Britomart's next encounter introduces the curious and impressive episode of Malbecco and Hellenore, the jealous miser and his light-minded wife. Britomart, seeking shelter, meets and challenges Satyrane and Paridell who are in like case and will not share the shed they have found near Malbecco's inhospitable door. Paridell accepts the challenge and is, of course, struck down, but strangely enough Britomart and her horse are brought to the ground too, though she remains uninjured. Satyrane, the man of the world, reconciles them, and all three agree to force Malbecco to open the castle gate. Paridell's character does not appear immediately; yet it is strange to see Britomart, even casually, on friendly terms with the type of the seducer who is about to corrupt Hellenore, and of whom it is later said:

> But Paridell of love did make no threasure
> But lusted after all that did him move . . .

His character is well sketched in even at this first encounter. He attacks Britomart like a fierce wind—comparisons to wind and water are no compliments in Spenser—but when they have entered the castle and her sex appears, 'the fairest woman wight that eye did ever see', fair, but 'like as Minerva', Paridell is won. But when Hellenore appears the experienced Paridell immediately turns his attention to the more likely object.

Spenser's brilliant description of the communication of the two under the eye of the jealous husband evinces the same satiric power, and the same ironic observation, as appear in *Mother Hubberd's Tale*. The same realism is noticeable in the later conversation when Paridell:

> . . . in whom a kindly pryde
> Of gracious speech and skill his words to frame

abounded, describes his own descent from Paris, and speaks of the Fall of Troy, which Britomart takes up, and they own themselves related as being both of Trojan origin. Britomart, ancestress of Elizabeth, must obviously claim descent from Brut himself. Meanwhile, Hellenore hangs on the speakers' words as Desdemona will on those of Othello. Spenser had too much experience not to know what weight Paridell's just claim to consideration as a knight and courtier added to his pretensions as a lover. Hellenore's virtue at this stage might have been proof against a Braggadochio, but Paridell, whom Richardson will call Lovelace, and Jane Austen, Crawford, and Thackeray, Steyne, she cannot resist. He will be seen again, and will be always true to the character here given him and to his descent from Paris the marriage-breaker.

Perhaps this scene has withdrawn Spenser's interest temporarily from Britomart's allegorical character; otherwise her amicable conversation with the seducer is hard to understand. Had she not seen, or not understood, what the poet so vividly describes? Or has she, a princess experienced in the ways of courts, learned to ignore the goings-on of those who cannot be saved because they will not try to save themselves? So had she treated the lady of delight.

It is worth while noting that Britomart's combats are progressive. Her skirmish with Gardante and his companions at Joyous Gard, resulted in no real harm on either side: Marinell's blow,

> . . . made her downe
> Decline her head and touch her crouper with her crowne;

Paridell's stroke brings horse and rider to the ground momentarily stunned, Busyrane, the next encounter, for the unnatural Ollyphant flies from her, actually draws blood, though slightly and as it were by surprise. But this is the furthest extent of her peril, the fights with Scudamour and Artegall are another matter, and when she meets Radigund in a later book she fights in another character. When Claribell, Blandamour, Druon, and Paridell combine against Scudamour and Britomart, the two hold their own with ease. Prince Arthur's intervention stops the encounter, but 'the good' were never in danger.

This progressive sequence corresponds to the allegory; Gardante and his companions, as names like Basciante and Jocante make evident, represent no more than what are called by moralists 'dangerous occasions', circumstances which are not sinful in themselves but which, in the given case, might predispose to sin, as convivial company might be to an alcoholic. Neither knight has wilfully sought trouble, and neither is harmed. But the more serious encounter within the castle is Spenser's warning to Britomart on the danger of staying in bad company. Chastity had helped Holiness when incitements to which human weakness is prone were directed against his fidelity to Una ('the pure, the undefiled, who is but one'). Now Holiness flies to the aid of Chastity when it is assailed in its turn; the exchange is just.

Next comes the fight on the Rich Strand. Marinell shakes Britomart for the moment; but the attitude of timorousness and refusal is no real danger to her militant virtue. Paridell represents an opposite temptation, that of the professional charmer armed with all the tricks of the trade. The victory is not in doubt, but it costs a real effort, and she has learned that she could be weak. Busyrane whose character under all the courtly affectations of his masque is sheer lust, pricks Britomart's bodily nature into sudden response; her virtue would be no virtue if she were not flesh and blood. But the prick acts like a spur to the effort which subdues the enchanter entirely and renders him obedient. Amoret's own tendency to exceed is checked, and due balance restored; this is symbolized by the healing of her wounded heart.

This analysis has led us away from the tale of Malbecco and Hellenore; but of this I have already said something in the second chapter, and the comment of Sir Satyrane, that good, honest, man of the world, is apposite enough:

> Extremely mad the man I surely deeme,
> That weenes with watch and hard restraint to stay
> A woman's will which is disposd to go astray.

The picture of crabbed age and youth had perhaps remained in Spenser's mind from his reading of Chaucer, *The Merchant's Tale*; but he needs no literary source for what experience must have shown him. Hellenore with her rapid but quite self-satisfied descent from Paridell to the satyrs, who are, indeed, more innocent, is a type, here indicated by secure touches, to which Shakespeare gave the names of Cressida and Gertrude, and whom Jane Austen, within the restrictions of her ladylike entourage, knew as Lydia.

Malbecco represents a more subtle study in Spenser's symbolized psychology. Malbecco is a miser who keeps his wife as he keeps his gold. Indeed, when the one is escaping and the other burning, he behaves like Shylock himself lamenting both his ducats and his daughter. But his frenzied sense of possession has eaten away the control of reason; his emotions waste him. There follow his long, useless, wanderings, his encounter with Braggadochio, who deceives him as easily as Archimago: 'Bigge looking like a doughtie Doucepere'; his weak man's boasting what he would do, when there seems no likelihood of his being called on to make his words good, as proved in his craven meeting with Paridell's shameless indifference, and his 'pale-eyed dread' of monsters in the forest. His trembling visit to the satyr's camp destroys his long sustained pathetic illusion about Hellenore, and everything witnesses to his rapid moral disintegration as it becomes clearer and clearer that he has never really loved anyone but himself. Hellenore had only been his thing. His false courage Braggadochio flees, his buried treasure is lost, his obsession intensifies, so that finally it destroys the last traces of his humanity; his inflated ego which had filled his world has been punctured like a toy balloon, and as it shrinks it loses shape, and Malbecco becomes irrecoverably insane. Spenser symbolizes this in the wonderful description of his transformation into an owl, the figure of jealousy, clinging with crooked claws to the face of the precipice.

It is after leaving the house of jealousy and infidelity that Britomart sees Ollyphant, the giant, who seems to represent unnatural vice. She sees him only, and from a distance, for her mere presence is enough to drive him away. There can be no conflict here; certain vices are so completely incompatible with chastity that where one is the other cannot be, as Satan's toad-form cannot resist Ithuriel's spear. In his capacity as story-teller, a function in which the poet seems to take ever-increasing delight, Spenser uses this incident to separate Britomart from Satyrane, that remarkable and attractive figure, always on the side of right, always coming into contact with the highest virtues, and being their friend, always valiant, and yet never quite achieving anything. It is at this juncture that Britomart, possessed by her lofty idealistic passion for a shadow only seen in a mirror, having rejected various base imitations of love and purity, besides the passing glimpse of Florimell, first encounters true, pure, if imperfect, human love, the knight Sir Scudamour.

The story of Britomart's rescue of Scudamour's bride, Amoret, has already been commented on in other connexions, and also the reason why their story does not really end with the third book. It would certainly have been a premature ending. Amoret, though her wound has been healed, is still prone to stray into danger, and Scudamour still possesses the frailty which had disabled him, who had struck down twenty knights, from passing the circle of fire. Jealousy troubles him, Care torments him, Discord deceives him. Not till he has recognized Britomart and become her friend can he love Amoret as she should be loved. But Amoret's story itself is not ended, and Scudamour himself, as a virtue, is involved in the common destiny which forbids them all to attain secure happiness until Arthur has met Gloriana.

Britomart's rescue of Amoret concludes Spenser's treatment of the first part of his subject, in which he is chiefly concerned with chastity as it affects the relations of persons of the opposite sex, and in the marriage bond. He now enters upon a second, more complex, development of his general theme, which will treat love in the various relations of friendship. His groups of friends, both true and false, will still include both men and women, and there will seem a definite pattern in their oppositions, like the countering movements of line and group in the dances of the time. Britomart certainly still has a great part to play for, though going from strength to strength, she has not yet so much as met Artegall in the flesh; she is still striving, not indeed to acquire her virtue of which the habit has been infused by grace as a fruit of the Spirit, but for her complement, without which she — cannot be at rest. She is so dominant a personality that she rather takes the substance from the group which should hold the centre of the stage, the group representing Friendship, or Concord, made up of Cambell, Triamond, and their wives Canacee and Cambina. These have set against them a shifting group, of which the nucleus is the old enemy, Duessa, reinforced by Ate. Here belong Paridell and Blandamour, false friends and false lovers, sometimes accompanied by Druon, hard and loveless, and Claribell, less corrupt, but marked by the company he keeps. Allied with them, as far as alliance can be where there is neither love nor truth, is Braggadochio with false Florimell, against whom the pair on the opposite side seems to be Britomart with Amoret. But these groups change; they are joined by others; people pass to and fro; at times the whole *corps de ballet* disappears and we are left with the customary knight errant, riding through the forest, or else, with an Amoret or an Aemyllia in distress. The central, stable, group, that of Cambell and Triamond, does not even appear until Book Four is well on its way.

The interweaving of these two books clearly illustrates the fact that Spenser had conceived his story, complex as it is, in one whole. It is therefore less surprising if, having his eye on that whole, and directing the part towards it, he should be at times inconsistent in his treatment of some less essential detail, or should make some slip in his use of a name. Since Book Three is the last in the section first published, Spenser did well to carry on the story with so smooth a transition.

The poet tells us, in his introduction to Book Four, that he had been criticized for writing so much of love. One might say that love and truth are the main motives of the whole poem, and that they sound as a continuous undertone, even when he is apparently occupied with something else, an undertone like that rippling sound he imagines throughout the *Prothalamion* 'Sweet Thames run softly till I end my song'. He begins Book Four quite unrepentant, and fully determined to take as high a view of the love of friendship as he had taken of the love of marriage. He shows his colours at once by reverting immediately to the beginning of Amoret's story, swiftly sketching her abduction, not fully explained before, and passing on with his quiet, veiled humour to describe the situation which develops between Amoret and Britomart; the one desperately embarrassed by such close association with a knight to whom she owes so much, but who is not Scudamour; the other refusing to reveal her sex. It is by a pretty touch that it is the real kindness of Britomart towards the honest, foolish boy who challenged her, that reveals her true character to Amoret, who henceforth does not fear the virtue which she sees so lovely.

Thus Britomart and Amoret become a type of pure and faithful friendship between woman and woman where there is full trust and full confidence, and each is more concerned

for the other's good than for her own. This is contrasted with
that other well-assorted pair, Duessa and Ate, now accompanied by Blandamour and Paridell, and making a pretty
picture of worldly, simulated friendship:

> Faithless Duessa and false Paridell,
> That whether were more false, full hard it is to tell.
>
> (IV. I. 32)

Blandamour represents an artistic, egoistic, romantic, sort
of love, like that of Fitzpiers in Hardy's *Woodlanders*. He
loves, as Spenser says elsewhere, passionately, even sincerely,
but not for long. He challenges Chastity and receives a much
harder fall, given at much less cost, than Paridell's. As Ollyphant was too gross, so is Blandamour too slight for a real
conflict with Britomart's virtue; having struck him down she
passes on indifferently, as one who has brushed aside a fly;
thus leaving the stage clear for the action special to the fourth
book.

The friends unfriends proceed, and now meet Scudamour,
as yet unaware of the issue of Britomart's adventure. Both
Fickle Love and False Love are enemies of true; but it is
Paridell who attacks. Scudamour, though not yet perfected,
is still more than a match for one who knows no real love
at all, and passes onward, but not before hideous Ate and
false-spoken Duessa had uttered their poisoned words. For
Scudamour has not yet learned Britomart's reality.

Spenser is under no delusions. Both Amoret and Scudamour tend to slip away from the guardianship of chastity and
get into bad company, thus putting off their union in true
marriage. But Amoret at least knows the beauty and sweetness which are hidden by Britomart's armoured exterior; her
further troubles come from carelessness arising from over-
security, which again is true to life. Scudamour has still to
learn that the spirit of chastity has an office even between him
and his wife, and that it will intensify love, rather than
diminish it.

Spenser is setting on foot a game of cross-purposes whereby both Justice and Love will become temporarily opposed
to Chastity; but out of this opposition will arise friendship
and love. Meanwhile, he is concerned with demonstrating

the fragility of such friendships as are based on casual encounter and self-interest in which, as Paridell says, 'the left hand rubs the right'. Blandamour by a hasty, half-intended, cheat, has got possession of false Florimell, for whom any man will do, and she, professional that she is, can beat either Blandamour or Paridell at their chosen game of *ars amatoria*: 'so great a mistress of her art she was'. Spenser is at his old task of contrasting the false and true; this 'fayned friendship' soon breaks up into a furious, jealous, quarrel, both parties egged on by the women.

Duessa with Ate beside her is showing herself indeed, 'the daughter of debate that eke discord did sow' that Mary Stuart was called in the well-known lines attributed to Queen Elizabeth I. Spenser's lines describing Discord are notably similar, and express the horror of the breakers of public peace with which his own experience, whether in England or Ireland, had evidently inspired in him:

> Her name was Ate, mother of Debate,
> And all dissension which doth dayly grow
> Amongst fraile men, that many a publike state
> And many a priuate oft doth overthrow.
> Her false Duessa who full well did know
> To be most fit to trouble noble knights;
> Which hunt for honour, raised from below,
> Out of the dwellings of the damned sprights,
> Where she in darknes wastes her cursed days and nights.

> Hard by the gates of Hell her dwelling is,
> There whereas all the plagues and harmes abound,
> Which punish wicked man that walke amisse,
> It is a darksome delue farre underground,
> With thornes and barren brakes environd round,
> That none the same may easily out win;
> Yet many waies to enter may be found
> But none to issue forth when one is in;
> For discord harder is to end than to begin.   (IV. i. 19, 20)

Not only the poet, but the civil servant speaks here, the secretary to Grey and to Norris, and to the Council of Munster.

I have quoted these lines not only to illustrate the special horror which so many Elizabethans had reason to feel for the figure of public discord, but also to emphasize the poetic skill displayed in depicting that mean and miserable scene. In all his various portrayals of hell and hellish scenery Spenser looks backward to Dante rather than forward to Milton. Not for him the sombre, impressive, vagueness of the Miltonic underworld. He sees the Evil One as having become something much less than archangel ruined, a gargoyle figure dwelling in no magnificent Pandemonium, but in the very material mud and misery of Dante's *Inferno*. The heavy alliteration, and dragging vowel sounds, produce a parallel effect to that in the description of Despair, to which there is much similarity; while the grotesque figure of Ate herself, with her 'double eares and double tongue', besides its evident symbolism, illustrates again the poet's habitual association of evil with deformity and disease.

That not very admirable person the Squire of Dames, finally pacifies the quarrel with the argument, appropriate to such company, that it will pay them better to combine against the common enemy than to fight each other, and perceiving this as clearly as if they were financiers or leaders of political minorities, they reswear their forsworn friendship and set off for Sir Satyrane's tournament. Then as they ride, 'in close disguise of fayned love', they overtake the real protagonists of this Book of Friendship:

> Courageous Cambell and stout Triamond,
> With Canacee and Cambine lincked in louely bond.

The two groups are carefully balanced, four against four.

It is curious that Spenser, to whom friendship had meant so much from the time he first met Gabriel Harvey or Sidney, to the day Sir Walter Raleigh came to him in Ireland, and who was himself so faithful a friend, should paint these types of friendship in colours so much less clear and bright than those which bring the other knights so vividly before us. The Red Cross Knight and Una, Guyon, Sir Artegall, Sir Calidore, Britomart, all these come before us as individuals with distinct personalities. Even personages of the second rank are seen, as it were, in the round, some more, some less; Satyrane, Florimell, the disreputable Paridell, Phaedria. But not every attentive reader of the *Faerie Queene* could be certain of recalling off-hand all the names of the four faithful friends; or the odd tales of the origin of their friendship. They are by no means the most prominent figure of the book which is their Legend, and their actions are not essential in the forwarding of the story as a whole. They are static like a picture, or a group of statuary, which illustrates a theme but does not elucidate it. They alone are on no special quest, though still *in via*. When they appear their friendship has been already achieved; they have only to remain as they are; their story, though it is recalled, is only a vivid memory; it was finished long ago. It is their lack of vitality or distinctive action, supplied but once during the tournament, that makes the restless activity of the unfriends so remarkable.

Yet if it does nothing else, the first appearance of Cambell and Triamond gives Spenser occasion for one of his most fervent invocations of his master, Chaucer, with whom he has more in common than the believers in the 'moon-Spenser' are always ready to admit. It was from the *Squire's Tale* that he took the characters of Cambell and Canacee, though he ignores the others, omits the flying horse, and changes the character of the magic ring. It is from this invocation that the oft-quoted, 'Chaucer, pure well of English undefiled', is taken.

Perhaps the most remarkable characteristic of the beginning of this legend of perfect friendship is the decisive part that women play in the story, and the detail with which their intellectual powers and achievements are described: Canacee

> That was the learnedst lady of her dayes,
> Well seen in every science that mote bee,
> And every secret worke of natures wayes . . .

Cambina is

> . . . a Ladie passing faire
> And bright that seemed borne of Angels' brood.

Like Canacee, she is as good as she is fair, and as learned as she is good:

> Thereto she learned was in Magicke leare
> And all the artes that subtill wits discouer . . .

Agape, mother of the three brethren whom Spenser presents

as such an example of family affection, is 'right faire' . . . and
had the skill

> Of secret things, and all the powres of nature
> Which she by arte could use vnto her will.

It is not by chance that the poet who had written the hymns
to earthly and heavenly love, gives command of the powers
of nature to Agape, Motherly love, or that he should show
her affection, together with the fraternal love of her three
sons, as symbolically stronger than death. For if this be not
the significance of the strange little story in which Agape
persuades the Fates to allow the life of those who die to pass
into the survivor, I do not know what it may be.[1] It is good
folk-lore; but of a savage kind not so commonly found in a
poem as civilized as the *Faerie Queene*. For the rest, Spenser's
poetic fancy plays gracefully round this picture of friends
'lovely and pleasant in their lives . . . and in their deaths not
divided'. Even the love of Canacee had not divided them;
theirs had been the love 'passing the love of women' and,

> . . . whilest they liued none did euer see
> More happie creatures than they seemed to bee,
> Nor more ennobled for their courtesie.

Spenser tells us all this; but he does not show us those
happy brothers except at the moment when two are to die;
and even then the narrative is a throw-back to events which
have already happened outside the action of the poem. One
thing is clear, the friendship is made by the women. It is
Agape's wisdom which has been taught to Cambina, and
which operates when reasoning has failed. By its power injuries are less forgiven than forgotten as having no longer
any relevance to the new situation. Cambina's chariot is
drawn by lions, their tameness symbolizing the subduing
power of chaste love, Spenser cannot have been unaware how
this symbol would evoke the figure of Una, and she carries
the serpent-entwined rod:

> Like to the rod which Maia's son doth wield
> Wherewith the hellish fiends she doth confound.

---

[1] The hint is from Virgil, *Æneid*, viii, ll. 564–5.

If the symbolism of the lions recalls Una, that of the snake brings back Fidelia. In her face goodness shines as brightly as beauty. Canacee is less clearly seen than this majestic figure; she is a wonder for her knowledge and her chaste reserve; but she does not love, and her refusal to choose a partner has caused so many dissensions that her brother resolves to end them by a sort of ordeal by battle, which occasions his fights with the brothers. Canacee perhaps represents a wisdom which is not perfect until it has learned something of Cambina's lore of the heart. She yields readily enough to Agape's son. Thus love stills the combat in which neither side has prevailed, leaving behind not even the remembrance of grievance. And, with wisdom, love makes the final bond which unites this group now trebly bound, brother to sister, husband to wife, friend to friend. Their strife, however fierce at the moment, had been of the kind described by the poet in Canto IV;

> For enmities that of no ill proceeds
> But of occasion, with th' occasion ends.

Why the four should be thus riding through the forest does not appear. A fate seems to be on Chaucer's unfinished story, so that even Spenser, taking it up, leaves it incomplete. Cambuscan perhaps has died, and Algarsife may be king of Tartary in his place, upon which Cambell and Canacee may have set forth to seek another kingdom. Triamond, son of a fay whose home was the whole forest, is less difficult to explain. This, however, is fancy. What is clear, is that Spenser, in the moving pattern of his story, has set these two groups, the one of faithful friends and lovers, the other of false, over against each other. And in passing it may be noted that Spenser's grouping would imply that he did not believe a false lover could be a faithful friend. It is clear, too, that the true-hearted remain as much as possible at peace with all, whereas the others are quarrelsome. Blandamour, who is like a stag or a bull in springtime, is ready to challenge any man whose wife is beside him; this occasions the first quarrel, which is pacified by Cambina; the second, set off by Braggadochio's arrival, is checked by Cambell; thus they all arrive at the tournament.

It is at this point in the story that Spenser brings together, at least for the moment, the two threads of narrative which ran through Book Three, the stories of Britomart and Florimell. This tournament has been arranged by Satyrane, natural goodness, in honour of the vanished Florimell, Innocence. Her girdle, which is one of many folk-story tests of chastity, is to be the prize of the most fair. This is the appropriate contest which will bring Britomart and Artegall together into the same place for the first time. But they will not recognize each other, for this conflict, in spite of its high and chivalrous intention, is a picture of the cross-purposes and confusions of this world. Triamond, son of Agape, and model of friendship, hastens to the help of Blandamour and Paridell, and he, after valiant deeds, falls to Satyrane's prowess, on whose side he should have been while Cambell, out of friendship for Triamond, levels his spear against the knights of Maydenhede. Each friend, after being adjudged victor of the day, vindicates his title by yielding the honour to the other. Yet the protagonists of the Book of Friendship are singular in this also, that they are not victors in their principal action. Good men and good friends may, out of mistaken friendship, sometimes take the wrong side; but Spenser cannot let that side win, or permit the defeat of Gloriana's Order, even though Justice disguised, Artegall under the semblance of the Saluage Knight, should, under the chivalrous error of defending the weaker, strike for once against it.

It was doubtless the interests of the historical allegory which suggested this general post of knights, some of the minor combatants have names but thinly disguised; but Friendship and Justice have certainly lost their way, when they are found fighting on behalf of the Blandamours, Paridells, Braggadochios. That Britomart, a heavenly grace, should enter and redress the balance overset by Artegall's misplaced valour becomes inevitable, and it can be theologically contended that the infused virtue should be stronger than the natural one. Nevertheless, the whole scene, like that later of the awarding the girdle to the false Florimell who cannot wear it, is one of misunderstanding and confusion. Discord has prevailed. Everything goes by contraries: the wise Cambina, Canacee, Cambell, Triamond, have all

vanished, not to be seen again; while love and justice, in
the persons of Scudamour and Artegall, seek revenge on
Chastity. It is a vivid picture of the moral confusions of this
world; and it has apparently happened because the false
Florimell has been taken for the true, and has deceived even
Satyrane, faithful lover. Was Spenser remembering how
often he had seen virtue and honour on the side that seemed
to him the wrong one? However, there will be another tournament where the true Florimell will be honoured, and these
mistakes will be set right; but not yet.

Spenser takes occasion here for one of his thrusts at art if
regarded as the sham of nature, the authentic creatrix. Florimell, the false imitation, is so like her model as if anything,
to surpass her, like the false ivy in the Bower of Bliss. But,
whatever she looks like on the outside, there is frozen death
within, and, given her choice, she chooses the only one of all
that crowd of bad and good who is not a knight at all, Braggadochio, himself a sham. With this is contrasted Artegall's
appearance as a symbol of nature:

> For all his armour was like saluage weed,
> With woody moss bedight, and all his steed
> With oaken leaves attrapt, that seemed fit
> For saluage wight . . . (IV. iv. 39)

In such guise Justice first appears in the poem, and he
carries all before him until Britomart intervenes with a
weapon beyond nature's reach.

Scudamour's quarrel with Britomart is an excellent example of dissension sown by evil tongues, and as he pursues
it, hounded on by his angry thoughts, he comes on the house
of Care. The description of his restless night, the iteration of
the same hateful idea vividly represented by the recurrent
hammering, his uneasy movements, his painful dreams,
Care's red-hot pinch at his heart as he wakes from his unrest-
ful sleep, his heavy rising, all this is described as picturesquely
as accurately. The next day's reaction from angry excitement
to deep depression is equally well indicated and equally true
to nature:

> Who having left that restlesse house of Care,
> The next day, as he on his way did ride

> Full of melancholie and sad misfare,
> Through misconceipt . . . (IV. vi. 2)

He has not yet learned what chastity really is.

The general state of confusion leads Artegall, still disguised, to level his spear at Scudamour. But Justice is not so far gone in misunderstanding as not on a nearer view, to recognize Love, and Love equally is still enough himself to make quick accord with Justice; between these two only brief and mistaken warfare is possible.

And now justice and love both imagine that chastity, which they misconceive to be what its outward appearance suggests, is wronging them by coming between love and love, Artegall has seen false Florimell, Scudamour claims Amoret. The quarrel so stated is evidently not an uncommon one. Overhasty Love is easily disposed of, it is but half itself until chastity is known to it; the combat with Justice is prolonged and serious; that is due to both. The first time Britomart had been victorious: Spenser must now redress the balance, for neither justice nor chastity can be subject to final defeat. Britomart, then, is dismounted, the enchanted spear is useless, while Artegall has the sword Chrysaor. The stroke of that sword reveals Britomart for what she is, and it is enough. Chastity clearly seen is irresistible, both to Love and to Justice. Britomart's quest is over; her very human character will be more evident from now on, for though she has attained her own fulfilment in this almost casual manner, her adventures are not ended, nor can be until Artegall's own quest has been achieved. Meanwhile, Scudamour, though disabused as to Britomart, is still as far from Amoret as ever. This time it is she innocently unguarded, who has strayed away, and has been seized by a monstrous passion from which – innocence is no protection.

It is at the end of this canto that Britomart shows herself so truly a woman in her resistance to Artegall's leaving her, even to finish his quest, and in her seeking for excuses to delay his departure.

Book Four, however, does not confine itself to one interest; but is rather made up of various episodes, all carefully connected, in which various aspects of love and friendship are displayed.

The instability of interested friendship was shown as Blandamour and his company journeyed towards the tournament; the mutual loyalty and devotion of Cambell and Triamond are demonstrated during the tournament itself; how 'evil tongues can poison truth' was illustrated by the goings-on of Ate, and their effect on Scudamour; the pair to Cambell and Triamond's masculine friendship is found in the mutual affection and confidence of Britomart and Amoret, and, when once the misunderstanding is cleared up, Amoret brings Scudamour and Britomart together in a noble equality of friendship between man and woman. Later on Arthur, travelling with Amoret and Aemylia, will show another beautiful type of friendship where protective care on one side is answered by perfect trust on the other.

But a whole group of human relationships has as yet been left almost untouched, except by the charming study of Britomart and Glauce, and this is composed of what may conveniently be called 'unequal friendships', friendship and affection arising where there is a marked difference whether of age, or rank, or some other quality. Like the musical themes suggested in an overture, this has been already shown, early on in the book, by the shrewd, realistic, yet touching statement of Glauce's relations with the young princess Britomart, not yet a knight errant, and in her continued fidelity. But a study of nurse and nurseling does not exhaust the possibilities. Moreover, Spenser has left aside for some time the subject he had stated in making Amoret, the foster child of Venus, the younger twin of Belphoebe, foster-child of Diana. Nor can his treatment of chastity be considered complete without something more than the passing glimpses he has so far given of virginity. We left Belphoebe ministering to Timias (Honourable) wounded in defence of Innocence; and Spenser now returns to this subject, making the losing of Amoret the structural link between Belphoebe in her remote forest fastness, and the other personages of the story.

Amoret, the loving wife, has not yet learned the whole of her lesson. She has reached an interior knowledge of chastity which goes far beyond the mere material keeping of a commandment, essential though that be; but she has not learned prudence. She wanders away from Britomart sleeping, 'of naught afeard', when fear would have been the beginning of wisdom. It has not struck her that, even while not tempted herself, she might be a temptation to others. Thus it comes about, and she is swept off in the clutches of a manlike beast, or a beastlike man,

> It was, to weet a wilde and saluage man,
> Yet was no man, but only like in shape . . .

Timias saves Amoret, an appropriate protector, but only Belphoebe herself, with arrows more deadly than Britomart's 'heben speare', can kill the monster.

Very likely in the historical allegory, the quarrel which results between Belphoebe and Timias on account of Amoret, represents Queen Elizabeth's anger at Raleigh's marriage with Elizabeth Throckmorton, and the carryings-on of Timias are not an extravagant version of Raleigh's real behaviour. But the situation as given by Spenser has a human value which is quite independent of this; recalling at one point the meeting of Troilus with the leper Criseyde whom he does not recognize in Henryson's sequel to Chaucer's poem. For when Arthur encounters his lost squire by chance, he too does not recognize him, though he pities the wretch he sees. Indeed, such is the miserable change made in him that Belphoebe herself does not know him. And yet the poet, careful to observe all the forms of courtly compliment, all the same gives a clear hint that Timias would do better to follow 'his owne deare Lord', the ideal friend Arthur, than even remain in that restored happy state where for the moment he leaves him, having said his say on courtly love when innocent.

And now Spenser leads into the motive of the sixth book. The old hag Sclaunder, worse and more abhorrent even than Ate, miscalls prince Arthur who is escorting the rescued Amoret and Aemylia, and this causes the poet to break out into a beautiful apostrophe to those antique times when men and women had exercised the freedom Guyon had fought for, and had seen in Alma's castle, man's nature ruled in the liberty of right reason:

> But antique age yet in the infancie
> Of time, did live then like an innocent.

> Of simple truth and blameless chastitie,
> Ne then of guyle had made experiment,
> But voide of vile and treacherous intent,
> Held vertue for itself in soveraine awe . . . (IV. vii. 30)

Spenser does not duplicate his figures. Sclaunder, seeing evil where none is, can annoy, 'and wound the soul itself with griefe unkind', but she has not the Blatant Beast's power to pursue, and she cannot bite with poisoned teeth.

The episode of Corflambo, the basilisk-eyed pagan who stands for 'the lust of the eye', restores Arthur to his role of deliverer, and illustrates the faithful, resourceful, friendship between the squires Amyas and Placidas. Moreover, since this is the Legend of Friendship, in which mutual good offices play a considerable part, Arthur can, in that capacity, join even Britomart.

And now Spenser opens his mind on those three forms of love which he has been treating in this middle section of his poem.

> Hard is the doubt, and difficult to deeme,
> When all three kinds of love together meet,
> And doe dispart the hart with powre extreme,
> Whether shall weigh the balance downe; to weete
> The deare affection unto kindred sweete,
> Or raging fire of loue to woman kind,
> But of them all the band of vertuous mind
> Me seemes the gentle hart should most assured bind.

> For naturall affection soone doth cesse,
> And quenched is with Cupid's greater flame:
> But faithfull friendship doth them both suppresse,
> And them with maystring discipline doth tame
> Through thoughts aspyring to eternall fame.
> For as the soule doth rule the earthly masse,
> And all the seruice of the bodie frame,
> So loue of soul doth loue of bodie passe,
> No less then perfect gold surmounts the meanest brass.
>
> (IV. ix. 1, 2)

Spenser himself had proved his friendship enough to dare say this, and never does the power of his art show to more advantage than in such passages where he uses it not to evoke a picture or a mood, supremely as he can do both, but to tell his thought clearly and persuasively, as though his ideas presented themselves spontaneously and without effort in the complex form of his stanza.

In pursuing the path through which the ideal of perfect manhood is to be attained, the poet has now dealt with a well-known sequence; but in reverse order; 'the lust of the flesh, — the lust of the eye, and the pride of life'. The last of these was a main theme in Book One, the first has been exhaustively treated in Books Two and Three, and here, in Book Four, has been finally disposed of by Belphoebe; the second, Arthur has now destroyed; without this clearance neither — justice nor courtesy, which are to follow, would be possible. Yet before he leaves this subject, Spenser, in ending the Book of Concord, has one more thing to say. Paena, daughter of Corflambo, is beautiful and gifted. Her music is so sweet that it almost moves Arthur himself from his purpose: 'Yet she it all did mar with cruelty and pride.' She had, moreover, been her father's daughter in her mode of life. Brought up where and how she had been, what else could be expected of her? And now the deprivation of her lands and lordship gives her angry spirit something real to feed on, 'a bitter corsive'. Yet there is good in her, and Arthur's kindness softens her; she realizes his care for her interests, the choked back seed of virtue begins to spring, and she who could do nothing by halves, becomes in time as strong in good as once in evil:

> And she whom Nature did so faire create,
> That she mote match the fairest of her daies,
> Had it defaste; thenceforth reformed her waies,
> That all men much admired her change and spoke her praise.
>
> (IV. ix. 16)

Spenser knew his New Testament too well not to add to his portrait of Hellenore, this shadow of the Magdalen.

Amoret now falls to the care of this perfect friend, in whom not a thought contrary to honour can arise; there is, however, no friendship between them, but reserve on his part and distrust on hers. Perhaps it is natural that Amoret, who has suffered so much from her want of prudence, should now go to the opposite extreme, and Arthur does not know who she is. The next event in her history is mysterious, even allowing for the abrupt transitions Spenser could have learned from Ariosto.

The precious group of friends whose troubled journeys began this part of the story, is now encountered again, all furiously quarrelling over the loss of false Florimell. Druon who would not love at all, Claribell who loved too rashly 'out of measure', Blandamour passionate and changeable, Paridell, loveless as Druon, passionate as Claribell, changeable as Blandamour. These are struggling furiously together when Scudamour and Britomart, who are seeking Amoret, appear. At once, as one would expect, the four turn on them temporarily forgetting their other grievance, and pairing as would be natural, Druon and Paridell against Scudamour, Blandamour and Claribell against Britomart. Theirs, however, is the fury of the weak; neither of the virtues is in any real danger, and when Arthur arrives and intervenes it is not to rescue, but first to impose peace by force, and then to reconcile the parties by persuasion. And now, here should be Britomart with Scudamour, Arthur with Amoret. But where is Amoret? She has disappeared; Arthur has apparently forgotten he was escorting a lady, and Scudamour, quite unaware that his love has come so near him, is still lamenting 'this present lucklesse howre'.

Spenser, who must have meant at some later point to explain Amoret's vanishing (it is not the first time it has happened), masks it to the reader by at once introducing Scudamour's story of his courtship, his winning Amoret in the Temple of Venus, and having thus drawn the reader's attention away from the main story, which remains suspended, he reverts to the tale of the true Florimell, all this time imprisoned under sea by Proteus's unlawful love. Here the poet immediately brings in the famous description of the marriage of Thames and Medway, perhaps a revised version of a piece of old work *The Epithalamion Thamesis*. Structurally this episode is justified by its providing the occasion of bringing Marinell, who as a sea-nymph's son is present at the wedding, celebrated in the hall of Proteus, into contact with Florimell, whom he is now able to love. But Spenser might have achieved that end more simply if he had not been concerned to mask the abrupt change in his pattern by a piece of heavy embroidery. He will end this book by bringing together Florimell and Marinell, whose story had filled so much of Book Three, and when he resumes the main narrative in Book Five, he will take it up at another point. In the poem as we have it we never see Amoret again.

Spenser's famous descriptive passages, of which this marriage of Thames and Medway is one, usually belong to one of two kinds: they are either scene-settings, such as the description of the house of Morpheus, or the cave of Mammon, or the various gardens, or the abodes of Discord, or of Despair; or else they are masque-like processions or pageants, such as Lucifera's ceremonial drive with the other deadly sins, or the Maske of Cupid, or the procession of the Seasons and Months in the Mutability fragment. In the first case, they build up mood and atmosphere, and may also be symbolic. In the second, they are always organically connected with the action; but they serve too, as an ornament, enriching the material and covering transitions. In this particular procession there are introduced not only the English rivers, but also the Irish ones the poet loved so well and even, 'though but knowen late', both Orinoco and Amazon. A notable characteristic of this procession is that it should have so slight a pictorial element, and so strong an auditory one. It is true that many of the rivers are characterized by an epithet or a phrase, as are the sea-nymphs, or the trees in the Wandering Wood; but the suggestion of colour and form, which Spenser can give so perfectly when he pleases, is largely absent, and there is substituted the sound of the flowing of those many waters, a sound which his stanza, in his hands, was so well adapted to give. This effect is partly cumulative, and the quotation of a single verse cannot therefore give it fully; perhaps the 29th, which also illustrates his touches of colour, may serve as an example.

> And round about him many a pretty page
> Attended duly, ready to obay;
> All little Riuers, which owe vassallage
> To him, as to their Lord, and tribute pay:
> The chaulky Kennet, and the Thetis gray,
> The morish Cole, and the soft sliding Breane,
> The wanton Lee, that oft doth loose his way,
> And the still Darent in whose waters cleane
> Ten thousand fishes play, and deck his pleasant streame.
>
> (IV. xi. 29)

The long, but not heavy vowels, the liquid *r*s and *l*s, ripple along in this verse like the waters themselves, leaving us at the end to rest by that still Darent, whose waters are so clear.[1]

Nothing now remains but brief characterization of these two books as a whole. Throughout both, the poet has been concerned with love in its various aspects, and he has not yet reached a conclusion. Structurally, each book is dovetailed into the other, and into the fifth book, since the conclusion of Britomart's quest, and Scudamour's, as far as it is concluded, are found at different points in Book Four, while the Florimell story is only ended in Book Five. Book Four, moreover, unlike the other books, has no major quest of its own; its theme is illustrated by a number of smaller stories, and single episodes, the whole having rather the character of an elaborate dance, or ballet, than of a regular narrative. Groups, pairs, single figures, come forward, perform their part, are lost among the crowd of others, reappear, perhaps may be finally lost again. But with all this interchange of his moving pattern, Spenser never loses sight of his theme, and he admits nothing which does not contribute to illustrate it.

In spite of the importance given to Florimell, Scudamour, and others in these two books by this method, there is still in them a single dominating figure whose presence acts as a sort of touchstone to reveal others in their true character. This figure is Britomart, chaste lover, true friend, and beautiful woman. All love, all friendship, is tried in relation to her; if it be not chaste, it is not true love or true friendship, at all. This chastity is to be found not simply in striking down its rude obvious assailants, but also, and even more, in regulating those who have all the rights that love can give, who must yet remember that the soul counts for more than the body. Like poor Malvolio, Spenser thinks nobly of the soul, and will not permit that it be held down to a lower level. Love is the ordering power of the whole earth, by which everything is formed, preserved, directed, and those who seek to wrench it away from its proper end to serve their own selfish pleasure and purpose, do so at their own peril, as proved by Amoret's wounded heart, Scudamour's long pro-

[1] The last canto is treated of in chap. iv where the whole story of Marinell and Florimell is discussed.

stration, and the falls of Hellenore, Paridell, Corflambo. But for all that, they are wrong who would reject love because of this danger:

> For it of honour and all virtue is
> .The roots, and brings forth glorious flowres of fame,
> That croune true louers with immortall blisse,
> The meede of them that loue, and do not liue amisse. (IV. i)

VI

JUSTICE AND EQUITY

BOOK Five belongs on the whole, to the knight it is assigned to, Artegall; a severe figure, of character akin to Guyon's, but lacking the sweetness which is one of Guyon's qualities. Was Spenser simply writing as a psychologist, or should we read an allegorical significance into Britomart's lack of sure confidence in Artegall's fidelity? As a theologian, the poet might have remembered that justice was precisely the virtue specially attacked by the original sin of man; and he may well have thought it the one most to seek in human, social, political, relations as he knew them by experience. It is true also that Artegall shadows Lord Grey of Wilton, and that Lord Grey was credited with an early sympathy for Mary Queen of Scots, which is figured in Artegall's captivity to Radigund.[1] In the whole of this book the historical allegory is much more evident and continuous than in any of the others, thus of course influencing the course of the story. Yet, allowing for this, and in spite of Talus, Artegall appears less strong in his aim, less single-minded in his purpose, than Guyon is. Were it not for Britomart he would not have achieved his quest, and he needs Arthur's help as well.

There remains a possible explanation. Guyon's virtue resides primarily in the will. Of course, since virtue is a habit formed by repeated acts, if not there would be no meaning in Spenser's narratives, reason and will must co-operate; reason to propose the act as good, will thereupon to perform it. But Guyon's virtue of self-discipline requires one original act of reason, and then that the will should persist in its decision without ever flagging. The palmer's office is to recognize temptation as such, and to procure help at the moment of extreme physical weakness and depression. Guyon's battles are fought in the field of emotion and sense, and his last enemies are all illusions, phantasms of the imagination, the

---

[1] J. C. Smith and De Selincourt, *Poetical Works*, p. iii. Froude gives Ridolfi's list *Reign of Eliz. IV*, p. 158.

strange visions which rise from that deep sea underneath man's conscious self, where Acrasia has her secret dwelling. Artegall is in another position. His office takes the task of Temperance for granted, for if self mastery were not attained, his price might be found; but it is primarily an intellectual function: his problem is not to do what is right, he has Talus for that, but to know what is right. Justice, says the definition, is that virtue which gives to each his due; it derives from an act of judgement. But if its decrees are not to remain merely abstract, academic, decisions, without influence on the real course of events, there must also exist a physical force sufficient to bring them to effect. That force is typified by Talus the iron man, well did Spenser know his necessity, and the decrees themselves are represented by Chrysaor, the sword with which kings are girded, which cannot be broken or lose its edge. But as the danger of the will is that it may be weak, so the danger of the judgement is that it may be deceived. Artegall's subjection to Radigund is an instance of this, when the bewildered judgement is turned back upon itself, and, in Lancelot's paradox:

> His honour rooted in dishonour stood
> And faith unfaithful made him falsely true.[1]

And then Britomart herself, who rescues Artegall from this entanglement in a legal mesh by sheer forthrightness, is she to be regarded as precisely the Britomart of Book Three? Spenser takes a great deal of pains to make it clear that Artegall's fault, if fault at all, and not merely a disastrous error of judgement, is not one that affects the virtue of chastity; and Radigund, whom Britomart overcomes, represents, it is fairly evident, Tyranny[2] who only by guile has made herself gaoler of Justice, and tyranny is no enemy of Britomart in her original character.

It might be that Spenser, now that Britomart's personal

---

[1] Radigund having cheated, Artegall was no longer bound in *justice*, only by a legal scruple: it is the situation where law does not do justice which therefore equity is called in to redress.

[2] It is suggested (cf. A. B. Gough: Introd. V. iv) that Radigund more especially represents 'the monstrous regiment of women'. But a poem so largely honouring a Queen, and in which so many good queens appear, can hardly condemn female sovereignty as such, but only if usurped.

quest has been achieved, and her other care, Amoret and Scudamour, both mysteriously removed from the scene, no longer regards her as an allegorical figure, but simply as the personage of the story to whom it would naturally fall to rescue Artegall. But this would be to disregard Arthur's role as the general deliverer. Moreover, her adventures on the journey seem to show her as still a person in an allegory. It is now that Dolon, Guile, seeks to betray her. Perhaps the poet has expanded his view. If he regards chastity as a super-natural grace it must appertain to the soul even more than to the body, and chastity, perfected by exercise, will become only one aspect of a more comprehensive virtue, purity of heart. Then Britomart will represent, on a higher plane than Burke's, that 'chastity of honour which feels a stain,—that is, a sin—like a wound'. It is thus that like a lightning flash, she blasts the two sons of Dolon, and thus, that like a thunder-bolt, she falls upon Radigund and by sheer straightness, con-sumes the bewilderments of Artegall's reason. Artegall's pauses and deviations on his quests, and these are nearly disastrous, form another proof that it is the guiding judge-ment which has to be perfected.

Yet neither is Artegall regarded as entirely a creature of earth. Justice, perfect justice is in heaven, teaches Spenser, using for this purpose the old myth of Astraea; it is not achieved by any clumsy, human reasoning of sharing alike, that crude, schoolboy equity of equal parts, which would seem to have dictated such a recent communistic experiment as that of Robert Kett in East Anglia, and which must have circulated much, if vaguely, before producing such an effect. As the emissary of heaven, there is about Artegall something of the remoteness and clear hardness of the angel who led the Israelites: 'Take notice of him and hear his voice, and do not think him one to be contemned: for he will not forgive when thou hast sinned, and my name is in him' (Exod. xxiii. 21).

Also, and perhaps because of his very simplicity, there is, except at moments, less of human attraction in Artegall than even in Guyon. From this point of view it may be rather his misfortune to be associated so closely with the warm, breath-ing, figure of Britomart, whose reception of the bad news of his captivity, is narrated by Spenser with so much psychological observation. It was possibly with a recognition of this that Spenser never leaves them long together, and also insists so much on his bringing up, so remote from family affection or even natural human kindness.

Like all the knights closely associated with a figure of Queen Elizabeth I, Artegall is not of faerie birth or, from the allegorical point of view, can he be, for fayerye is the realm of glamour, of illusion. Yet that his task will lie mainly in Faerie land is equally apparent, since it is those very illusions, as they relate to justice, that his task is to destroy. The communistic giant, or Malengin with his shape-shifting, or the tricked-out wickedness of Munera, are illusions more dangerous than many realities. But this analysis must not be pressed too far. Faerie land, historically considered, is also Gloriana-Elizabeth's kingdom, which to treat as illusory might hold some peril. And of all the knightly counsellors who stand round Gloriana's throne, Sophy and Artegall are the highest in place. Wisdom and Justice are Gloriana's guardians, and Guyon, himself not unimportant in that hierarchy, can imagine nothing higher for Arthur himself than that he should be as they are (II. ix. 6).

Artegall, therefore, is first mentioned as far back as Book Two. But the first description of him is in Book Three, where Britomart sees his face in the magic mirror. Perhaps there is something symbolic in this suggestion that Justice in full and lovable beauty can be seen on earth only in vision. Artegall's personal beauty is more dwelt upon than that of any other of the knightly heroes, not only here, but also in Book Four when Britomart sees him for the first time in the flesh. This beauty is indeed a sort of outward symbol or sacramental form of the virtue within. For it is becoming that he who must deal to all others what is due, should have himself received an appearance without fault. At the first seeing of him, he looks out of the mirror 'like Phoebus from the east', and Spenser refers at other times to the beauty of his countenance, 'Virtue in her face how lovely.' But yet an air of sadness hangs over this conquering knight with his golden sword and his iron man, a sadness arising perhaps from Spenser's own public experience, and proper to him in whom he had seen the embodiment of justice, Lord Grey de

Wilton. To Artegall is granted no such complete, lasting, success as the others achieve. He does what he has to do; strikes down the oppressor and sets up a just authority. But it will not remain long when once his face is turned, and, called away prematurely, he will see the Blatant Beast as he goes. It is true that in this Spenser was shadowing what he had seen in Ireland when Grey was governor. But he would not have used this material if he had not believed that the fate of the justice he was considering in a more universal context, was really concretely illustrated in it. And, in Spenser's version, a cloud of melancholy mystery hangs over both the beginning and the end of the story. Merlin tells Glauce and Britomart that Artegall, though believed a faerie knight, is really a son of Gorlois King of Cornwall—hence related to Arthur through his mother—'by false faries stolne away' while yet in his cradle, so that he himself does not know who he is. When Britomart brings him back to his native land, so the wizard continues, he will defend it gloriously. But he will die young, treacherously murdered. True, that here again, Merlin is prophesying future history, and Spenser is playing the British Virgil. But again, he would not have used this material in this context if it had not been congruous with his conception of justice. Brief and rare are the visitations of perfect justice in the affairs of men. In his short sojourn he will do all things well, and leave behind a true model, but none of the other knights is a stranger and sojourner as Artegall is.

The Red Cross Knight, himself a changeling, has been brought up to the soil, and is at home in his English patronage. Guyon is 'An Elfin borne of noble state, and mickle worship in his native land': he also has his own place and people. Britomart is the daughter of the king of South Wales; we know the castle which is her home, and she has lived there like any other young princess, except for her love of arms. Cambell and Triamond are securely established amid wife and sister, brother and friend; Calidore is loving and beloved wherever he goes. But Artegall, like and unlike Rousseau's 'Emile', has been brought up by Astraea in solitude, carried off a second time even from his faerie companions:

. . . So thence him farre she brought
Into a cave from companie exilde,
In which she noursled him till yeares he raught,
And all the discipline of justice there him taught.

There she him taught to weigh both right and wrong
In equall ballance with due recompence,
And equitee to measure out along,
According to the line of conscience
When so it needs with rigour to dispense . . .

Thus she him trayned and thus she him taught
In all the skill of deeming wrong and right,
Until the ripeness of man's yeares he raught;
That euen wild beasts did feare his awfull sight
And men admyred his ouerruling might. (v. i. 6, 7, 8)

Spenser's reason for this isolation is evident. Artegall is to be excluded from such ties, or unties, as might affect his judgement. His virtue is understood in the strictest sense of its definition. Exiled, orphaned, without home, family, friends, country, he has ridden on his way abandoned even by Astraea now set in heaven, known to the world by his golden sword and his iron man; but, till he met Britomart, known to no one by 'his louely face'. Such is Spenser's conception of the Knight of Justice; such only can be his character and his mission in this fayerye land, or land of glamour, which stands for the world as it is.

Spenser's change from the usual pattern of his narratives, in which we are first shown the knight travelling on his quest, and are then by some opportunity, told his earlier history, is more apparent than real. It is true that Book Five begins with the story of Astraea adopting and training 'the gentle child', procuring him the sword with which Jove had smitten the Titans, and then quitting the earth, leaving him her task and her iron man. But Artegall, without Talus, has already played some considerable part in the narrative, and has already found, in Britomart, the law of purity within, the complement of himself. The third, fourth and fifth books have been woven together with such care that Artegall's thread has been worked into the general pattern some time before its colour is due to predominate. But he is now for the first time the principal actor on the stage.

Why Artegall, who had been already appointed to Irena's quest before he met Britomart, should not then have been attended by Talus, and where the iron man has now appeared from, seem questions that might indicate a want of smoothness in the narrative. But the leading knights when they appear in contests not their own, are usually found without the special appanages of their virtue; not that they cease to represent it; but that these adjuncts are not called for except in their own quests. So Guyon, appearing in Books Three and Five, is without the palmer; Britomart, fighting for Artegall, is without the enchanted spear.

Artegall's story is taken up at a point apparently some time after his parting from Britomart, and we see him exercising the various functions of his virtue.

The tasks that fall to him usually have one of two characters: either to break the power of the evil-doer, or to make some difficult decision between contending parties. In the first episode, both these functions are combined. Sir Sanglier is a criminal who has murdered his own lady, and carried off another from a defenceless squire. At Satyrane's tournament Artegall, then disguised as the Salvage Knight, had not disdained to joust with Sir Sanglier. But he does not touch him now. It is Talus, irresistible strength at the service of law, who holds him a helpless captive, while Artegall, having recourse to Solomon's famous stratagem, convicts him of his evil deed, and dismisses him to his punishment 'like a rated Spaniell'.

Since Spenser has left various threads hanging from previous stories, at this point he works these ends into the pattern by inserting here the festival of Florimell's wedding. In particular, the strange adventure of false Florimell is now to be concluded, and here Artegall's wisdom will be needed. Even he will turn aside for the happy ending of true Florimell's adventures for, if 'all the world rejoiced in Florimell', so too did he.

The allegory of the knight's various encounters on the way is simple enough. In fact, Artegall's story is, on many counts, the simplest of all, even simpler than Guyon's, and is certainly a marked contrast with the two books immediately preceding. His virtue is a straightforward eye for eye

and tooth for tooth activity; but the poet takes the opportunity, possible not without some risk, of attacking not only
Sir Sanglier, the private lawbreaker, but also those who do
their evil under form of law. His next enemy represents
those who use their official position to enrich themselves and
oppress the weak, typified in the given case by Florimell's
dwarf, Dony. In fact, the poet has made a good collection of
villains at this first bridge; the 'groome of evil guize', the
little jack in office who avenges his own servitude on those
still weaker, and Pollente, strong enough 'upon the rich to
tyrannize', a tyrant, and also a cheat, as shown by the traps
in his bridge.

In the background, more fatal than all with her golden
hands and her silver feet, lurks Bribery, Munera, daughter
of Pollente, corruption deriving from abuse of power. Spenser is thinking here of those who corruptly take, not of those
who give what in the case posed, they dare not deny. If St.
Thomas More's integrity as a judge had not been excep-
tional, it would not have impressed his contemporaries so
much, and that the evil custom had continued is proved by
Bacon's later case.

Why does the poet use the somewhat bizarre device of
making Artegall and Pollente leap down the oubliette on the
bridge and fight in the water? The river is named at stanza
19, 'His corps was carried down along the Lee', and there is
a very vivid, if gruesome, touch where Spenser tells how the
head, struck off at one blow by Artegall,

> . . . tumbling on the strand
> It bit the earth for very fell despight,
> And gnashed with his teeth. . . (v. ii. 18)

Doubtless Spenser's contemporaries in Ireland easily guessed
what fight it was that had taken place at the fords of the Lee,
and whose head was 'pitched upon a pole' by the stern
justice of Lord Grey de Wilton. However, critics have identified Pollente with Charles IX of France, and his evil doings
as the Massacre of St. Bartholomew, in which case the
'groome of evil guize' would be the Duke of Guise. But in
that case, why mention the river Lee? Moreover there is no
resemblance between the episodes.

Those who do evil under form of law are not fought with but punished; it is Talus, the rigour of the law, unshaken by offered bribes, who first makes way into the castle of Munera, and Talus who, able to scent evil like a hound his quarry, drags out that figure of corruption and destroys her, her treasures, and her castle; Artegall is here only the judge.

The next encounter (v. ii. 30) has a special interest in the twentieth century. It is not now a question of crime; but of the imposition, presumably by force, of a new social order, a savage egalitarianism which insists that all should have less, to prevent any having more. Artegall's line of argument against the giant of communism, who wants to deal out earth and sea, riches and rank, in equal shares by weight, is interesting. He first asserts the superiority of the existing order of nature as being the one ordained by God according to heavenly justice, in which all know their place and their part. This divinely decreed order of nature, order as law, and order as arrangement, was indeed the world scheme as the Elizabethans still saw it.[1] Artegall has no notion of the upheaval which the popularization of the Copernican system would give to the securely walled-in Ptolemaic universe he himself describes. But even had he known that the planet Earth was the centre neither of the universe nor of the solar system, Artegall-Spenser was too good a Platonist to give such superabundant importance to the material arrangements of the world of the senses. Indeed, his argument would need but little change to fit it to the entire universe, rather than the earth only to which he applies it:

> In vaine therefore doest thou now take in hand,
> To call to count or weight his workes anew,
> Whose counsels depths thou canst not vnderstand,
> Sith of things subject to thy daily vew
> Thou doest not know the causes, nor their courses dew. (v. ii. 42)

The inequalities in the existing order are therefore included in the divine appointment from which it is wrong to diverge. The force of the further series of experiments in using the

---

[1] No doubt Spenser's attention had been drawn to these social problems by the communistic doctrines and experiments which were a powerful element in the revolutionary movement in Germany from 1525 onwards: cf. *Camb. Mod. History*, i. 62.

giant's balance seems to be directed to show that, in the first place, material and moral values are not subject to the same scale of measurement, and they cannot be calculated against each other. But, if we confine ourselves to moral values, wrong and falsehood, which are negative, cannot be compared with truth and right in which being resides. Aristotle too had taught that virtue and vice are incommensurable like truth and falsehood. However, if wrong be weighed against wrong, right will be found poised between. Here is Spenser's old principle of Book Two; virtue is in the mean and the opposite of a vice is not therefore a virtue. But, significant fact, the discomfited giant is not really seeking the right, he wants to be able to destroy the one extreme, to benefit the other, and if that is not right, so much the worse for right. And now another curious fact. This huge giant who has gathered all the peoples about him in expectation of their gain when he has succeeded in levelling everything down, has in himself so little of real substance that the mere pressure of contact with rightful law and order flings him off his height to wreckage down below. Be it noted that this is a righteous law and order, subject to true, heaven-inspired justice, an ideal order, free from weakness or corruption.

But now the peoples, misled, disappointed of their hoped-for riches, prepare for violence. These Talus disperses with his flail like a swarm of flies. They rush into hiding as ducks, startled by a falcon, scatter among the reeds. Spenser often delights us with these vivid thumbnail sketches. There he leaves the problem; he had seen social extremes enough in Ireland and in England; for it was Elizabeth I herself who introduced legislation to deal with the indigent poor, and yet such immense mansions as Knowle were being erected by her ministers. Probably too, he had heard of the wild attempts of the Anabaptists at Munster. He could not foresee how grisly a spectre would rise from the giant's 'timbered bones', and how much less effective would be the flail of Talus after that early death of Artegall which Merlin had foretold.

So far the Knight of Justice has used the sword Chrysaor only against Pollente, Oppression armed with a robber baron's power; the iron hand of Talus, the ordinary force of law, had dealt with all the other cases of evil-doers, whether private or public, or of turbulent enthusiasts whose crazy theories thrust inconsiderately into practice, endanger public peace. But Artegall is now going to honour the wedding tournament of Florimell. This is a private occasion, and the police, though not absent, will be left outside the door.

Elizabeth's courtiers probably amused themselves for an evening in identifying of the six knights who with Marinell undertake to uphold the peerless beauty of Florimell. Marinell himself has often been identified with Lord Howard of Effingham, the High Admiral, who defended that rich strand, the shore of England. But this is of less interest now than the bearing of the whole episode on the general course and purpose of the poem. It serves as a kind of provisional climax, disposing of many lesser threads of narrative which could not be carried further without cluttering up the flow of the poem and impeding the new train of events, allegorical and actual, which were to exemplify the qualities of justice and courtesy.

Of the story of Marinell and Florimell it is only requisite here to recall how the first confronting of the true and false Florimell results in the immediate destruction of falsehood 'Truth is a touchstone'. Spenser had already glanced at this favourite thought, when the giant with all his strength could not put falsehood into the opposite scale to truth. Perhaps false Florimell and her going from knight to knight, did stand for Mary of Scotland, her much publicized intrigues, and her possible French or Spanish marriage: that Braggadochio and Trompart were originally Anjou and the ambassador Simier is fairly evident. But Spenser was a brave man if, in a poem to be laid before Queen Elizabeth, he so insisted on the beauty and charm of her rival, still more so if the true Florimell is meant for Mary 'on her good side', as some have suggested. That he had the necessary courage is shown by his steadfast support of the unpopular Grey, and of Leicester, in spite of Burleigh's hostility. But that for no reason of honour or loyalty, and contradictory to his perfectly sincere cult of the great Queen, he should thus have flown in her face, seems much less credible.

It is more to the present purpose to examine Artegall's doings. In his character as knight errant he enters the tournament in disguise; but later we find him functioning like an embodied principle of equity, as arbiter of problems that the law cannot touch.

He begins by rushing to the aid of the weaker, Marinell, victorious till now, and only overcome by numbers. He overcomes a hundred knights—no one but Love fights at such odds as Justice—but when the victors are proclaimed he withdraws, as though in penance for his behaviour at the first tournament, and at first allows Braggadochio, whose shield he had borrowed, to claim his prize. It is only when the boaster attacks Florimell and advances his own false companion, that Artegall, to authorize his intervention on her behalf, makes good his own claim to be victor.

Justice, like Holiness, is allied to Humility and, still more, to Disinterestedness; it does not seek its own reputation, and will not struggle for its own rights, until those of others are involved. But Justice is then both swift and practical. Evidence is quickly brought to prove Braggadochio's imposture, and then Artegall approaches the more important matter at issue by proposing that the two Florimells should be confronted. When the innocent is placed beside the shameless, no doubt remains where true beauty is. Artegall shows the same practical wisdom in the matter of Guyon's horse, now at last to be returned to his owner in a pretty recognition scene. But fiery Justice needs the restraint of Temperance when his verdict is disputed. Justice and Temperance, these Elizabeth herself had claimed as the chief virtues of a governor.[1] Thus exposed, Braggadochio and Trompart become a mere police affair, and Talus, who has remained behind the scenes till now, deals with them. It is one of Spenser's special points that justice is to be proclaimed only where there is power to enforce it. Idealist as he shows himself, he was still too much of a practical man of affairs, and had seen too much in Ireland, to suppose that people would be moved from their own interests by the mere abstract statement of what is just:

> Who so vpon himselfe will take the skill
> True Iustice vnto people to diuide,

[1] Cf. *Letter to Leycester* quoted in Chap. IV.

> Had neede haue mightie hands, for to fulfill
> That, which he doth with righteous doome decide,
> And for to maister wrong and puissant pride.
> For vaine it is to deeme of things aright,
> And makes wrong doers iustice to deride,
> Vnlesse it be performed with dreadlesse might,
> For powre is the right hand of Justice truely hight. (v. iv. i)

If politicians were as realistic as poets, some pages of recent history might have been written in ink less red.

Artegall's next encounter, the problems of the islands and the treasure, seems to illustrate the folk wisdom of the old proverb, that what is sauce for the goose is sauce for the gander. It is, moreover, a warning requisite at that time, that the judge's decision must not be affected by any consideration of wealth or power in the disputants. However, Gough quotes legal authority, both in English and Roman law for Artegall's decision.[1]

It must be noted that Artegall does not fight his way like the other knights. Only when he has to do with Tyranny above, or against, the law, does he draw his own sword. This next occurs when his meeting with Terpine leads to his unlucky fight with Radigund, in whom, it may be, Lord Grey encountered Mary Queen of Scots, though in view of the slightness of connexion with her and the unlikelihood that Spenser would stress it; it seems probable that the historical allegory may be in abeyance at this moment. But Artegall in any case encountered Tyranny itself, irresponsible Power, to Justice, most deadly enemy.

It is in fighting Radigund that Artegall encounters his first serious temptation, and suffers that one moment of weakness from which so few of Spenser's knights are altogether exempt. Indeed, it is only Britomart who can never yield at all, since in her virtue, what is once lost is wholly lost, not indeed, without remedy, but without recall.

Artegall's weakness is compassion, which a just judge may and should feel, but not so that emotion should make him fail in his duty. No doubt Grey's Irish difficulties are hinted at here, for Spenser certainly supported his severe policy and regarded the conciliatory one of his opponents as

[1] A. B. Gough ed. Bk. V: notes to Canto IV.

fatal.[1] Artegall's fall is the most disastrous of all the knights';
the most shameful to himself, the most fatal to others; for the
fault of the Red Cross Knight, or Guyon, or Calidore if fault
it were, hurts no one but themselves, whereas that of Artegall brings to shameful death the knight who had trusted
him, and whom he had undertaken to save. Not only so, but
the one false step, however pardonable in itself, for compassion is a noble quality, and more excusable in excess than
in defect, carries with it inevitable consequences, a blurring
of the moral judgement, till now so clear; so that Artegall
believes his knightly honour binds him to keep his pledge
to Radigund however treacherous had been her means of
gaining it, forgetting that no pledge can bind him to what
is wrong in itself. His first error, owing perhaps to over-
confidence, had been making the pledge at all. However,
this said, all is said. Artegall in defeat is dignified, patient,
ready to use honourable means to gain his freedom; but firm
in his private faith to Britomart. 'Absolute power corrupts
absolutely.' Spenser is insisting on the evil of Radigund's
irresponsible power, and on the basic necessity of unshakeable justice, when he draws such serious consequences from
the momentary yielding of the reason of the judge to the
heart of a man.

Spenser's portrait of Britomart fretting over Artegall's
prolonged absence is full of life, truth, and even of humour,
and so is his narrative of her reception of the news that
Talus brings her; her too-hasty believing of the worst; her
returning to Talus for a fuller account when her emotion has
exhausted itself, and her setting forth to the rescue, all her
wrath concentrated on Radigund. But in what character is
she riding when she meets Dolon?

Britomart's old quality of chastity as deliverer, hardly
suits the present occasion even in the wider sense I have
suggested for it. Artegall is already admirably exercising
this virtue and, if that could save him, would already be free.
Moreover, Dolon's plot is formed in the belief that the
wandering knight is Artegall, and that he may thus avenge
the death of Guizor his son. In fact Britomart, having
escaped the first snare, meets and destroys the two remaining

[1] Cf. *View of the Present State of Ireland,* passim.

brothers on the very bridge where Artegall had fought Pollente and, as he believed, had destroyed the evil customs. Further, Isis, in the Temple which Britomart now visits, represents, the poet tells us, 'that part of Iustice which is Equity', though the priests indeed must serve in chastity, and by Britomart's dream there she is confirmed in her trust in Artegall, who is symbolized by the crocodile of Osiris, god of justice; for so the chief priest affirms. Britomart, then, would correspond to Isis herself, Equity, and this interpretation is supported by her subsequent conduct. For the principle of equity enables even law to be set aside when, by some circumstance, it becomes clear that slavish insistence on the literal legal position would defeat the ends of real justice. Artegall, like the other knights who fought Radigund, is bound by a contract though, actually, he was cheated. Britomart refuses the bargain proposed—a princess may refuse a queen when a knight cannot—and will not be held but by the bonds of common law. In the fight she uses a sword, not the enchanted spear for, though still deriving her strength from her purity, it is not a combat of chastity as such. Thus fights the common reason of humanity, the source of equity, against the selfish predominance of irresponsible tyranny, with all the system that Radigund typifies. Britomart victorious kills Radigund. Spenser was too wise to kill a woman, even a Radigund, by other than a woman, and proceeds to the release of the captives, restraining, 'for very ruth', equity can be allowed to pity when the law is over severe, the ferocious retributions of Talus. Now follows a natural touch; when she sees Artegall in his trouble she sets aside jealous suspicion and thinks only of comforting him, while he receives her help as generously as it is given.

And now Britomart, since this Amazon state is organized legally but not justly, 'did true Iustice deale', redressing injuries and restoring order. But Britomart too has learned something, and when Artegall proposes to set out again on his original quest, she does not repeat her attempt to delay him; she acknowledges his obligation, and she restrains her grief. She has come close enough to justice now to know that there are times when personal interests, the highest and purest, must yield to duty.

It may be worth noting in passing the singular restraint and relative austerity of Spenser's style in this book, even in such a passage as the description of the temple of Isis; the flow of his music remains; but the diction is sobered to suit a sober theme.

Perhaps it is poetic justice that Artegall, whose habit of disguise, still characteristic of his virtue, had originally caused his first meeting with Britomart to be a fight, should now be mistakenly assaulted by Arthur, who has long been left in obscurity, when both are seeking to save Samient from her enemies. But one of the most charming qualities of Spenser's knights is their readiness to own their mistakes. Arthur and Artegall are soon friends, and with this encounter, Arthur comes back to his position as the prowest knight of all the world, and the great deliverer he in whom all good qualities are at the heroic level.

Mercilla, the royal mistress of Samient,[1] is the figure of Elizabeth in this part of the book, and is seen in a more gentle and feminine aspect than she has usually appeared in either in the character of Britomart or of Belphoebe. The political allegory, however, hardly becomes prominent till the trial scene; the next encounter, though undertaken to help Mercilla indirectly, is a conflict with an abstract evil, Adicia, Injustice, companion and guide of 'a mighty man and Souldan', Philip II presumably, on the historical plane, but, on the universal, the supreme enemy whom Artegall must encounter as the Red Cross Knight encountered Pride, Guyon, Passion, and Britomart, Busyrane, Arthur's challenge to the Souldan 'in behalfe or wronged weake', alludes to the Netherlands attempt, historically, Arthur is here Leicester, but the actual history is modified to suit the moral allegory in which justice must triumph. In reality Elizabeth's armed intervention in the Netherlands was by no means wholly successful although the poet seems to include the Armada victory with it, if Upton and others are right in associating Arthur's contest with the Souldan fighting from a chariot in which the prince cannot reach him, with that battle. Yet not by human means does Arthur vanquish the Soldan, the political and military power of Spain, standing for those material

[1] The critics are not agreed in their identification of this figure.

forces which in this world seem to support the rule of the un-
just. Only the unveiling of the shield, the symbol in Arthur's
own case, of supernatural aid, gives him the victory, and
even then it is not he who slays his enemy, but the bolting
horses that dash the chariot to pieces, i.e. the fortunate wind
that scattered the Spanish fleet. This is all the victory the
poet can dwell on since, though the Protestant regions of the
Netherlands did gain their freedom eventually, it was not by
means of Leicester's expedition, or Elizabeth. On the moral
plane this conflict is represented by the encounter of Artegall,
who has got by stratagem into the castle of Injustice, and
Adicia. The latter escapes, and by her furious despair is
transformed into a tigress; but Artegall succeeds in defeating all those who had submitted to her. Spenser is well aware
that injustice in itself cannot be destroyed, until all evil is no
more. In fact, he is distinguishing rather carefully between
those concrete wrongs which can be done away with, such as
Radigund, Tyranny, or the giant Communism, and the ideal
evils, Injustice, Intemperance, which can only be denied
activity and remedied in their effects.

Perhaps in the encounter with Guile, Malengin, Spenser
on the factual plane, had in mind the plots, real and con-
cocted, against Elizabeth and her power in Ireland and
elsewhere, though it is Maleger in Book Two who more precisely represents the kernes. In Dolon's attack on Britomart,
he seems to have been also glancing at French intrigue more
particularly; but, in the moral allegory, Malengin, though a
pair to Dolon, is not his duplicate. Spenser never repeats
exactly. Dolon, an old man of respectable and even dignified
appearance, living with all the outward semblance of honour
and prosperity, invites Britomart to his house with apparent
kindness, and then would have murdered her. This is the
treachery in the intimacy of family and social life, of which
the Psalmist speaks: 'For if an enemy had done this I might
have borne it but it was thou, my familiar friend in whom I
trusted: we took sweet counsel together: we walked in the
house of God as friends.' In that era of Renaissance states-
manship, there were enough politicians to fill the character
whether on the one side or the other, and Spenser may also
have had in mind the English plots against Elizabeth; Dolon

being a figure for conspiracy. The Homeric Dolon was a spy who betrayed his own side, but this may be coincidence.

Malengin in the moral allegory is an Ishmael, a savage preying on society like a wolf, unscrupulous, ready to murder, or steal, or commit any other crime, a gangster, admitting no law but his own interest, an adept at all the tricks whereby fools are deceived, a professional criminal, living in hiding, and thence pouncing on his victims:

> Als at his backe a great wyde net he bore,
> With which he seldom fished at the brooke,
> But vsd to fish for fooles on the dry shore
> Of which he in faire weather, wont to take great store (v. ix. 11)

And now, justice guards the ways, but Talus, all the material means which a state can use to enforce its laws, hunts down the criminal through flight and disguise, until the capture is made. But Spenser tells this in language straight from folklore, the old tales of the wicked wizard who changes his form and must be gripped in each until he has finished the sequence and his power is exhausted. Through such a series Tamlane passes before he can be rescued and restored to human living. Even then, Artegall cannot hold Malengin. It is Talus who beats the life out of one who, as Spenser shrewdly says, was primarily a self-deceiver who thought he would always get away with it; other criminals might betray themselves, but not he: 'So did deceipt the self-deceiver fayle.' Granted Spenser's religious sympathies he might have been alluding to the devices and disguises of the recusants. But the 'View' does not show Spenser as holding extreme views about the Catholics as individuals, the Sydney entourage in Ireland does not seem to have done so, Campion lived peacefully among them, and he may also have been referring to, or including, the whole crew of political cum religious informers and spies of which the correspondence of the time reveals so many everywhere, and who so often mingled their betrayals with lofty professions of faith and loyalty.

Now Injustice has been driven away, and treacherous crime destroyed, the palace of Mercy may be approached, for mercy is then only possible to the ruler when leniency is not dangerous to the innocent. This palace is guarded by moral force, not physical. Awe is sentinel at the gate, and Order controls the crowd within. Warlike array is 'straunge there to se', where peace, fostered by just judgement reigned. Yet this idyllic scene includes the figure of a poet[1] who for attacking 'Mercilla-Elizabeth', has been nailed by the tongue to a post. Perhaps to none of Spenser's first readers did this seem an incongruous piece of savagery. Yet the twentieth century can hardly reproach the sixteenth, for 'those who live in glass houses should not throw stones'.

One may well suppose that in a narrative here so closely corresponding to the contemporary scene, Spenser did not insist so much on the long peace of Mercilla's domains without adverting to the lines ascribed to Elizabeth herself about Mary Queen of Scots:

> The daughter of debate
> That eke discord did sow,
> Shall reap no gain where former rule
> Hath taught still peace to grow . . .

In this book the trial of Duessa-Mary is about to be represented before Mercilla-Elizabeth; and in Book Four, Duessa was shown riding in company with Ate, and doing her best to foment quarrels, in particular between Britomart and Scudamour. Those who have remarked the different light which recent historical research has thrown upon the Babington plot in particular, and the figures of Burleigh and Walsingham in general,[2] might be inclined to quarrel with Spenser for the view he clearly takes in this Book, as elsewhere. But, in his position, he could not be wiser than his contemporaries, and even if he had had his suspicions, of the parts played by agent provocateurs—Mary accused Walsingham in Burleigh's presence of rigging Babington's plot, this poem was not the place for them.

The description of Mercilla in state, which may be contrasted with that of Lucifera in Book One, is one of the few highly wrought passages in a book otherwise singularly austere; the canopy above her throne seems to reach the clouds of heaven, and angels are seen clustering about it;

---

[1] Identified by Gough with one Fulwell a political satirist who had attacked Elizabeth.

[2] Cf. Devlin, *Life of Robert Southwell*, Longmans, 1956.

while others are grouped round her throne itself, and she herself is angel-like, Spenser's favourite compliment to a woman. On the steps of the throne are ranged, under the image of a 'beuie of faire Virgins clad in white', the Ideas of those attributes which should attend sovereignty. That they are universals is seen in the fact that justice is shown among them, and temperance also. They are all powers of conciliation and clemency:

> And often treat for pardon and remission
> For suppliants, through frayltie which offend. (v. ix. 32)

Is it too fanciful to suggest that Spenser's insistence on mercy as the primary attribute of the righteous sovereign whom he pictures surrounded by angels, was remembered by Shakespeare when he composed Portia's famous oration about the mercy which droppeth as the gentle dew from heaven from such clouds as canopied Mercilla's throne, which becomes the throned monarch better than his crown, and which is enthroned in the hearts of kings? Had not Spenser already written:

> . . . in th' Almighties euerlasting seat
> She first was bred, and borne of heauenly race,
> From thence poured downe on men, by influence of grace.
>
> (v. x. 1)

Too many parallels can be traced between Shakespeare and Spenser for it not to be apparent that the dramatist well knew the *Faerie Queene*. Indeed, how should it be otherwise? It would be impossible that such a poem could be published by a poet of the reputation Spenser already had and Shakespeare not read it, were it only to see what plots he could get from it. Two ideas the two poets certainly had in common; this belief in mercy and conciliation as the wisest and most worthy policy of kings; and the hatred for war in itself. As to this, there are passages in Book Four and elsewhere, as, for example, in this description of Mercilla, which might be set beside Shakespeare's principal reference in *Henry V*.

But in the trial about to be continued, the merciful Queen places pure justice beside her, 'and neare them none'. That a trial should be one of the central scenes of the Book of Justice is clearly appropriate, and if so, granted the persons and the circumstances, it was inevitable that it should be Queen Mary's. Spenser had been already preparing for this when he associated Paridell and Blandamour with Ate and Duessa in the quarrel scene of Book Four; since these two are generally accepted to stand for Westmorland and Northumberland, Lords both implicated with Mary. Besides, Lord Grey really was one of the Commission against Mary.

But, also, the theme of the book required that Spenser should set forth his conception of a just trial, nor had signs been wanting that such a lesson might be needed. Doubtless Spenser did believe Mary as guilty as Duessa; doubtless there were others of another opinion, whom he might have been concerned to convince; the whole truth was certainly not known then, and has hardly been fully revealed now. The description shows the trial as it should have been rather than as it actually was. Spenser's ideal trial is public, impartial, with full liberty to witnesses and advocates on either side, with no sign of violence of any kind, and with judges exact to determine guilt, but slow to punish it, and reluctant to go to extremes. With his usual tact the poet refrains from describing, or even mentioning, except by implication, the unhappy scene of Fotheringay. Indeed, from the point of view of the moral allegory, he cannot describe it, for Duessa in that represents Falsehood, and falsehood cannot be eliminated from the human combat any more than injustice; Duessa can no more die now than when Una spared her in the first book. Had Spenser continued his poem to the length originally proposed, how would he have managed without this personage who has been more active through five books than the chief villain Archimago? Perhaps, like Adicia, she would have been transformed into an animal; certainly the poet must and would have found another symbolic form, moral and historical. Intrigue did not die with Mary, and Falsehood can take as many forms as Malengin. Meanwhile, the narrative returns to Arthur.

Even when Arthur is not required to act as deliverer, he must in each book approve himself by some great symbolic action, except, indeed, in that part of the narrative where Britomart assumes his role. To Philip Sidney, the Netherlands war had been a high adventure; such an expedition as an Arthur-Leicester might fairly lead, and illustrate thereby why, and how, a just war might be fought in defence of the weak and oppressed, at their invitation, and without harm to non-combatants. Moreover, such a war will not be ended by a mere destruction of the enemy, the deaths of the seneschal and the *gyant* himself, but the institutions set up by the invaders, through which their oppression was exercised, must also be done away with, and this is seen in the destruction of the monster. Readers of the life of St. Teresa of Avila, a generation older than Spenser, will know what a dread the Inquisition, in the time of Philip II, inspired even in Spaniards themselves, of whose orthodoxy there could be no question. At a later age, Spenser's inquisition dragon would still have represented the subtle inner tyranny which seeks to control the liberty of mind and will, but its material counterpart would be found, many times multiplied, in the various political, economic, national, international, organizations which now lay their heavy yoke on the necks of their members.

Thus does Arthur-Leicester liberate Belge and her seven sons, and the soul, from the fear of interior or exterior restraint of just liberty. Despite the retained name of Belge, Spenser has dropped the historical allegory here; he only needs literal facts when they illustrate moral and spiritual truth; when they cannot be interpreted as he wants, he abandons them. Arthur, ever triumphant, can never rest, the soul, even perfected, must always go forward in this world. Gloriana's knights, who have come from Cleopolis, could presumably have instructed Arthur, their benefactor, how to reach it. But Cleopolis still has its character of an enchanted dwelling, the stranger cannot enter it, or even find it, except at the appointed time. Arthur, therefore, goes his way.

Artegall, after his various obstacles and delays, is now approaching the end of his personal quest, in which he can be helped neither by Arthur nor by Britomart. For whatever part Spenser gives to the deliverers, and sometimes it may seem greater than that of the protagonists, the last and decisive act each must perform alone. True, Guyon is helped, even at the last, by his palmer guide. But he is a projection of his own reason and moral judgement, from which he cannot now be separated, and which must be instrumental to the final conquest, since reason, not merely force, must subdue rebellious desire.

Artegall's delay, that fatal confusion of his faith with Radigund has gravely compromised the success of his quest, and has caused Irena to fall a prisoner to Grantorto. I surmise that by this name, Irena, which Spenser also uses in his *View of the Present State of Ireland*, he intended a double meaning, one the object of the historical allegory, the other of the moral. Lord Grey, indeed, was to drive the Spanish out of Ireland, but the Knight of Justice must destroy that evil which is the enemy of public peace. Peace is the good which the just queen, Mercilla, has obtained for her kingdom; peace, Spenser held, was the one essential requisite for Ireland, without which nothing else would avail; peace was a principal object of Elizabeth's tortuous policy; and, where there is perfect justice, there should be perfect peace. A little later than Spenser, another poet, Vaughan, of mind not altogether unlike, would write of the City which the Red Cross Knight saw from the Mount of Contemplation, and would say of it that the plant of peace grew there. What greater wrong can an enemy from without do a country, or a false and selfish faction from within, or both together, as Spenser supposes it, than subvert by violence and intrigue, that 'tranquillity of order' which is the definition of peace? Philip II as Gerioneo was doing more powerfully and thoroughly, because more powerful and thorough, what every sovereign more or less at that time, was striving to do, namely, impose his will on dominions he regarded as his. He had pressed his right beyond the limits permitted to man, therefore just war might be waged against him; but that there had been in the first instance, a right, the thought of the age, and of the people who still lamented Calais, could not well deny.

But Philip II, as Grantorto, or alternatively, the Papacy as a political power, was in another position. Here he was intervening by intrigue and conspiracy in a country where he had no trace of sovereign claim, and the purpose of those intrigues, of that conspiracy, was war. That there might be a parallel between Protestant Gloriana intervening in the

Netherlands on behalf of her co-religionists, and Catholic Grantorto intervening in Ireland on behalf of his co-religionists, was a possibility that no servant of Elizabeth, himself a protestant, could be expected to perceive. Spenser, planter at Kilcolman, with his wife and young family there, was certain that peace was what the country needed above all. Those who broke it, for whatever reason, were those who wronged her, but he who wronged her most was he who thrust in from without, careless of peasant or cottage, house or farmland, to destroy that peace as a mere incident in a larger policy. Such was Grantorto, Artegall's enemy.

Before this last combat, however, Artegall meets Burbon, Henry IV, ready to buy Paris with a Mass, fighting for his throne, Flourdelis, France. Artegall admits his legitimate claim, but reproves the policy of crooked means:

> Fie on such forgerie (said Artegall),
> Vnder one hood to shelter faces twaine,
> Knights ought be true, and truth is one in all:
> Of all things to dissemble fouly may befall (v. xi. 56)

The admonition might be just; but it applied to the policies of Walsingham and Burleigh quite enough to explain the poet's unpopularity in that quarter.

In describing the last fight between Artegall and Grantorto, the poet spares no pains to give the Knight of Justice a worthy opponent. Grantorto is not only of giant strength, but a skilled and courageous fighter. And it is true that material wrong is often so heavy, as it were, so well established, that it is hard to find where to strike it without seeming to do more harm than good, armoured as it is in vested interests, and disposing apparently, of endless resources. Artegall defends himself with skill; but it is not by skill or policy, but by sheer straightforward hitting, that he defeats Grantorto.

This is the first, the destructive phase, of the work of Justice. Historically, Lord Grey could not proceed much further in the time allowed him; but Spenser cannot let Artegall stop at this point; he gives him time:

> . . . that he did there remaine
> His studie was true justice how to deale.

And day and night employed his busie paine
How to reforme that ragged commonweale: (v. xii. 26)

In spite of the name Artegall-Grey acquired for severity, he
is shown by Spenser here as in the *View*, as often checking
the rigour of Talus, the material force of the law.

In ending this book, Spenser was treading on thin ice.
The course of his narrative was perfectly clear, much clearer
to his first readers perhaps, but not obscure even to us,
so that it seems that Queen Elizabeth and Burleigh are
rather to be praised for magnanimity than blamed for parsi-
mony, when one considers that the poet got away with his
outspoken criticism of Grey's withdrawal from Ireland 'ere
he could reforme it thoroughly', his virtue obscured by
'enuie's cloude', and his homeward path troubled by the two
hags Enuie and Detraction, painted with the whole power of
Spenser's descriptive genius:

> The one of them that elder did appeare,
> With her dull eyes does seeme to looke askew,
> That her mis-shape much helpt; and her foule heare
> Hung loose and loathsomely: thereto her hew
> Was wan and leane, that all her teeth arew,
> And all her bones might through her cheekes be red:
> Her lips were like raw lether, pale and blew,
> And as she spake, therewith she slauered:
> Yet spake she seldom but thought more the lesse she sed.
>
> (v. xii. 29)

Probably both queen and minister realized that to show
anger would be to admit the force of the criticism, and
Elizabeth herself could hardly be too severe with the section
of the whole poem in which she appeared as Mercilla. Indeed, Spenser's outspokenness gave a value to his compliments which nothing else could have conferred upon them,
and the queen could well appreciate this.

Friendship might have led Spenser to introduce his vivid
portraits of Envy and Detraction at this point; but he was
too much of an artist not to work them neatly into the pattern.
Calumny is the enemy of the next book, the book of Calidore
and the Blatant Beast, and the two hideous figures he has
now created, are the very ones to bring this last monster

appropriately on the scene; where envy and detraction are, calumny will not be far behind. This makes the structural contact with the next book, where, according to his usual method, the poet brings the new protagonist into contact with the one just passing off the scene.

The cordial greetings and felicitations of Calidore, sincere as doubtless they were, do not dissipate the air of sadness that clings round the figure of Artegall, his triumph not complete, the shadow of his early death already upon him. It is true that his legend is conditioned by the historical mould in which, more than in any other of the narratives, Spenser chose to cast it. But it still remains true that the historical allegory is secondary. Spenser took what seemed to him to exemplify his moral theme, and he would not have used those events to illustrate the perfecting of justice, if he had not recognized that, in the world as it is, he could not truly represent any human institution as being permanently administered according to perfect justice. Adverse circumstances, human ill will, human frailty, all these will enter, and whether it be Plato's Republic, or More's Utopia, or the City of the Sun, or the new Atlantis, or any other attempt at a perfect state upon earth, the writing is already on the wall: 'Here we have no abiding city.' But still, it is demanded of the steward that he be found faithful, and in the hurly burly amid which the virtue of justice must be exercised, it will be much if the ruler, though not succeeding as he desires, yet retains his personal virtue. This Artegall does; he has done justice and shown mercy, and after the brief encounter with Calidore, in which he proves himself not embittered, he passes away into the forest from which at first he had mysteriously appeared:

> A man's reach should exceed his grasp,
> Or what's a heaven for?

VII

COURTESY: THE MUTABILITY
FRAGMENT

NONE of the first rank of English poets, unless it may have been Chaucer, has had to cope with the practical difficulties which beset Edmund Spenser. The conditions in which Shakespeare worked militated against careful finish; but they made for inspiration, and his art was his profession, he had not to serve two masters. If Milton deferred his major work to his later years, it was by his choice, and the environment in which he lived, his own daily activity, were all favourable. Wordsworth, Coleridge, Keats, Shelley, Tennyson, Browning, were all professional writers, and several had means to write at leisure; while many of the greater names of the twentieth century have enjoyed the advantages of a literary environment almost to excess. Spenser's situation was very different; it was very much what used to be that of an Indian Civil Servant in a frontier province where guerrilla warfare prevailed. Had he been chiefly a lyric poet, or one who got his material mainly by exploiting his own personality and varying moods, this might have been of little importance; or such experiences might have been a valuable source of inspiration. But it was not so. Spenser is not a lyric poet in the usual sense of the word, though he could and did write lyrically in the wider sense which that word can bear. He is moreover no more subjective than anyone else was at that objective period. It is true that he sometimes writes of his own experiences, and sometimes makes himself a personage of his own poem; but this is not done subjectively, any more than Dante's part in the *Divina Commedia* is. The lyric cry was not his medium; to compare him with the kindred art of music, he was rather the conductor than the soloist; he required the complex response of an orchestra or choir, not that of a single instrument. For such a poet, whose works exact a long sustained effort of intellect

and imagination, and whose characteristic prosody is equally
sustained and complex, the possibility or certainty, of being
called away by absorbing active duties, which might occupy
him for weeks or months on end, take him, perhaps, far from
his books and papers, and fill his mind with considerations
of a character very far from being congenial, formed such an
impediment to artistic composition as few poets of his type
have had to contend with, or could have contended with. It
is a wonder that the inconsistencies and discrepancies which
really do exist in the *Faerie Queene* are not much more
numerous and much more serious than they are. From the
date when Harvey was already criticizing some beginning,
or the first form, of the *Faerie Queene*, and his letter was
printed in 1580, to the date of the publication of the second
part, sixteen years had passed. Spenser would not have been
the practical man he clearly was, if he had not realized that
the chance of being able to complete his original plan was
remote, unless indeed, he could have been transferred to
England; but he could not have taken the line he did in the
Legend of Sir Artegall without at least guessing that there
could be little hope of that. Even reasoning from the more
than sixteen years that had already elapsed, he must have
known that the Book of Sir Calidore, the sixth book, would
stand as the last for years, if not for ever. In the event it has
stood for ever. It must have been this consideration, at least
in part, which dictated the choice of the virtue of courtesy
from the seven still remaining on his list.

In composing Book Six, Spenser has taken up something
of the tone and spirit of Book One. Calidore, usually exemplified on the factual plane by Sir Philip Sidney, has
something of the charm and elevation of the Red Cross
Knight. He is not better than Guyon or Sir Artegall in the
sense of being more virtuous, but he is more beautiful and
more beloved. Alone of all the knights he has at no time an
official guide or companion. Even Britomart had Glauce,
and though she passes into oblivion in the fourth book,
she performed an essential function in the beginning of
Britomart's adventures. For the others, the Red Cross Knight
has Una, Guyon has the palmer, Triamond has wife and
friend, Scudamour has Britomart, Artegall has Talus; but

the Knight of Courtesy is alone. What, then, is there in the
quality he represents, to make him thus self-dependent?

It is only necessary to notice the character of even the
earliest adventures of Calidore, to realize that Spenser comprised much more in his idea of courtesy than the modern
use of the word would suggest; though that still remains
richer in content than its would-be synonym politeness. Calidore's place in the sequence would by itself imply this. That
sequence is not a chance one. In the process of forming the
'gentleman or noble person' it will first be requisite that the
soul be set right with God; the whole personality thus
receives its due orientation towards heaven as its end. This
done there follows the next step, whereby man strives to
regain his lost sovereignty over himself. Only then will pure
and noble human love, whether in friendship or marriage,
become possible. But man also has relationships of many
kinds with other human beings; relationships governed
neither by the love of family nor of friends in the usual sense.
Here, one fundamental virtue is necessary, and it is possible
to him who is king over himself; the virtue of justice whereby
each is given his due. But by making Artegall himself a lover,
Spenser has recognized that for perfect human intercourse,
justice alone is not enough. Justice was the virtue of the old
Law; but, in Spenser's world, a new commandment reigns.
Even under the old law, man had been enjoined to love his
neighbour as himself; he had since been taught that neighbourhood does not depend on geographical, or even on
racial, propinquity alone. When the man went down from
Jerusalem to Jericho, his neighbour proved to be not the
man of his own town, or his own people, but the Samaritan
'he that showed mercy'. It is thus that Calidore must follow
Artegall as being that love which is the fulfilment of the
law, neighbourly charity. As such, he will need no other
guide; for charity is a law to itself. 'Love, and do what you
like', says St. Augustine, and the group of books which
began with holiness, the love of God, is becomingly completed by courtesy, the Christian love of man. But how far
can this reasoning be substantiated by the text itself?

In the prefatory stanzas to Book Six, Spenser speaks of the
flowers of virtue which grow in the heavenly garden:

> Amongst them all growes not a fayrer flowre,
> Then is the bloosme of comely courtesie,

But this virtue, he laments, has now become a mere matter of exterior behaviour: 'Fashioned to please the eies of them that pass' and is thus but a 'forgerie' compared with what it had anciently been, for:

> Virtues seat is deepe within the mynd,
> And not in outward shows, but inward thoughts defyned.

Courtesy then, if it is a virtue, is an interior habit, not a conformity with any exterior social code. We shall find various examples in the book itself of those who, though circumstances have forbidden their acquiring the outward modes of courtesy, nevertheless possess it as a virtue, as an interior habit of conduct. Of Calidore himself the poet, giving the reasons why he is so beloved, mentions first, 'his gentleness of spright', and 'manners myld', which are not mere manners in the restricted modern sense, but in that of the old Winchester motto, 'Manners makyth man.' From this root springs 'comely guize' and 'gracious speech'. Anything insincere is abhorrent to him, 'he loathed leasing and base flattery', 'and loved simple truth and stedfast honesty'. This distinguishes his virtue from its false semblance in such as Paridell. He is, moreover, no carpet knight but tall and strong, famous for his prowess in battle. Indeed, both in description and behaviour, he is so nearly the 'gentleman or noble person' whose formation it had been Spenser's purpose to portray, as to confirm the impression that the whole book was intended as at least a provisional conclusion. Further evidence of his habitual, practical concern for the good of others will appear as we proceed.

At Calidore's meeting with Artegall, for this book has the usual structural link, he tries tactfully to comfort that knight, 'yet halfe sad' at the cutting short of his work. Then as he explains the nature of his own quest, which is to find and conquer the Blatant Beast, the monster sent into the wicked world 'to be the plague and scourge of wretched men', its altruistic nature becomes evident. He is not trying to help or avenge any individual, Una, Ruddymanes, Scudamour, Irena, but people in general, and while all the knights hasten

readily to the help of the unfortunate, this seems to be Calidore's characteristic occupation, and it is no interruption to
his other duty, as sometimes in Artegall's case it seems to be,
because the enemy he is seeking is everywhere, he may
appear anywhere, having no fixed place, and only to be found
by the desolation he leaves behind.

Yet, 'flowre' of the court as Calidore is, his adventures
are just as near the substance of folk-lore as are the stories of
the other knights. His first adventure after leaving Artegall
is derived from the old ballad story which appears in various
forms, of the mantle trimmed with human hair. Briana and
Crudor are shown as the originators of an evil custom whereby overbearing arrogance and cruelty oppress anyone weaker,
and the cutting off of hair and beard is an apt enough symbol
of that kind of savage selfishness which treats other persons
solely as utilities, an unpardonable insult. But Calidore is no
mere partisan avenger. Though he fights for the hopeless
squire and lady with the fury of a torrent released by the dam
that held it, breaks into the castle and drives off its defenders
as easily as a steer brushes away flies with his long tail (vi. i.
21); he treats Briana, now the weaker, with forbearance.
When, after conceding him every advantage, he defeats
Crudor, and yet, to be harsh and overbearing is so inherent
in our fallen nature that even Calidore is wounded in this
conflict, his first care is not vengeance, however justified it
might seem, for, as he says himself:

> Who will not mercie vnto others shew,
> How can he mercie euer hope to haue?

but to heal the disorder by removing the cause, and making
Briana happy, and good because happy. Thus those whom he
had broken by his strength, he wins by his kindness; the injured are compensated, and all are friends.

Of the next adventure,[1] 'chyld Tristram', always a magic
name, is at first the hero. He, equipped only as a hunter,
with a hunter's weapons, has killed an evil knight, another
Crudor, who attacked an unarmed man, and then maltreated
his own lady. Tristram is nobly born, son and heir to a king,
and bred to 'noble thewes', though in the forest; but Spenser

[1] Cf. vi. ii. 3.

is perhaps insisting on the necessity of nature as well as nurture, when he makes Tristram's conduct contrast so acutely with the helplessness of the former squire. He further illustrates in Calidore that generous character which delights as much in the good qualities of another as in his own. And as the story thus begun advances, Calidore does not hesitate to put aside his knightly dignity and help to carry a wounded man where he may find succour. Lancelot, as Chretien de Troyes, and the middle ages conceived him, might not have ventured so much; but Calidore's position does not suffer. Still, there is a more real problem before him (VI. iii). Priscilla, the lady of this knight, Aladine, is now in danger of her reputation, since the necessity of tending his wound has prevented her from returning home in due time. Calidore concerns himself with this too, and goes to a good deal of trouble to ensure that she shall return home in such a manner as not to be blamed. In fact, to keep Aladine's part in the escapade from being known, he manipulates the truth in a way that the supporters of the doctrine of equivocation, so much controverted at that time, might hardly have thought justified. The two lovers deserved his help, for each thought first of the other's good. In this way Spenser is able to contrast his first selfish lovers with these, purer and nobler. But Calidore had found the way to help both.

Spenser's next step in the exposition of this virtue, an exposition which proceeds in a series of pictures, is to put Calidore himself into the position in which the knight whom Tristram killed, had been. As he travels on, he comes on a knight and a lady who had made a rendezvous in the forest.[1] These two are Serena and Calepine, henceforward to play some considerable part in the narrative. Calepine at some moments seems to double the part of Calidore, and his final rescue of Serena from the savages is one of the most famous episodes in the sixth book. His name would suggest that he represents the sweetness of speech which is certainly one aspect of courtesy, and which the false courtier, Paridell, possesses, but uses for evil ends when corrupting Hellenore. Serena who has many of the qualities of Amoret, like her, lets the boldness of her innocence verge upon rashness, and

[1] VI. iii. 20.

when Calidore, with sincere regret, has apologized for his intrusion, and the two knights are talking, she, too, wanders off alone. A Serena rambling alone in the forest may seem to resemble a Hellenore abandoned; the Blatant Beast of Scandal appears and seizes her; he is blatant because he blares forth evil. The knights rush to her rescue, and Calidore, the swifter, drives the monster off and pursues it; thus leaving the stage to Calepine and the wounded Serena. He has now seen in the very act the evil he had come out to destroy.

The story turns to the other pair. The wounds inflicted by Scandal which have prostrated Serena, have left Calepine so much at a disadvantage, that even his sweet tongue cannot extricate him from his difficulties. When he seeks refuge at a house of worldly society he is taunted by Turpine as he is crossing the river, and is subsequently rejected with contumely. Shame pursues the unlucky pair even into hiding, and Calepine, on foot and almost defenceless against a rider with a spear, is reduced to the deepest humiliation, even hiding behind Serena. This is the way of the world; but it is not the way of nature. Calepine is rescued by the natural inborn courage and humanity of the Salvage Man, one of Spenser's most interesting conceptions, whose first contact of civilization, in Spenser's sense, is experienced through his compassion at the sight of Calepine's troubles. The poet seems to suggest that the Salvage Man first realizes that he is a man and not an animal, through this feeling of pity, his first touch of Calidore's virtue, of which compassion, issuing in practical deeds of loving kindness—a beautiful word, invented in Spenser's age—seems to be the foundation.

The speed, strength, skill in herbs, and plantlore, which characterize the Salvage Man, are qualities that Spenser in that age of explorers would easily find in traveller's tales; there were also folk-lore figures to help him when he began to work out what a primitive man, or one brought up without any human society, might be like. How fascinating a figure this is has been proved by the popularity of much more recent attempts at a similar delineation. But the first sketch having been made, the poet proceeds to add significant details, and first, that the Salvage Man has been invulnerable from birth. In fact, Sir Turpine's spear-thrust rebounds from his breast without piercing it. Some tale of savage or Red Indian stoicism might have suggested this trait to Spenser; but the prominence he gives it shows that it had a special significance for him, apart from the possible wish to explain the Salvage Man's survival in the forest. It is Serena who has been wounded by Scandal; but Calepine, by trying to protect her, has been involved himself, and if Scandal has not attacked him, Shame has.[1] But the spear which has pierced him is useless against the Salvage Man. For he, if he is ignorant of the graces and utilities of civilized life (he is unclad, he cannot speak, he does not build, or hunt, or till the ground, or tame animals, or cook, he is such a food-gatherer as the Stone Age historians tell us about), is unaware also of civilized vice and corruption. But though he is uninjured, he feels intuitively the malice of the blow and Turpine's ugliness and evil, and is enraged by them so terribly that the latter is panic-stricken by his attack and flees shrieking: 'a thing uncomely in a knight', as Spenser comments drily.

It is the rebellion of the natural good in man against the evil of which his own perversion has been the cause. Shelley counted on it to bring about the brave new world which Prometheus, unbound, was to see. Rousseau thought Emile could be educated into it; Peter the Hermit set it to recapture the Holy Places. Many a politician has roused it, and used it for a lesser end, even a bad one; for it is a blind fury, and may in error do more harm than the evil it is trying to destroy. In the individual it operates in the phenomenon called conversion, and thus it might have acted on Turpine, if he had not been so thoroughly corrupt. But for him the sudden vision of the humanity he has outraged, in its naked elements, is unbearably frightening; he flees from it to other crimes and to final destruction.

Calepine and Serena are in a different situation. Social corruption has wounded them, but they themselves are not corrupt. Calepine's grace of kindly tactful speech is not

---

[1] Calepine's dodging Turpine, while it may allude to some fact lost to us, may also have been suggested by Homer, where even a Hector behaves no more heroically at moments.

false; Serena's gentleness is not a superficial trick of manner, like Blandina's. For them the first sight of the Salvage Man springing on an armed knight, and driving him away by the fury of his onset, is startling; just as the satyrs startled Una when they rescued her from Sansloy. But, like Una, they quickly recognized the 'very virtue of compassion' which informed this rage. And indeed primitive man (by the attribute of vegetarianism Spenser indicates that he has in mind man as shown in the Biblical ages before the Flood) soon proves this by his deeds. He does not hunt or till the ground, but he knows plants and their virtues, and quickly heals the knight's wound, there in 'his wonning'

> Farre in the forest by a hollow glade,
> Covered with mossie shrubs, which spredding brode
> Did vnderneath them make a gloomy shade;
> Where foot of living creature neuer trode,
> Ne scarse wyld beasts durst come, there was this wight's abode.
>
> (VI. iv. 13)

The wound of Turpine's spear is easily healed in the Salvage Man's dwelling, remote from venomed tongues, pointing fingers, and peeping eyes. But Serena is another matter. The wound given by the Blatant Beast is 'inwardly unsound'. Time and natural means will not cure it; something more is needed that the Salvage Man cannot give. Spenser may also be recognizing here the greater psychological and social harm that Scandal does to a woman.

After this[1] there follows the charming story of the Child and the Bear. Calepine, walking in the forest, sees a bear carrying off a baby. He gives chase and eventually saves the child, killing the bear with his bare hands and a stone he picks up. He is then in difficulties how to deal with the baby, and here Spenser's quiet humour is felt, as also where he describes the bear trying to swallow the stone Calepine has thrust down its throat. Fortunately, he meets the childless Matilda, and the lines describing her acceptance of the infant have often been admired for their delicate truth to nature:

> And having over it a little wept
> She bore it thence and ever as her own it kept.

[1] VI. iii. 17.

Probably this incident owes its existence, in part at least, to Spenser's perception of the necessity of showing that Calepine was, after all, a man of his hands, who might himself have given a good account of Turpine if they had met on equal terms. Besides, the plot requires that Calepine and Serena should be separated. From the point of view of the allegory, it demonstrated that Calepine's virtue was not only a matter of fair words, but that fair deeds accompanied them. 'Right glad was Calepine to be so rid of his young charge.' But this good deed has made him lose the way back to the dwelling of the Salvage Man, where Serena still is. His true being, like Calidore's, is social, he was made to do good, the peace of remoteness from the human struggle, delightful as it might be in itself, cannot be his for long, the first cry of human distress has led him away from it, he has saved both the child and Matilda; but the way back to that forest hut is lost for ever.

It would be interesting to know whether Shakespeare, when devising who should dwell in Prospero's island, resolved to make a Salvage Man in reverse, and thus created Caliban. Spenser insists that the Salvage Man's good qualities came from his having inherited a good nature (VI. v. 2), though till now no occasion had called them forth. Pastoral poet though he was, he does not suggest that living 'with nature', or remote from society, will of themselves make a good man. Shakespeare insists that Caliban had evil inborn; there was that in him that good natures could not abide to be with, and that in spite of the society of Miranda, and the instructions of Prospero. The Salvage Man is strong, brave, quick to compassion, generous, and loyalty itself to Serena; besides being of a good judgement that distinguishes at once a Turpine from an Arthur. His appearance is not described, but it was certainly human, his inarticulate speech was soft and murmuring. Caliban is brutish, full of superstitious fears, hard-hearted, sensual. He has a poet's imagination; but not judgement to see through Trinculo and Stefano; his appearance is monstrous, and he fears pain. So precise a reversal can hardly be accidental; it holds even as to speech for though in a drama Caliban must necessarily speak, and Prospero has taught him how, his profit on't is he knows how to curse, whereas the Salvage Man's murmurs are beneficent. Spenser himself contrasts the Salvage Man with the ferocious and superstitious cannibals who afterwards capture Serena, among whom Caliban might have found himself at home.

Serena's conduct when Calepine so mysteriously vanishes (Canto V) forms a marked contrast with that of Una in similar circumstances, and shows plainly enough why the wound inflicted by the Blatant Beast is inwardly unsound and will not heal. Unlike her name, she is full of impatience, bitterness, distrust, uncontrolled agitation. Indeed, the Salvage Man's behaviour, as he plays her trusty squire, is more civilized, in Spenser's sense, than hers.

When the rightful exponent of any virtue in its normal functioning is helpless or elsewhere, it is the moment for Arthur, the helper from heaven. The Salvage Man has reached the limit of his own possibilities, and as for Calepine, they may find him, but he cannot return to them. Therefore, riding along the forest path come Arthur, perfected Courtesy, with his squire Timias, Honour, who has now joined him again.

Timias was last left restored to the friendship of Belphoebe, Virginity, and in that devotion, forgetful apparently of his faith to Arthur. But Belphoebe on the historical plane is Queen Elizabeth, whose service must be allowed the supreme claim; moreover, Arthur, whether as Leicester, Essex, or England, must certainly acknowledge that he who serves Elizabeth, is serving him also. But Timias cannot keep up this troubadour devotion for ever.

'Be thou as chaste as ice, as pure as snow, thou shalt not escape calumny', Hamlet was to say. Timias is hated by three mighty enemies, 'Despetto', 'Decetto', 'Defetto', Malice, Deceit, Detraction. Certainly no court favourite, no favourite anywhere, could expect to escape such enmity. They bring the Blatant Beast in his way, and though he drives it off, he does not escape a wound, illustrating the popular proverb that if you throw mud enough some of it will stick. Spenser draws a vivid picture of the squire, whose conduct has not always been manly in our sense, though it was that of a true lover in Lancelot's, standing with his back against a tree fighting his three enemies, who now attack him together, 'like a wylde Bull bayted by a mastiffe, a hound, and a curre dog' Deceit and Detraction always trying to reach him from behind. The poet had seen the plunging bull 'that in his chauffe digs the trampled ground, And threats his hornes', and there could be no better illustration of the infuriating effects of malicious tongues. Certainly, if perfect fraternal charity is ever needed, it is at such a moment. The neigh of Arthur's horse is heard, and at first sight of the rider, the foes of Timias flee. Thus are reunited the two who were separated when Arthur pursued Florimell and Timias remained behind to fight her enemies.

Arthur meets his errant squire with gladness, affectionate inquiries, but no reproach, for 'charity thinketh no evil', and when Timias gives him no explanation, he does not insist. It is thus that riding on together, they find the Salvage Man trying to arrange the harness on Serena's horse.

Arthur and the Salvage Man with his 'so milde humanity and perfect gentle mind', have been untouched by the Blatant Beast. Both are in their different ways invulnerable to such wounds, and in such company the other two soon find their way to healing. It comes from Religion, figured as a

> Hermite which his life here led
> In streight observance of religious vowe,

who is found in prayer, and is the truth of Archimago's sham. This hermit the poet describes as profoundly versed in human nature. He, searching the interior wounds, quickly perceives the 'stubborne rage of passion' which poisons them and, like a good director of souls, he sets them to cure themselves of the faults which had enabled the Blatant Beast to reach them and to bite; he who had only barked at Artegall, and had fled from the first sight of Calidore. It is treatment of the same sort as that which had cured the Red Cross Knight of his more deep-seated malaise:

> The best (sayd he) that I can you advize,
> Is to avoide the occasion of the ill . . .
> Abstaine from pleasure and restraine your will,
> Subdve desire and bridle loose delight,
> Vse scanted diet and forbeare your fill,
> Shun secresie, and talke in open sight:
> So shall you soone repaire your present euill plight. (VI. vi. 14)

While they follow this excellent counsel, confirmed by fifteen hundred years of experience, it is Arthur's part to deal with Turpine and Blandina, of whose conduct Serena has told him. The Salvage Man, with his unfailing intuition of what is noblest, will not leave him.

Turpine and Blandina, Shame and Flattery, are well housed together. Shame is almost the only coward among even the evil knights; he is the bully of the weak, but he relies on his wife's tongue to save him from the strong. Three times Spenser shows him fighting, always against unarmed, or virtually unarmed, antagonists, and twice running away, because twice effectively resisted. Blandina's smooth tongue wins even upon Arthur; hers is the false use of Calepine's gift of pleasing speech, and, remarks the poet, she could weep to order. He adds, with some irony, that he does not know if women have this gift by nature, or whether they learn it. Spenser is usually an idealist about women. Those to whom he gives human personality, as he does not give it to Duessa or Acrasia, he usually treats gently even in their ill doing. Phaedria has no vice in her, and neither Briana or Paena is bad at heart. But, in the figures of Hellenore and Blandina, he has portrayed, in the first, the natural prostitute, for whom any man will do, and in the second, the more common type, the woman who will say anything to get her own way, and get herself out of trouble.

While Arthur is dealing with Turpine and Blandina, the Salvage Man is making easy prey of all the garrison of Turpine's castle. He who knows nothing of moral convention or social usage, is not easily hurt by the tribe of peeping Toms, whisperers, gossipers, evil thinkers, evil sayers, rejoicers in iniquity, however numerous; nor will the followers of Turpine in real life exert themselves much for their master when his own short-comings come to light. Arthur hastened to the Salvage Man's rescue; but it was this rabble rather that needed rescue from humanity without human respect.

There follows an incident (Canto VII) that one would take to be based upon some factual happening; that of the two young knights, friends, to whom Turpine accuses Arthur, of 'great discourtisie' and who agreed to attack him. Youth, Sir Enias (Spenser names him later on) and Inexperience are easily led into fiery partisanship by a fancied tale of wrong. Both together they assail the prince. Youth misses his aim, and flashes by:

> Like to that heauenly sparke,
> Which glyding through the ayre lights all the heauens darke.

It is clear the poet feels no anger against generous, hotheaded, Youth. But Inexperience strikes, and is killed by the blow Arthur returns. That too is true to life. Youth may survive the encounter in which he has been deceived into taking the wrong side; inexperience cannot, it necessarily dies in the very act of experiencing. Youth too, on a second attack, is struck down; but when he sees Arthur above him, sword in hand, he realizes in one flash that this man is true, and Turpine is the traitor. In such flashes youth does recognize its heroes. Arthur is too just to punish an honest mistake; but though in this book he stands for perfect courtesy, or neighbourly charity, that does not make him sentimental; it is no charity to let the Turpines of this world go free to injure the innocent. The young knight is sent to find and bring the traitor and, doubtless with natural pleasure in the stratagem, he does bring him to see Arthur's body. It is said of charity that it thinketh no evil. In spite of what has happened Arthur is asleep, and the Salvage Man has wandered off on some forest employment:

> The whyles his Lord in silver slumber lay,
> Like to the Euening starre adorned with deawy ray.

Arthur is at all times the child of light, and even in sleep there is brightness about him. One might say that Spenser had designed this whole poem to illustrate the Gospel sayings about those whose deeds are done in light, and those who love the darkness because their deeds are evil, so absolute is his distinction between the faithful light and the perfidious dark. There is such a contrast now between Arthur asleep, shining like a star, and dark Turpine whispering to the knight to stab and make all sure. Treachery is usually a sin of maturity

> . . . the gentle knight
> Would not be tempted to such villanie,

R

Regarding more his faith which he did plight,
All were it to his mortal enemie,
Then to entrap him by false treacherie. (VI. vii. 23)

And then one of Spenser's flashing pictures, the Salvage
Man throwing down his gathered fruit and brandishing like
a hazel wand, the young oak tree he has uprooted. But
neither staff nor sword, for Arthur is now roused, is to be
sullied by Turpine's blood. He is hung up by the heels, a
warning to others, and, in the same breath, Spenser returns
us to Serena and Timias, who had just met 'the ladie riding
on an asse and led by a carle'.

Spenser often makes use of an inset episode to illustrate
an aspect of the virtue or vice which he is treating, to which
the course of the chosen knight's adventures would not easily
lend itself. Florimell's story is such an inset on a large scale.
He now shows us the god of love in a different character
from the one he had borne in Busyrane's masque. Mirabell
is young, and though not of noble birth, has become the
centre of admiration for her extraordinary beauty. She is, in
fact, the glamour girl of the moment, and as has happened to
other glamour girls, her success has gone to her head and,
like a parvenu intoxicated by unaccustomed money, her own
inflated ego fills her world, she is in fact, the cruel beauty of
the conventional sonnet sequences.[1]

And now we see the Cupid of the Courts of Love giving
audience on St. Valentine's Day, as if he had been Dame
Nature in Chaucer's *Parlement of Fowles*. The ironic tone in
which Spenser narrates the whole process of Mirabell's trial,
and his use of legal terms, suggests a satire on the trials
which he, as Secretary, must sometimes have witnessed.
Cupid, here the Cupid of the Garden of Adonis, 'who is
myld by kynd', imposed on the proud self-centred beauty a
penance like that of the Squire of Dames, the very correct
obligation to make restitution for the ill done, by helping as
many lovers as her pride had injured, and Disdain and Scorn
should see that she did it. Timias, with rash chivalry, rushes
on carle and fool; but is struck down by Disdain's iron club
and made prisoner himself, the usual fate of those who burst

---

[1] Like Professor de Selincourt (cf. Introd., *Oxford Spenser* pl. note l), I cannot
accept the identification of Mirabell and Rosalind; it is quite out of character.

heedlessly into other people's quarrels. Spenser does not leave his personages at the lower rank of squire unless because they are not capable of the greater conflicts, Tristram is only an apparent exception. It is an odd thing, if Timias really stands historically for Raleigh, as many critics think, that Spenser should seem to make rather a habit of leaving his magnificent and perhaps rather overwhelming friend some- what at a disadvantage. But Timias is probably only Raleigh at moments; he seems very often to stand simply for the type of courtly lover.[1]

With his unfailing feeling for the places where the different elements of his complex pattern come into contact, Spenser takes advantage of this encounter to set Serena off on the wandering line which will eventually bring her back to Cale- pine. It will be in a darkness in which he will not know her, but happier than Amoret, or Britomart, she will at least be permitted to meet her lover again. Meanwhile Timias has been rescued by Arthur.

It is usually the story-teller's practice to give Arthur one of the principal enemies of the virtue in question to defeat, generally one who, like Maleger, would hardly yield to the virtue except on the higher plane where only Arthur stands. It is worth while therefore to inquire why the rough carle Disdain should be so dangerous that no virtue less than Arthur's can defeat him, and not even Arthur's do away with him altogether. He is a remarkable figure with some points of resemblance to the Salvage Man; he wears no armour, he fights with a club, fatal to whomso- ever receives its blow full, blood cannot be drawn from him. Enias, courteous and loyal, though making a good fight for it, is overthrown, for Scorn helps Disdain, and few can bear being laughed at. But the strength of disdain is that it abashes others; it assumes that the other is of no value, and what he can do is of no importance. Nothing can be more wounding than that assumption, when false, except that assumption when true, and Disdain will always find the chink in our armour. Arthur's blow brings him down, for in Arthur there is no weakness, but Disdain sheds no blood, if he could

[1] Actually, if Serena is Elizabeth Throgmorton as some suggest, it must be Calepine who is Raleigh in this book.

bleed, even for himself, he would not be Disdain. He stands upon golden feet, and comforts himself by looking at them, for this is that ignoble disdain which supports itself on mere meaningless material differences. Mirabell's cry saves his life, for none can save us altogether from the moral consequences of our own actions, and it is these which she is suffering. The Salvage Man, single-handed, has dealt with Scorn, who is often more stupid and ignorant than malicious, and can be lashed with his own whip by those who are quick enough and calm enough to seize it from him.

Mirabell, then, goes her way; there is no short remedy even for the repentant, who have sinned through pride and hardness; the consequences of their actions follow them until they have lived down their old character and lived into a new one. The story leaves her and follows Serena.

Spenser makes a very definite portrait study of Serena. Gentle and sweet when all is going well, even courageous in emergency, she seems not to have the moral fibre to resist adversity; she is a dead weight on all those who try to help her. Complaining and querulous, she is sure it is all Calepine's fault:

> And euermore she blamed Calepine
> The good Sir Calepine her owne true Knight,
> As th' only author of her woeful tine
> For being of his loue to her so light
> As her to leaue in such a piteous plight. (vi. viii. 33)

And then, completely disregarding the perils of the forest, of which she already has ample experience, she proceeds to lie down and go to sleep. Yet all her troubles and Calepine's were caused, in the first instance, by her wandering away and being wounded by the Blatant Beast. However, she has the courage of love; she kept between her unarmed knight and Turpine's spear; and she has 'the genius to be loved'. Is Spenser punishing her for her want of trust, and the taint of selfishness in her love; or giving her one of those great trials which sometimes raise and purify a complaining nature, or simply giving her proof of Sir Calepine's real faith and courage, or doing all three? At least it is the timid, helpless, unthinking, Serena who is captured by savages, fierce, pagan, cannibal.

This may be merely an effective episode in the story, in which Spenser shows that he knows very well that all savages are not like the Salvage Man, and in which he eventually joins up two ends of his pattern in a scene which has been often and justly admired. But these elaborate episodes usually have some further meaning, and here the very character of the book itself suggests one; for Spenser is dealing with the whole subject of scandal evil-speaking.

Throughout the book various aspects of fraternal charity and its contrary, have been touched upon. Briana is guilty of inhospitality and, with Crudor, of selfish unkindness and insult. The knight whom Tristram kills has been brutal and faithless to his own lady, and has attacked an unarmed and unoffending adversary; nor would he have assailed Tristram if he had not thought him defenceless. Turpine too is an armoured hooligan and bully, brutal to the weak, insolent when he thinks himself safe, treacherous and cowardly in danger. Blandina, who, however, has some good impulses to her credit, is the flatterer whose manners are put on with her best clothes, and who is, in an expressive phrase, adept at 'getting round people', 'Yet were her words but wind, and all her tears but water'. But most of these very recognizable social types are strong to hurt only where Scandal, the Blatant Beast, has bitten with his poisoned teeth. Serena's wound made Turpine's attack on Calepine possible; Timias would not have crossed the path of Disdain and Scorn but for a similar injury, and now Serena, healed of the actual wound, but flying from its consequences, Disdain and Scorn, falls upon this savage tribe, eaters of human flesh. But will one who has been a principal, even innocently, in a public scandal ever escape again from the gossipers and scandalmongers? Spenser did not know the name of Mrs. Grundy, but he was well aware of her social function. Scandalmongers are really a species of cannibal; they devour the character and reputation which are more precious than bodily flesh, and nothing but violence can rescue their victim. And it is Calepine, whose gift is 'good-speaking', who rescues her.

Be all this as it may, the episode, regarded simply as a

story, is an admirable piece of work; the savages creeping on
the sleeping girl, gloating over her, and planning how to get
the most from their windfall; her sudden awakening and
their howls of glee as they rush upon her, like provincial
tattlers when someone has found out the newcomer's story,
the hasty building of a turf altar, the priest with his knife
and magic formulae; 'To what strange altar O mysterious
priest?', and then, in a glade of the forest, the knight roused
by the outcry, seeking for its cause, and, 'by th'vncertain
glims of starry night, And by the twinkling of their sacred
fire', perceiving what was going on, though not clearly
enough to recognize the victim; his rushing to the rescue and
Serena, saved yet ashamed to answer lest he should know her
voice, and dreading the moment when the light would be
strong enough to show him her face; for she knows him even
in his armour. It was not thus that Serena, who had thought
herself badly treated by Calepine, would have chosen to meet
him again. That he does know her when daylight comes,
Spenser tells us; but takes the tale no further. Perhaps in
Book Seven or Eight we were to have seen the morning of
that day; in the meantime the poet, having shown what
happens to one who, even innocently, gives occasion to
scandal, returns to someone whom he has ignored, though
not forgotten, for some six cantos, Sir Calidore himself (vi.
ix).

The Knight of Courtesy, who was last seen driving the
Blatant Beast away from Serena, has not been idle all this
time. He has chased Scandal from court to city, from city to
town, from town to country, to farm and open field, until he
reaches the place:

> Whereas the Heardes were keeping of their neat,
> And shepheards singing to their flockes, that fed
> Layes of sweet loue and youthes delightful heat— (vi. ix. 4)

It would be strange, seeing that Calidore is believed to stand
for Sir Philip Sidney, if his admiring friend had not let his
quest bring him back to Arcadia.

Calidore, by his zealous pursuing of his quest, has so far
succeeded as to have liberated court, city, country town, and
'private farm' of the pest. Now he has reached the shepherd

country, the traditional abiding place of simplicity and innocence, recommended both to Sidney and to Spenser as scholars and artists, by classical and renaissance pastoralism, and, as Biblical Christians of the type both were, if by nothing else, by the fact that David, the shepherd king, was himself a pastoral poet.

It might be very natural and graceful that Spenser, having got Sir Calidore among the shepherds, should make an Arcadian idyll of Philip Sidney's marriage with Frances Walsingham, however little Meliboeus in his rural retirement, and his deliberate rejection of the ways of court and city, might resemble her politician father. But this alone would not be enough to justify so long and important an episode interrupting, if it does interrupt, the main thread of narrative so recently resumed. But is not such an episode, not always so long certainly, part of the structure of most of the other books? In whatever way, and for whatever reason, nearly all the knights whose quest is treated in full, are at some point set aside from pursuing it, and this usually just before the ultimate victory. Moreover, in the other cases, the delay is formative, and the knights are better equipped for their conflict after it than before. Indeed in the Red Cross Knight's case, the final victory seems to have depended on it.

In saying this, I set aside the Knights of Friendship, Cambell and Triamond. Their trial is summarized for us only after its completion and in the real action of the poem, they appear only for a moment, when they are already confirmed in their distinctive virtue. Britomart's case too is somewhat different. Chastity as an infused supernatural grace is an all or nothing sort of virtue, indeed it must always be so, not subject to piecemeal increase or diminution. Yet, in the long delay between her finding Artegall and their actual union, she learns something, as we see in her contrasted behaviour at her two partings. In the second she reveals a patience and sweetness in submitting which are certainly not hers before her painful wait and distressed journey. Guyon's profit by his sojourn in the House of Alma I have already mentioned; while Scudamour certainly serves his probation in his long association with Britomart while they

search for Amoret. There he learns the mystery of those
flames which had separated him from her. Artegall, truly,
had time enough in Radigund's dungeon, to ponder the
difference between a slavish literalism and the free spirit of
real justice. It would be strange if Calidore alone had nothing
further to learn, no practical experiment to make.

'Love had he found in huts where poor men lie', like
Wordsworth's Shepherd Earl, and this love must certainly
teach him something, advance him to a higher plane of
achievement. If Pastorella had been but a pretty Arcadian
doll, she could not have become, as surely she was, the not
remote ancestress of Perdita. In fact, her character is quickly
shown; she is not at all dazzled by the splendid homage of
the stranger knight; he must meet her on her own ground
if he wants her favour; she will accept no King Cophetua; it
must always be the woman who condescends. Calidore, the
more won, doubtless by the firmness beneath the simplicity
which had charmed him, becomes, as Florizel afterwards, a
shepherd for her sake.

Simplicity would seem to be the virtue Pastorella stands
for, the simplicity which goes with an innocence as real as
Florimell's, but perhaps more courageous, more compatible
with the experience that the peasant's daughter could not be
without. If Florimell's purity recalls Ben Jonson's lyric:

> Have you seen but the bright lily grow
> Before rude hands have touched it?
> Have you marked but the fall of the snow
> Before the soil hath smutch'd it?

Pastorella's resembles the white swans of Spenser's own
Prothalamion on which soilure could not stick:

> So purely white they were,
> That euen the gentle stream, the which them bare,
> Seem'd foule to them,

Especially granted the Arcadianism of the day, simplicity
might well seem the point of perfection in which Calidore,
the darling of the court, still needed schooling. And that
simplicity, not ignorance, which remains precisely what it is,
and takes other people exactly as they are, without any of
the affectation or embarrassment which arise from self-

consciousness and social insecurity, really is a virtue of the country rather than the town and, in the country, of the mountain rather than the plain. Spenser may have noticed this on his visits to the north, or among the Irish hills he alludes to so affectionately. For the countryside he seems to have in mind here is of open fields, indeed, but rising slopes: 'The Heards were keeping of their neat' in the one, while the shepherds watched their flocks among 'the budded brooms', on the second. Calidore had pursued his quarry across the plain, up to the sheeplands, and there it had vanished:

> They answer'd him that no such beast they saw
> Nor any wicked feend that mote offend
> Their happie flockes, nor daunger to them draw:
> But if that such there were (as none they kend)
> They prayd high God him farre from them to send (vi. ix. 6)

What wonder if the hunter thought that here he might well rest a little?

And now the Knight of Courtesy finds himself breathing far other air than that which lay heavy on the castle of Briana, though purged of evil custom, or in the bower of the soft-spoken Blandina, with her coaxing wiles, and easy emotions. Spenser has not forgotten the art which first gained him the fame of poet, when, in the *Shepheardes Calender*, he gave life to Cuddy and Willye and Thomalin, and the other dwellers in that Arcady of more northerly latitude where he first assumed the name of Colin Clout, his use of which has so completely blotted out Skelton's share in the invention. It would indeed have been strange if, having so felicitously restored Sidney-Calidore to that Arcadia where 'the shepherd boy piped as though he should never be old', Colin Clout should not have been there to meet him. There was to be one more meeting in 'Faerie land' with that friend whom he would not see on common earth again. But Colin Clout dwells on Acidale, and Calidore has not yet found the way thither.

Whether by happy chance, or happy invention, several events have disposed Calidore to appreciate the simplicity and honesty he now encounters. For if he can, on the one hand, contrast Crudor and Briana's churlishness and inhospitality with the ready welcome that is here offered him, the untaught knightliness of Tristram had given him a hint already that the graces of person and character in which the essence of civilization, civility if the word had not been ruined, consists, are not learned only at court. And the reader, who has followed Arthur's path as well as Calidore's has seen in Blandina an admirable foil to the straightforward, sincere, Pastorella.

The romance of the wandering knight who loves the simple maiden was no invention of Spenser's. Perhaps he even knew Greene's version of it in *Friar Bacon and Friar Bungay*. But certainly the theme was never touched more gracefully than by Spenser, as he describes the knight's first sight of that 'faire damzel', and traces the various steps by which the idyll develops. There is no Lord of Burleigh business about this courtship. Pastorella tending her sheep, or taking away the table at evening when the cottage meal is over—one of Spenser's realistic touches—has her own dignity; she is not to be had for the mere asking. Calidore must learn their life and accept it as it is, before her heart is given. Meliboeus too, when it comes to the point, shows himself a sturdy British yeoman, whose flock is his own, who calls no man master, and whose respect for the gentry is mingled with a due regard for his own independence. The means at his disposal may be limited; but he can be as generous with them as Calidore with his gold. Indeed, there is a certain tone of reproof in his dignified refusal of this:

> Sir Knight your bounteous proffer
> Be farre fro me, to whom ye ill display
> That mucky masse, the cause of men's decay,
> That mote empaire my peace with daungers dread.
> But if ye algates couet to assay
> This simple sort of life that shepheards lead,
> Be it your owne: our rudenesse to your selfe areed (vi. ix. 33)

The poet demonstrates Calidore's real virtue in showing him adapting himself to these new circumstances. Like the Red Cross Knight in the house of Coelia, he is receiving his last formation, and, as Holiness on the Mount of Contemplation longed to lay aside the earthly struggle with evil and gain at once the joys of eternal rest, so his companion and similar, for the second commandment is like the first, having found people living in a society so simple, so unworldly, so pure, that scandal is not known in it by sight, or even by name, would fain abide there for ever. If the Red Cross Knight looked from afar at the heavenly city, Calidore is seeing from within, something very like the innocent earthly life which might have been led in Eden. And in his praise of it there is something of the spirit of the song which another than Sidney's shepherd boy, would sing in after years:

> He that is down need fear no fall,
> He that is low, no pride.
> He that is lowly ever shall
> Have God to be his guide

So sang the shepherd boy in *Pilgrim's Progress*, almost the last voice of that genuine pastoralism which gave so authentic a ring to so much Elizabethan poetry, and not least to the nostalgic melody of Spenser's own lines:

> That euen I which daily doe behold
> The glorie of the great, mongst whom I won,
> And now haue proued what happiness ye hold
> In this small spot of your dominion,
> Now loath great Lordship and ambition;
> And wish the heauens so much had graced mee,
> As graunt me live in like condition;
> Or that my fortunes might transposed bee
> From pitch of higher place vnto this low degree (vi. ix. 28)

Like Guyon in the House of Alma, Calidore is seeing what that society is like in which his own virtue rules supreme.

But there underlies all Spenser's imaginations, symbols, dreamlike melody, a strong sense of the reality of things. Indeed his poem in being an allegory is an attempt to clothe that reality in a concrete form which shall express its character more vividly, and with less alloy, than factual conditions allow it. It is Meliboeus himself, who has both sought and abandoned the world, who answers with a thought echoed consciously or not, from Marlowe's *Faustus*, and sounding again in Hamlet's voice and Milton's:

> It is the mynd that maketh good or ill,
> That maketh wretch or happie, rich or poore—

> For some that hath abundance at his will,
> Hath not enough but wants in greatest store;
> And other that hath little, askes no more
> But in that little is both rich and wise,
> For wisedom is most riches; fooles therefore
> They are, which virtues doe by vowes devize,
> Sith each vnto himselfe his life may fortunize (VI. ix. 30)

If Calidore learns his lesson, he may carry his Arcadia within him.

But even this happy place, where scandal is not known, is not really paradise; it is still the world where no one can win without somebody losing, so that Calidore's increasing joy in Pastorella's favour means Coridon's increasing sorrow. And it is still an earthly place, whose very poverty will not protect it from thieves that break in and steal. The Arcadian interlude is not meant to last; when its work is done, if Calidore does not leave it, it will leave him.

Before that happens Spenser gives us a charming picture of Calidore among the shepherds, putting aside his armour for Pastorella's sake, and conforming his sword-hand to the crook. But beside the pretty idyll of the girl's gradual yielding as she realizes Calidore's worth and attraction even by Arcadian standards, there is the contrast of the uneasiness and jealousy of Coridon, who before had hoped for her favour, with Calidore's patience, sweetness and generosity of practising steady, day to day, goodness and neighbourly love.

As far as the allegory is concerned when Calidore has once achieved this, and has gained the love of Pastorella, attained the perfect simplicity which presents so polished a surface that scandal will not stick, whether giving or taking, he has no place more in this rural retreat as Spenser hints at the beginning of Canto X. But, like the Red Cross Knight, before his return to the earthly conflict, he is granted a vision, the strange and singularly imaginative vision which he sees on Mount Acidale.

There is nothing in the whole poem more completely of the stuff of the fairy-tale, yet more shot through with hints of deeper meaning, than Calidore's adventure of Mount Acidale. Ballad and folk-tale are full of benighted travellers who come unawares on the fairy ride, or the fairy dance, when the hillside stands open, and the night is as light as day. But the traveller must neither be heard or seen, or else the vision will disappear in a flash.

In the explanation which Spenser puts into the mouth of Colin Clout, his *alter ego*, these hundred dancing maidens whom Calidore has caught sight of, and the three, still more fair, in the midst of the circle, are called by classical names; they are the handmaids of Venus; this mountain is one of her resorts, the three leaders are her Graces, Euphrosyne, Thalia, Aglaia. But the winds of Greece never blew on that mountain top. A colder, more northerly, air breathed on it, coming from uplands where gorse blooms all the year round. Nymphs and oreads do not vanish like the fairies.

Yet one may also wonder if some traveller's tale of unknown dancers surprised at some rite, had lurked in Spenser's memory until the occasion called it forth. The rhythmic beating of feet upon the ground which Calidore hears from a distance, and which arouses his curiosity, is a strangely realistic touch in the dreamlike scene.

Few women, even the brides of poets, have received praises as magnificent as those Spenser lavished on Elizabeth Boyle. Perhaps, in the magical scene where Calidore breaks in on Colin Clout playing while the hundred maidens, and the three Graces dance, almost ritually, about the Fourth Grace, Colin's wife, and they all disappear, fairylike, at the interruption, the poet only meant to utter those praises, and complete Calidore's formation by giving him this glimpse of good feeling as it is among those whose task is to inspire the unbought grace of life. Colin Clout's explanation would suggest this, and moreover, it throws much light on Spenser's conception of courtesy, the distinctive, essential, virtue of civilization:

> These three on men all gracious gifts bestow,
> Which decke the body or adorne the mynde,
> To make them louely and well-favoured show,
> As comely carriage, entertainement kynde,
> Sweet semblaunt, friendly offices that bynde,
> And all the complements of curtesie:
> They teach vs, how to each degree and kynde

We should our selves demeane, to low, to hie;
To friends, to foes, which skill men call Ciuility.

Therefore they alwaies smoothly seeme to smile,
That we likewise should mylde and gentle be,
And also naked are, that without guile
Or false dissemblaunce all them plaine may see,
Simple and true from couert malice free:
And eek them selves so in their daunce they bore
That two of them still forward seem'd to bee
But one still towards show'd her selfe afore;
That good should from us goe, them come in greater store.

                                            (VI. X. 23, 24)

Colin Clout speaks for his maker, and his maker's mind is
clear on this. Courtesy equals 'ciuility', and 'ciuility' com-
prises the exterior gracious sweetness, together with the interior sincere kindness, and readiness to good offices, which
distinguishes the civilized man from the savage as Spenser
conceives of things. For him an advance in luxury or com-
modity is not a note of civilization, Archimago, who can
travel on the wings of the north wind, is not more civilized
thereby, nor are Lucifera in her palace, nor Philotime on her
throne, civilized, but Meliboeus is civilized when he receives
Calidore in his hut with generous hospitality, and the Graces
are civilized when they honour the surpassing beauty and
virtue of the 'countrey lasse', and dance to a mortal's music.

At various points Spenser has shown us glimpses of this
courtesy. Blandina had possessed the outward grace, but not
the inward virtue; the Salvage Man had all the inward virtue
and good actions; but so far, lacked the 'sweet semblaunt';
Calepine was pleasing in speech and kind in deed, Meliboeus
and Pastorella, besides their solid goodness have the natural
good breeding of simplicity without vanity, affectation, or
social ambition. Calidore has exemplified everything from the
beginning, when we first meet him tactfully comforting
Artegall. All through the book he has never raised his hand
for himself; but has been ready, daring, resourceful, gracious,
and sympathetic in his dealings with others, and he has
driven the Blatant Beast so far away that he can hear no
sound of it. Now he seems to have set aside the further
quest, and to place his love for Pastorella before every other

claim. Yet this desire to abandon court and camp and live in pastoral seclusion, simplicity, and innocence, if it be a temptation, is one that only the good can feel. It is a dream that reality will dispel, as he himself has dispelled this other dream which, if vision to him, was reality to Colin Clout.

Is there another side to this experience? This was an act of poetic creation, this playing of Colin Clout's pipe for the dance of nymphs and Graces; an act, apparently, of lyric creation, which could not well be renewed if interrupted, any more than Coleridge could continue the tale of Xanadu when once it had been broken off. Perhaps at that moment Calidore represented not Sidney, but Raleigh, who had come to him in Ireland, his Arcadia, if also a scene of battle-grounds, and had awakened in him again the ambition of the court, dispelling who knows what other poetic projects. He must have realized the advantage of getting some, at least, of the *Faerie Queene* into print. But still he would no longer be playing to the fairy maidens and Elizabeth, a fitter audience, perhaps, than the one he found.

From this scene Calidore returns unwillingly even to Arcadia. Only his love is a stronger attraction than the beauty of artistic creation. However, his steady kindness to his rival, Coridon, proves that he has learned Colin Clout's lesson. His formation is now complete; he has learned to live with all men as with brothers. But he has still to prove to Pastorella that his exterior graces cover strength, courage, and sincerity, while, at the same time, it appears that selfishness underlies Coridon's rougher manners; the 'tygre' that springs on Pastorella, when the three are in the forest, elicits both these facts, for Coridon flees while Calidore saves her with his shepherd's crook.

Now Pastorella and Calidore are united, and now Arcadia, its end achieved, is about to vanish; for though there be paradise still on earth it is permitted to no one to live there for ever. 'Thieves break in and steal', Brigantes, sophisticated, commercial,[1] savages worse than Serena's cannibals, break in with fire and murder, and Pastorella is carried off.

As a story-teller, Spenser needs some more active and exciting event, and one which will bring Calidore back to

---

[1] VI. x. 43.

his quest: as an allegorist he cannot leave his knight in a
fool's paradise: his quest is not finished, he had driven off the
Blatant Beast, but it is still at large; the world has not been
freed from the poison of evil tongues, and there is still active
the most potent source of strife among men, the love of
money, 'economic interests', serving to unify the false form
of human society, as love of the neighbour does the true.
Enter, then the Brigantes

> That never used to liue by plough and spade
> But fed on spoile and booty, which they made
> Vpon their neighbours, which did nigh them border . . . (VI. x. 39)

Calidore is absent at the moment of the raid; for when the
principal of true civilization is withdrawn, savagery and self-
interest have nothing to check them, and free society itself is
destroyed. It is not we of the twentieth century, who have
seen what we have seen, who can question Spenser's analysis.

Now, with the shepherds' cottages, the open fields, and
the budded broomes, is contrasted the underground den,
with its almost complete absence of light, sure sign that their
deeds are evil, of the robbers. In the introduction to the next
canto Spenser suggests that the robbers themselves stand for
the 'worldly chances' which are permitted to bring misfortune, so that men may not trust their happiness to earth, and
yet may realize how precious those glimpses are (VI. ii. 1).

In the darkness of the robber island Pastorella shines 'like
a good deed in a naughty world'. But beauty is there only a
cause of strife and contention, and a bond which is only of
interest, is easily broken:

> Thus as they words amongst them multiply . . .
> They fall to strokes, the fruits of too much talke,
> And the mad steele about doth fiercely fly . . .
>
> Like as a sort of hungry dogs ymet
> About some carcase by the common way
> Doe fall together stryuing each to get
> The greatest portion of the greedie pray . . .
> And snatch and byte and rend and tug and teare. (VI. xi. 16, 17)

In that struggle of frantic greed and fear between those who
want the lovely thing to sell, and him who wants it all for
himself, good and evil are killed without distinction, Coridon

who loved his neighbour, but not as himself, making good his escape. Spenser's point is sufficiently clear, and he returns to Calidore.

Yielding to the evil-doer is no part of Calidore's love of his neighbour; and it is not because he has no mind or will of his own that he is easy to get on with. Once guided to the right spot by the fugitive Coridon, afraid of going and afraid of staying, he bursts into the underground cave like a thunderbolt, and rages in it like an earthquake. The evildoers are destroyed, Pastorella is saved, flock and herd are regained; but the hillside where the wandering knight had first found the friendly shepherds 'among the budded broomes' is desolate. Calidore does the best he can when he brings the spirit of that unworldly place with him into the world in the person of Pastorella who, 'Had euer learn'd to loue the lowly things.' But he takes her to the castle of friends, where, like Una and Britomart, she must wait, and there after his departure, a pretty recognition scene restores to her a father and a mother; for it would be against the tradition of all the romances if she had been really of peasant descent.[1]

The Blatant Beast, so long left unmolested, is now easy to track by the damage he has done. Perhaps, too, Calidore, after his late experiences, is more clearsighted. Driven out of court, city, town, the monster has been raging among 'the estates', that is, the different conditions of men, and is now working havoc among the clergy. It is in a monastery that Calidore at last brings him to bay; he has broken into the church itself, blaspheming, says the poet, and casting down the images, 'for all their goodly hew'.

It would seem that the excesses to which puritanism might go were already apparent; irreparable damage had indeed been already done and Spenser has already made his lack of sympathy clear. He had been the Bishop of Rochester's secretary, and Young was no extremist. Moreover, phrases and allusions in his poetry make it evident that the poet tended towards what would now be called the High Church. Even apart from the passage now in question, it seems certain that he did not share the bitter zeal of those

[1] It has been suggested with some appearance of reason that Belgard Castle is Belvoir and Sir Bellamour the Earl of Rutland.

who shattered shrine and window, and burned statue and image. Even prescinding from their sacred character, he would have spared them 'for their goodly hew'. One of Una's assailants had been Kirkrapine, and the lion had struck him down, and the very introduction of his own wife into this poem, recalls how he had spoken in *Epithalamion*, published in that same year, of the high altar, the sacred ceremonies, the 'trembling steps and humble reuerence', proper to 'those holy places'.

In such surroundings, the Blatant Beast turned despairingly to attack his enemy. Two rows of iron teeth he had; but his chief weapon was his thousand tongues of dogs, cats, bears, tigers, but, says Spenser, in his expressive mournful cadence:

> . . . most of them were tongues of mortall men
> Which spake reprochfully, not caring where or when.

Even Calidore cannot kill the Blatant Beast. Almost alone of all the heroes, he has no sacred armour, no adamantine sword, no guarded shield, no enchanted spear; for none of these avail against evil speech. It is by sheer strength and resolution that the victory is won, the beast crushed down, the mouth forced shut and muzzled.

But though the poet alludes, briefly, to the triumphant leading of the captive monster 'through all Faery Land', the book ends, like Book Five, on a note of sadness. For the Blatant Beast was running free again in the countries Spenser knew, whether released by 'wicked fate' or 'fault of men':

> So now he raungeth through the world againe,
> And rageth sore in each degree and state;
> Ne any is that may him now restraine,
> He growen is so great and strong of late,
> Barking and biting all that him doe bate,
> Albe they worthy blame, or cleare of crime:
> Ne spareth he most learned wits to rate,
> Ne spareth he the gentle Poets rime,
> But rends without regard of person or of time. (VI. xii. 40)

That brief glimpse of Calidore and the captive monster in the streets of Faery land, with the people staring after him, is the last we see of the Knight of Courtesy. Like all the other knights, he is left *in via*, not yet returned to Gloriana, not yet reunited to Pastorella. Like Artegall, he had been given an impossible task; since, to succeed, he must make his virtue not only the law of his own being, but also of the world around him. Spenser, idealist as he might be, wore no glasses which distorted the view of things as they are. Yet one thing Calidore had gained, more than all the others, with love he had bought love. Spenser imagines him as one of those delightful characters that seem not to have sinned in Adam, so exact is the harmony between the graces of their inward virtues, and the charm of their persons and minds. Gloriana's court included the fine flower of 'goodly manners' and 'ciuil conversation':

> But mongst them all was none more courteous knight
> Than Calidore, beloued over all
> In whom it seems, that gentleness of spright
> And manners mylde were planted naturall . . .
> Whose euery deed and word that he did say,
> Was like enchantment that through both the eyes
> And both the eares did steale the hart away. (vi. i. 2; ii. 3)

One gets the impression that Spenser, too, had a tenderness for this, as it proved, his last creation:

> If in the rich vocabulary of love,
> Most dearest be a true superlative,

then such was Sidney–Calidore to Spenser–Colin Clout.

So ends Book Six, and if that were all, one could only add, as was added to another fragmentary romance a few years later, 'the rest was not perfected'. But that is not quite all.

In 1609 Matthew Lowmes published an edition of the *Faerie Queene* in which to the six books were joined two further cantos, 'which both for Forme and Matter appeare to be parcell of some following Booke of the Faerie Queene vnder the legend of Constancie'. Thus the famous 'Mutabilitie Cantos' were given to the world.

These two cantos tell an inset story, complete in itself, of how the Titaness, Mutabilitie, sought the throne of Olympus and was defeated by Nature's decision against her. Nor did Spenser ever write anything better than this story, whether we consider the poetic beauty of narration and description, or the breadth and power of the conception. That the knight of the book into which this story was to be inset, was to be Constancy, or Fortitude to keep up the apparent parallel with the group of cardinal virtues, seems a fair inference from the subject-matter. Yet, as I am not the first to perceive,[1] the more one tries to enter into Spenser's mind and follow his construction of the poem, the less likely it appears that this could have been part of a seventh book, or even part of a legend, strictly so called, at all.

That Constancie, to keep the accustomed name, was one of the virtues Spenser meant to treat is, in itself, extremely probable. He intended to include all the qualities proper to a perfect human character, and he certainly realized how important among these was the virtue on which perseverance to the end would depend. It would little avail that the ideal man should become holy, temperate, just, and so forth, if he did not persevere in that state to the end. But, as I have tried to show, Spenser was following a logical order in the sequence of his legends, and it would certainly appear illogical that Constancie should appear half-way through; its obvious position would be in Book Eleven. For Spenser meant to write twelve books of twelve private moral virtues, and the last of these would surely have been that of Magnificence itself, and Arthur would have been its hero. The whole structure of the poem points to this: the knights sent forth by Gloriana on the successive days of the feast must clearly return to her court to give account of their missions, and besides, Artegall's recall is a hint that Gloriana herself was to have a special need of all her knights. This too is suggested by the poet's leaving all the stories without their natural end. He may have learned the trick of suspending the final from Ariosto, but he makes his own use of it. Certainly, in the last book, and in the hour of Gloriana's need, Arthur was to reach Cleopolis and meet there the lady of his vision. Then would follow the last act in which both moral and historical allegory would be combined in a great final battle in which good would triumph over evil, and England over Spain. Spenser himself refers to this at the end of Book One, where

[1] Janet Spens, *Spenser's Faerie Queene*, Edwin Arnold, 1934.

he hints at a future battle, greater than that between the Red Cross Knight and the Dragon, which would take place: 'Twixt that great faery Queene and Paynim king.' Arthur would be the victor, and in his triumph all the other stories would also come to their happy close.

With these events occupying Book Twelve, five books remain unaccounted for. One, presumably, would have been that of Sophy, the knight whom Guyon speaks of as being, with Artegall, highest in Gloriana's favour.[1] Plato's list, in the *Republic*, adds to two virtues already treated by Spenser, Temperance and Justice, Courage and Wisdom. But that Courage could have been the theme of a special book seems unlikely, since all the knights possess this virtue in the highest degree. But Sophy's name points to a purposed Legend of Wisdom. Aristotle's urbanity, and his gentleness also, would seem to be both comprised in Spenser's Courtesy; but liberality and magnanimity remain, though liberality again is a virtue which has been already freely exercised. Aristotle's Modesty would seem to be that maiden Shamefastness who so powerfully affected Guyon in the House of Alma. Even if we hold it possible that Spenser had in mind those just mentioned, Wisdom, Magnanimity, Constancie, Magnificence and, possibly, Liberality, one place would still be vacant. Was he thinking of Aristotle's Righteous Anger? Or, since Aristotle's list clearly never supplied more than a general idea, would he have recurred to the place where he had already found a chastity which could be exalted above temperance, and where both courtesy and love are? These are questions which can never be answered, and meanwhile, the place of the Mutabilitie stanzas is still to be considered.

It would seem reasonable that a story culminating in the defeat of Mutabilitie, should illustrate a legend of Constancy, into which it might be inset as Scudamour's story is in Book Four. But there are objections to mutability being taken as a contrary of constancy. In the other books the contrary of the dominant virtue is a vice. Holiness is opposed by hypocrisy, false holiness, Truth by Falsehood, Temperance by intemperance, True Friendship by false, Justice by injustice, and so forth. But Mutability is not, to Spenser, evil

[1] II. ix. 6.

in that way; she is as bright and beautiful as the dwellers on Olympus:

> But when he (Jove) looked at her louely face
> In which faire beames of beautie did appeare,
> That could the greatest wrath soone turne to grace,
> (Such sway doth beauty euen in Heaven beare)
> He staide his hand . . . (VII. vi. 31)

It is true that the poet speaks of her 'bad dooings' while she subjugates the earth, and says that she has disturbed the order of nature, and exchanged justice for policy, and death for life:

> Since which all liuing wights have learn'd to die,
> And all this world is woxen daily worse.
> O pittious worke of Mutabilitie
> By which we all are subject to that curse,
> And death instead of life have sucked from our Nurse. (VII. vi. 6)

She comes, too, certainly of suspicious origin; she is the Earth's daughter, and we have already seen that in Spenser, chaos, darkness, disorder, decay, are associated with Earth, in contrast with Nature, who is the principle of order and generation. Indeed, this whole story is, at the last analysis, the full statement of the contrast between Earth and Nature which has been suggested throughout the poem. When Mutabilitie faces Jove, she calls herself:

> . . . a daughter by the mother's side,
> Of her that is Grandmother magnifide,
> Of all the Gods, great Earth, great Chaos' child. (VII. vi. 26)

But still, that doubtful origin, as Jove himself admits, has not impeded the exaltation of Hecate and Bellona who are her sisters and, however unmannerly her attack on the Moon, the brilliant description of which impressed the imagination of Keats, she behaves with dignity on Olympus where she appeals to Nature's God to vindicate her right.

Now it is quite certain that in Spenser none possess true beauty who are evil. 'False seeming' is the sure sign of a Duessa, a Blandina. His whole doctrine on this point, exposed at length in the *Fowre Hymnes* published in the same year as the six books, requires that real beauty should not be only a material semblance, but the manifestation of the spirit within, for:

> Beautie is not as fond men misdeeme,
> An outward show of things that onely seeme
> So euery spirit as it is most pure,
> And hath in it the more of heauenly light,
> So it the fairer bodie doth procure
> To habit in . . .

If then, Mutabilitie's beauty be great and real, there is good in her. Secondly, the vitality, the strength, of Mutabilitie, is real also, the Gods themselves recognize and fear it; she remains unaffected by Hermes'

> snaky-wreathed Mace, whose awfull power
> Doth make both Gods and hellish fiends affraid:

she deals with Jove as with an equal, and, though he dislikes her appeal to the God of Nature, he cannot set it aside. But Spenser's evil creatures are all in themselves, old, hideous, monstrous, deformed, sick, and dying, as Duessa in her true shape, and Maleger, exemplify, to say nothing of the various giants and monsters that cross the path of the knights. True, Mutabilitie has brought injury to the dwellers of earth. But they suffer rather as Rosencrantz and Guildenstern do, for coming between the collision of mighty opposites. Archimago and company make no appeal to Nature's God against their opponents; they belong to Gorgon the terrible shadow that underlies Spenser's evil actions and his hell. But, in fact, Mutabilitie is not a moral figure at all, though, from the point of view of the story, Spenser calls her proud and ambitious. She is a natural force, like Venus Genetrix herself, and there is so much justice in her claim that Nature herself hesitates before deciding against her. Even in that adverse decision she calls her daughter, and enjoins her to submit, not to Jove, but to her.

It is difficult to see what such an artist as Spenser could have been intending to do with so overwhelming an episode in a legend of Constancie. Spenser has many inset stories, but they are always subordinate to his main theme, and their action in some way depends upon it. But this story is complete in itself without any loose ends such as Spenser is wont to weave in with the threads of his principal narrative. He could, of course, have manipulated the beginning and ending as he did in other cases, if there had been any detachable threads; but the story is self-contained in the sense that there are no persons in it who could belong to the main narrative. It is, besides, much longer than Spenser's inset stories usually are. Its nearest parallel in character is Scudamour's story in Book Four, in which he recounts, in an abstract allegorical form, events which, on the factual narrative plane, had happened to occasion the main action of Book Three. Understood in this way, as giving the allegorical significance of the book in a similar manner, and as forming a background, and an abstract context, for the concrete factual narrative, these cantos might introduce a legend of Constancie, rather as the much slighter Astraea story introduces the Legend of Justice. Or there is one other imaginable context. If the Knight of Constancie were undergoing a formative period, like the other knights, he might read or be told this story, thus coming to a clearer notion of himself and his mission, as Guyon and Arthur read their chronicles in the Castle of Alma. But none of these suggestions remove one tremendous difficulty, that this splendid story, with its elaborate descriptions, which include the famous procession of the seasons and months, and in which Spenser's full genius is manifest, should be meant as merely a subordinate episode. When Spenser intends such a thing, he does it as he did the marriage of the Thames and Medway, not like this.

But if these cantos do not belong to a Constancy legend at all, what purpose could Spenser be imagined to have in composing them? One possibility is that, conscious as he always is of the transience of earthly things, he wrote the story for itself, trusting to find a good place for working it in, at some point in the six books still to be written. Such critics as those who have read so much between the lines of Shakespeare's dramatic development, might even imagine the poet, with the same spirit that bade him reject Essex's gift, using those last weeks in London, when his house had been burned, and his life's work as a man of action, apparently destroyed, to affirm in his own special way, his faith in the divine reality behind the changing shadow show, and in the guidance which was in fact leading him to the sabaoth he so ardently desired.

Another, and an attractive hypothesis is possible. Spenser did not leave the development of his poem to chance happy thoughts cropping up as he went along; though doubtless he did make use of windfalls when a good wind blew. In Book One he already foresees the culminating event of Book Twelve. Were these cantos, which work up to so magnificent a peroration, intended to be the conclusion of the whole poem?[1] Say that Arthur has found Gloriana, has overcome in the final battle, has entered Cleopolis, and with him the Knights of Maydenhede whose stories here terminate, for all this was evidently to happen. Say that Arthur also finds out his own mystery and assumes his own throne, as may well have been intended also, and what then? Cleopolis, however splendid, is still an earthly city. The reign of Arthur and Gloriana, however prosperous, peaceful, magnificent, is still an earthly reign. Spenser was too good a Platonist, too good a Christian, too thoroughly a man of the Renaissance not to be intensely aware, just when triumph reaches its apex, of the *sic transit gloria mundi*. Moreover, speaking practically, he needed an ending which would be artistically satisfying, and yet not too uncompromisingly final; since there remained his further plan of treating the virtues of Arthur after he was king. Would not this vision of Mutabilitie, leading its magnificent pageant of cloudland figures, which momentarily conceals 'the pillours of Eternity', have made just such an ending as the mood, the subject, and the form required?

The content of these cantos was treated when discussing Spenser's contrast between Nature and Earth, and his use of mythological divinities, which he fundamentally regards, as Camoens does, as personified natural forces.[2] But when taking the Mutabilitie cantos by themselves, these become secondary considerations.

In the following generation, Henry Vaughan was to write famous and often quoted lines:

> I saw eternity the other night,
> Like a great ring of pure and endless light,
> All calm as it was bright.

---

[1] Cf. Spens. op. cit., for this also.　　　　　[2] Cf. Chap. II.

> And round beneath it, Time in hours, days, years,
> Driven by the spheres
> Like a vast shadow moved: in which the world
> And all her train were hurled.

Such a vision, though reversed in order, Spenser shows us in these cantos. In them he makes an ascent like that he describes in the *Fowre Hymnes*, following the scale of being upwards, through the world of phenomena, until it reaches non-contingent reality, the unchanging is. The ascent, however, as it is set forth in the Hymns, is mainly conceptual. Here he tells it as an allegorical story. Mutabilitie, whom he also calls Change and Alteration, is represented as wilful, arbitrary, irrational, a spirit of lawlessness:

> For she the face of earthly things so changed
> That all which Nature had established first
> In good estate, and in meet order ranged
> She did pervert, and all their statutes burst. (VII. vi. 5)

From inanimate things, Mutabilitie passes into the moral world, creating the same disturbance, and then, following the Ptolemaic world-structure, mounts to the circle of the moon. Few of Spenser's narrative situations are more vivid than his evocation of the consternation on earth, and among the other planets, when the moon is eclipsed by Mutabilitie's highwayman tactics, and few things are more charming than the preceding picture of the Queen Moon:

> Her sitting on an iuory throne shee found,
> Drawne of two steeds, th' one black, the other white,
> Environd with tenne thousand starres around,
> That duly her attended day and night;
> And by her side there ran her Page that hight
> Vesper, whom we the Euening-starre intend:
> That with his Torche, still twinkling like twylight,
> Her lightened all the way where she should wend,
> And ioy to weary wandring trauailers did lend. (VII. vi. 9)

There is also a touch of mysterious suggestion, not common in Spenser, in the following stanza, where Mutabilitie resolves to seize 'The kingdom of the Night and waters by her wained'. There is a faint undertone of laughter when the stars stand paralysed with astonishment, and the other planets rush, 'with a great outcry' to the circle of Jupiter, as also when the Heavens' Herald, finding his magic staff powerless, and himself defied, prudently 'staid not to reply'. The experience of Grey's secretary has lent something to the description of the grave council interrupted by the bursting in of the rebel, at which sight the gods spring up in confusion while Jove, keeping his head, draws himself up in a dignified attitude, to overawe the intruder. Spenser's genius was not for the stage but, whatever the nine lost comedies might have lacked, it was probably not dramatic situations.

Mutabilitie has thus ascended from earth and the realms of men, through the circles of the planets. But there is a limit to her rebellion and her daring. She is no Lucifer defying the Omnipotent, she desires to go no higher than the sovereign natural power. Spenser's insertion at this point of the pretty fable of the river Molanna and Arlo-hill, serves the useful artistic purpose of interposing an interval which may give greater impressiveness to the assembling of the gods. These include all the powers of nature from earth, sea, and sky, even Pluto and Proserpina from the underground, but not 'th'infernall Powers', not, for example, mysterious Gorgon, nor Night in her iron car. Spenser distinquishes carefully: the theme of these cantos is not moral good and evil, but the philosophical conflict between Being and Becoming; he therefore excludes all the personages who have appeared in the moral contests of the *Faerie Queene* proper, and all who are necessarily associated with moral ideas. Nature herself, though she appears as the Demiurge, the intermediary between creatures and creator, through whom pure Spirit acts upon matter (Mutabilitie had appealed to God, not to Nature), is yet not represented as participating in divinity, or even as a heavenly being such as Guyon's angel is though in VII. vii, divinity is seen manifesting itself through her. Spenser, refusing to describe her, refers us back through Chaucer in the *Parlement of Fowles*, to Alan of Lille, who wrote *De Planctu Naturae*[1] where Nature is a personification of the ordered being of the total created universe as first created good. Nature's is that universal judgement from

---

[1] Alan of Lille, *De Planctu Naturae*; T. Wright, *Anglo-Latin Satirical Poets*, ii. 458.

which there is no further created appeal. She is the organizing One in which is comprised the activating Many, this in its turn, including Jove and all his hierarchy and, in her own place, Mutabilitie also. If one may give her another name than her own, she is Created Life, what Wordsworth calls Duty when he writes:

> Flowers laugh before her in their beds,
> And fragrance in her footing treads,
> She doth preserve the stars from wrong
> And the most ancient heavens through her are fresh and strong.

Judging from stanza 13, her place, in Spenser's allegorical use of the Ptolemaic system to stand for degrees of being, is that Primum Mobile: 'Still mouing, yet unmoued in her sted', but, as Alanus would tell us, high as she may be in the scale of being, she is yet far below the heaven of God: 'O Dei proles genetrisque rerum Natura, Dei gratia mundanae civitatis vicaria.'[1]

To her Mutabilitie sets forth her plea, appealing to experience to prove that in fact she already rules the four elements of which all things are made. As witness of this she calls forth that famous pageant of Seasons, Months, the Signs of the Zodiac, Day and Night, the Hours,

> And after all came Life and lastly Death;
> Death with most grim and griesly visage seene,
> Yet is he nought but parting of the breath;
> Ne ought to see, but like a shade to weene,
> Vnbodied, vnsoul'd, vnheard, vnseene.

Thus she claims to rule Time that rules 'this lower world'; and when Jove claims for himself and his fellow planets that overruling power which current astrology assigned to them, Mutabilitie retorts that even in the circle of the fixed stars there is motion 'as wizards saine'.

Long is Mutabilitie's argument, long the ensuing silence; but short the final answer: the universal flux is subject to Law; it is but potential being passing into act; phenomena changes, subject remains unchanged, changes themselves fulfil a

---

[1] Alan of Lille, *De Planctu Naturae*; T. Wright, *Anglo-Latin Satirical Poets*, ii. 458.

pattern by which mutability itself is controlled. So Spenser affirms this faith, that passes almost into vision in the following stanzas, in that Absolute and non-contingent Being he had proclaimed in the Hymns, whose wisdom

> rules the house of God on hye,
> And menageth the euer mouing sky
> And in the same these lower creatures all
> Subjected to her powre imperiall.

Artist that Spenser is, he does not end the canto with any blare of trumpets. Nature's words have evoked a glimpse of the Eternity of Vaughan's later vision, 'All calm as it was bright.' Reality for a moment shines through the world of phenomena, and silence falls on both plaintiff and defendant:

> Then was that whole assembly quite dismist
> And Nature's self did vanish, whither no man wist.

VIII

SPENSER'S POETIC WORLD

EDMUND SPENSER, the London schoolboy, whose headmaster was the enlightened Richard Mulcaster, lived from his childhood in an imaginative environment of which the reflections are seen in his work; and he received an intellectual formation which gave his genius the material it needed to work on. No poet has less to say about great cities; and the river he evidently loves was not the busy, wherry-laden, highway he could see not far from his school, silver-streaming though that river might still be in those days, but the quieter waters easily reached beyond the city, whose soft murmuring rhythm is heard not in the *Prothalamion* only but as an undertone at least, in all Spenser's verse: 'Sweet Thames run softly till I end my song', he had written, more prophetically than he knew, who did not know that when all his songs were ending, he would be back in London again.

Perhaps in Arthur's book, treating of the 'Legend of Magnificence', Spenser would have painted for us such a picture of Cleopolis, as would have made it as vivid to us as are Acidale or Arlo-hill; but though we have been deprived of this, there are many traces in his poetry of imaginative experiences which go back to the jostling, many-coloured life of the streets of London. Processions, gay pageants in bright costumes, sometimes in character, sometimes just gorgeous, made recurring episodes in that life, as the still surviving annual Lord Mayor's Show is witness. The trade guilds contributed each their special display, Spenser was still at Merchant Taylors' School, when the Merchant Taylor's Guild presented a group featuring St. John the Baptist in the show which was to honour Sir Thomas Roe in 1568.

One frequent figure, not only in these set pageants through the streets but in masks and dressings-up in general, was the 'wodewose', the wild man of the woods. Machyn's diary notes the appearance of 'ii gret wodyn with ii gret clubs all in gren', in a procession, and there are many other records. These passing glimpses left an impression which, in later years, would contribute to the brilliant portrait of the Salvage Man; though no doubt other factors played their part; the wild man only appeared as a figure in pageantry because he was already a figure in folk-lore, and he must also have received new life from the traveller's tales which the Elizabethan voyagers would bring back. As far as Spenser's own opportunities are concerned, Hakluyt's *Voyages* date from 1582, Raleigh's attempt on Virginia had been made in 1584, and he had visited Spenser in 1589, while a *Brief and true Report of the new land of Virginia* by Thomas Hariot was also available. Moreover, as T. D. Kendrick points out in *British Antiquity*, the antiquary set in which Spenser moved was interested in primitive man and various attempts had been made to reconstruct his possible appearance and behaviour. It is hardly possible to doubt the poet's acquaintance with these.

Spenser's boyhood had probably brought him some dramatic experience too. Mulcaster encouraged acting at his school; and the Merchant Taylors' boys even presented plays at court. Spenser must have been in contact with this activity even if he did not share it, as it is quite reasonable to suppose he may have done. That he originally had dramatic ambitions is clear from Harvey's allusion in the *Three Proper Wittie and Familiar Letters* to the nine comedies named after the nine Muses.

It would have been later, when he was with Leicester, or during his visits from Ireland, that he would have seen masking. This was one of the regular winter amusements at court; there are records of six or seven masks in one season. One, for example, showed the ubiquitous 'wild men', their costumes covered with moss and ivy. Accompanied by 'forsters' they appeared on New Year's Day 1573–4, during, that is, Spenser's Cambridge career. Simier, the French Ambassador, who was to be satirised as the monkey in *Mother Hubberd's Tale*, was officially entertained with a masque of six amazons and six knights.

Spenser's Mask of Cupid in Book Three is a combination

of the fantastic character figures of the mask with the processional movement of the pageant; but the mask in his time,
though there were already scenic effects, was less formal than
later, and usually ended by dissolving into a dance in which
the spectators also took part: in the rhythmic changes of the
various symbolic groups in Book Four, there is a sense of
pattern that might almost be transcribed back into the
medium of maskers dancing, and the dissolving away of his
pageants suggests this also.

This allusion to Book Four naturally leads to another and
very important feature of Spenser's narrative, the tournament, the groups I have just mentioned were on their way
to and from the tournament held by Satyrane for the prize
of Florimell's girdle. We look on the tilting and tourneying
of Spenser's knights as if it were entirely a piece of archaism
borrowed from Chaucer or Froissart, as out of touch with
reality as Beckford's make-believe medievalism and his
mimic Gothic castle. But there was a tiltyard in Spenser's
London in Whitehall, where the Changing of the Guard
takes place now. There were set tournaments at least
annually, from Queen's Day (17 November) in 1576 onwards. Leicester was a permanent challenger, the system
being that, for some special occasion, a group challenged all
comers, just as Marinell and his companions do when his
marriage with Florimell is being celebrated. Once a knight
presented himself disguised very much as Artegall was at
Satyrane's tournament, and in 1581, when Sidney was
among the challengers, but Spenser was already in Ireland;
Sir Henry Lee, the famous knight, came and went unknown,
like Artegall again, or Lancelot.

Tournaments were carried out with all the more elaboration because chivalry, which had already ceased to be a
practical method of warfare, was still being maintained as
a luxury, a game of skill. As the modern practice of show-
jumping is to riding, itself now a sport, so was tourneying to
chivalry in the days of Elizabeth I.

Spenser's single combats are criticized as too little realistic,
as when the blood that Arthur sheds is compared with a rose.
But he could assume a knowledge of such fights in his
readers, just as a reporter assumes a certain knowledge of

tennis in those for whom he writes his account of the match on the centre court at Wimbledon. His readers knew the reality; it was for him to make it beautiful and ideal as suited his theme. The technical words of tourneying are often given as examples of Spenser's archaisms. But some at least must have been still in use.

Other sports which have left their impression on Spenser's figurative language are bear and bull baiting, especially the latter. Characteristically, his sympathies are usually with the bull which for him is a noble courageous animal just as it was in the ancient world. It is Arthur fighting two enemies who is compared with 'a saluage Bull whom two fierce mastives bayt'. These and other allusions (cf. vi. vi. 37) have all the vividness of direct observation.

Pageant, procession, masking, tourney, baiting, Spenser had seen them all in London: but city life has left no other traces on his Faerie land, unless perhaps the allegorical pictures in the Emblem books affected him a little. But the loving portrait of Eumnestes and his room full of books, in Book Two seems a reminiscence of Cambridge days. Otherwise he has little to tell us of streets. Even Mercilla's palace seems remote from other houses, and of the appearance of Cleopolis we know nothing except the gleam of its crystal tower and brazen bridge. In *The Meaning of Spenser's Fairyland* there is a formidable array of possible sources for this crystal tower. But in fact Spenser could hardly read anything in romance and folk-lore without meeting such a structure. It was the proper thing to have.[1]

Country life and occupations are constantly alluded to, not in any vague, general, way, but with the precision of intimate experience. Even his Arcadia is no mere conventional landscape. Hunting, still more falconry, are frequent sources of similes, the ducks scuttling when the hawk's shadow falls on them, the fierce bird missing its 'souse', and mounting again (ii. xi. 36) the hounds trying to reach the hunted deer, turned to bay among the bushes, and dangerous with desperation. These sights, however, might have been observed by any of the courtiers who took part in the formal hunts of

---

[1] Spenser need have looked no further than the second sonnet of his own *Ruins of Rome* or *King Orfeo*.

a royal progress; but Spenser was equally familiar with more homely spectacles, the cloud of gnats rising above marshy ground after sunset, the cattle swishing off the flies with their tails, two hungry dogs fighting over a piece of meat, two bulls struggling for the leadership of the herd, moss growing on the branch of a tree, a tame squirrel, the shepherd's care to get his flock home before the dew was on their heavy fleece. All these are pictures as vivid in Spenser's mind as those of river and hill near Kilcolman, of rock and cataract in Dynevor, or of the wise woman working a folk charm to take away love.

I have tried to recall some of the pictures of real life which had stamped themselves on Spenser's retentive visual memory; but they were not always scenes of peace. The raiding savages who take refuge in their caves where the peasants dare not follow them, and carry on a regular traffic with unscrupulous merchants, are evidently as genuine as the motley crowd of kernes under Maleger that attacked Alma's castle, and also Kilcolman, and the scenes of desolation where Slander lived, or Care, or Ate, could serve as illustrations to the *View of the Present State of Ireland* which was being composed at much the same time.

In all these things Spenser was drawing on actual experience, but he had other sources, not only in his positive reading, but also in that less definable mental environment by which we acquire ideas we know not how, except that they are 'in the air'. Whether he shared the general belief in magic, black or white, in astrology, witchcraft, witches, fairies, is as impossible to say as in Shakespeare's case; but that he knew quite as much of such things as Shakespeare did, is equally certain, and when he chose the title *Faerie Queene* for his poem, and when he made Faerie land itself the scene of its happenings, he was as well aware as Shakespeare of the popular faith he could reckon on. As a story, the tale he had to tell was quite as credible and as fascinating to his readers as ever was *King Solomon's Mines*, or the works of Jules Verne, and more realistic than most of the modern wonder world of science fiction.

The modern reader's conception of fairy land is of a fantastic region where the fruit-trees produce jewels, where everything is as strange in form and substance, and where scientific rationality is abjured. It is definitely separated from our world, and its population largely consists of a jumble of grotesques, talking animals and spangled ballet dancers with butterfly wings. Now Spenser, though he often mentions 'Faerie Land', never gives a set description of it, and his incidental references show it as a familiar, though boundless, region of forest, river, plain, hill, and sea-shore, such as the poet had known in England and in Ireland. Indeed, both names and places may still, at times, be recognized. To find this strange is to misunderstand the whole character of Spenser's fairyland. And when once this is known it also becomes clear why he so names the scene of his poem.

The modern notion of fairyland is a literary fictitious one, made up of elements, some genuine enough in themselves, worked up in fancy and embroidered upon by those who make a profession of writing for children, or who seek an escape from the mass of matter and from mechanical techniques. From these fancies is derived the gauzy-winged queen with the silver wand whom Dan and Una so rightly repudiated, and whose proper home was the Christmas season stage. And yet her background, operatic and pantomimic, is in some ways the most genuine element in all the phantasmagoria conjured up by writers of a pretty fancy who saw in the anthologies of folk-lore the material for giving a sugar coat to 'the power that makes for righteousness'. For Spenser, Shakespeare, Gwynn ap Nudd, and Manannan MacLyrr themselves, would all have recognized in the pantomime transformation scene a praiseworthy attempt to show by art the land of faerie. For both are illusion. 'Strange sights like scenes of faerie.'

Shakespeare's incorrigible fancy, his Moths and Mustardseeds and the rest, is, presumably, responsible for the fragile crowd of flower-fairies and so forth of those who, when writing stories, have remembered that Ariel sucked where bees suck, and that Titania had some connexion with cowslips. Though indeed the spinning of literary cobwebs goes back to Drayton too. But Shakespeare at least was a countryman before he was a Londoner, and he inherited and used for the substance of *A Midsummer-Night's Dream* and *The Tempest*, a tradition on which Cobweb, Moth, and Mustard-seed make only a graceful embroidery. For Shakespeare's fairies travel from India and wander in a wood near Athens, they enter houses, they take changelings; or they live on an island which a ship sailing from Tunis to Naples might happen to ground upon, and where strange sounds and visions deceive the sailors when they land. Their earth is our common earth, but they have cast upon it the glamour which is their special gift. Under that glamour, bones are coral made, Ferdinand sees his ship full of demons; all the others, except those who already possess them, dream wild dreams of thrones and empires. Titania sees a donkey's head as beautiful as Antinous, and Helena acquires momentarily to the eyes of Lysander that perilous beauty which, in the real Helen, had:

> . . . sunk a thousand ships
> And burned the topless towers of Illion.

In the sixteenth century the word which has become 'fairy' was still as much an adjective as a noun. As an adjective it qualifies the name of a person or place in the state of fayerye, that is, in the possession, or under the control of those other inhabitants of the earth whom men cannot see, unless by some special gift. Elves was often their name in these islands. Their distinguishing power was that of casting the glamour, that is, of making things appear as they wished in the eyes of others. Thus the dry stick becomes a horse, the dead leaves, coin, the hairbrush thrown behind the fugitive, becomes a forest, the looking-glass a lake; the disused quarry may seem a palace, and one who has outlived the oak tree, a baby of three days. The magic of Oberon, Puck, and Ariel is true glamour, such as we find it in folk-tale or ballad.

In the witch trials of the same period, besides speaking of 'fairies' they speak of 'fairymen and fairywomen'. But elf is also a common term, especially when they are not speaking of changelings. Such allusions are reported in the trials of Isobel Goudie, Alysoun Pearson, Andro Man, all contemporary with Spenser, and with Shakespeare.

There is no substantial, geographical, difference between

the land of faerie and the land of humanity. It is the state
which is different. The forest of Arden, or the wood near
Athens, or Arlo-hill, are faerie land in the faerie presence.
No imaginative violence is required to conceive of England as
at once faerie land and the kingdom of Elizabeth, still less
if the hero be Arthur. For Lydgate knew that Arthur was
a king 'ycrowned in Faerie' and so in the romance of *Huon
of Bordeaux*, which Spenser alludes to (*F.Q.* ii. i. 6), Chaucer
too is aware of this association:

> In the olde dayes of the King Arthour,
> Of which the Britons speken greet honour,
> Al was this land fulfild of fayerye.
> The elf-queen with her joly companye
> Daunced ful oft in may a grene mede . . . (*Wife of Bath's Tale*)

Men too may be faerie for a time, or for ever. Huon of
Bordeaux had been a man, Tamlin was still human under the
glamour. If some of his knights are really not elves, but
faerie changelings, Spenser had good precedent for this.
Not only are tale of changelings widespread, but Thomas of
Ercildoune had been in fayerye, Arthur's sister was Morgan
le Fay, Welsh legend makes him all but faerie himself. In
fact the more he, through the Tudor legend popular at the
moment, and through his own cycle, is associated with
Wales, the more did he enter an enchanted region, preserved for us in such tales as those of the Mabinogion,
where human beings and faeries are in daily contact. Malory
himself, whose name perhaps is Welsh, connects Arthur
with the lake-dwellers who are so characteristic of Welsh
mythology. The allusions to Merlin's home, its locality and
character in Britomart's book, as well as his making her the
daughter of the King of South Wales, suggest, as do other
indications, that Spenser drew quite as much on local
mythologies and folk-lore as on literary sources in forming his conception. This was possibly the reason of Gabriel
Harvey's contempt for the first version of his friend's great
work.

In reading the *Faerie Queene* we must, then, prescind from
all subsequently acquired ideas and think of 'fairies' as
Spenser, Shakespeare, and their contemporaries thought of

them, and of 'Fairyland' as at our very doors and under our feet. But Spenser not only knew what was common know-ledge, and if I say common belief, I shall hardly exaggerate, about fayerye, glamour, and Arthur's connexion with both; he was also by way of being a Platonist, and for Plato the whole earth itself was little more than a fayerye vision. So indeed may Gloriana be at once true glory, the eternal idea enthroned in the heavens, and whatever men can conceive of as most fair and desirable, represented under the image of the Faerie Queene with whose excellent beauty Arthur is ravished; and also, as embodied in human form, may be 'the most excellent and glorious person of our soueraine the Queene'. And if indeed Spenser meant to portray the adven-ture of the Christian soul through the chances and changes of this mortal life, it must have been with a flash of joy like that more bruited one of Archimedes that he realized how that fayerye land that he had always known, was enriched and illuminated by Plato's philosophic imagination, and how perfect a scene it thereby became for his epic of the human soul, as being simultaneously the great globe itself, and yet the baseless fabric of a vision: 'For the fashion of this world passeth away.' 'This world, lordyngs, is but a faerye.'

Assiduous readers of fairy-tales will have noticed that, especially perhaps in Scotland, the famous 'glamour' covers a sufficiently poor reality. Legends tell us of visitors who have attained clear sight, and have perceived the palace to be a pit of red gravel, and the princely children, squalling mis-shapen brats. Spenser is aware of this aspect of things, and in his work glamour belongs chiefly to those who stand for falsehood and hypocrisy and are, in their own proper persons, hideous and vile, as Duessa unveiled is shown to be, or when, as with the snowy Florimel, there is no reality behind, and the appearance is all. But this is not the only vision; the mythology of Wales and of Ireland, the land which King Orfeo entered, need no such disguise, and the persons who move about them, though they may have stepped down from pagan altars to their fairy thrones, have remained not unworthy of their origin. It has already appeared that Spenser knew something of Wales, and his use of the name Guyon, even though it is also found in romances, may point the same way, as does the book which Arthur reads in Alma's castle, in which there are even Welsh words. It is true that Guyon, though a great lord, is not a king of the fairies, and even less a hunter of souls like Gwynn ap Nudd. But the borrowing of a name does not mean that Spenser wants all the character; the name of Britomartis has been borrowed in the same way from a classical source without obliging the heroine to adopt all the characteristics of her origin. Welsh mythology was in fact popular at the time, owing to a very natural desire to associate the Tudor dynasty with the ancient glories of the Welsh people rather than with the less pictur-esque movements of more recent politics. It seems at least reasonable to suppose that even before Spenser went to Ireland he knew enough of such beliefs (they were not con-fined to Wales itself) to recognize that the Sidhe were of the same kin; so that he used of this mythology also whatever served his purpose, that is, for instance, the chivalric organiza-tion of the fairy kingdom (there were two tributary fairy queens in Munster which is part of Spenser's Ireland), the dignity and high estate of the unfallen children of Danu, and certain episodes which suited his story.

It is clear that Spenser was a serious historian and anti-quary. His interest in ancient history appears incidentally in many of his minor poems, and in one, *The Ruins of Time*, he speaks in such warm terms of Camden as to suggest personal friendship and agreement in idea and opinion:

> Cambden the nourice of antiquitie,
> And lanterne unto late succeeding age,
> To see the light of simple veritie,
> Buried in ruines, through the great outrage
> Of her owne people led with warlike rage.
> Cambden, though time all moniments obscure
> Yet thy just labours ever shall endure.

This emphatic approval implies that the poet was definitely on Camden's side in the controversy relating to Geoffrey of Monmouth's *Historia Regum Angliae*, and other legendary collections relating to the origin of the British state. This in turn suggests that, though he uses Geoffrey as his main authority for the summaries of history given in Books Two and Three, he would not have taken him or his followers

seriously enough to justify quite so elaborate an interpretation as is given in the second chapter of *The Meaning of
Spenser's Fairyland*. Spenser was no dreamer in matters of
learning. The *View* shows that he had worked on the antiquities of Ireland with professional method; he had realized
the significance of place names, he had recognized that the
megalithic tombs were in fact burial places; he had not been
content simply to read, but had done what is now called
'field work' and had used Irish sources, though in translation, for his knowledge of poetry and legend.[1] He was
besides a member of the same circle of Dublin which, six
years before, when Sir Henry Sidney was governor, had
welcomed the convert Edmund Campion whose *History of
Ireland* he had read.

It is not then entirely fanciful to see certain traces of Irish
mythology and legend in *The Faerie Queene*. This mythology
is largely concerned with the perennial warfare between the
descendants of the Goddess Danu, who are gods of sun, of
light, of youth, of fertility, of arts and crafts, and the Fomorians, dwellers in the sea and the dark, giants, misshapen,
destroyers. Such a warfare is a commonplace of mythologies,
and can be traced south to Egypt, east to the Euphrates
plain and the Indus valley, north to Scandinavia, as well as
west to Wales and Ireland. But in the Irish version, the
antithesis between light and darkness is especially apparent,
and this is particularly a characteristic of Spenser's symbolism too, in which, for example, the old witch Night,
incapable of kindly feeling, is the aunt of Faithless, Lawless,
and Joyless, the sons of Blindness, and all of them friends
and allies of hell. Spenser's evil beings are deformed like the
Fomorians. No doubt the antithesis of light and darkness,
good and evil, is a natural one, and specially impressed on
the poet by the Biblical use of it. But it is more clearly
marked in the Irish than in the other mythologies accessible
to him. In such an episode as that where Britomart and
Marinell fight, his treatment of the sea, despite classical
terminology, suggests Fomorian deities rather than Greek
ones, as also do Marinell's whole character, Florimell's
undersea imprisonment, and the final marriage of the two.

[1] Cf. T. D. Kendrick, *British Antiquity*, Methuen, 1950.

Lugh the sungod was the offspring of a marriage between a deity of chaos, typified by the sea, and one of the organized world. There are of course many other tales, Scandinavian as well as Celtic, about marriages between people of land and water.

Besides this, Spenser's treatment of the fairy mistress theme as seen in Arthur's dream of Gloriana, followed by his search for her in waking reality, is singularly like the famous Irish version, the *Dream of Angus*, in which the Irish Eros is visited in sleep by a fairy maiden, and has no rest till he finds her again. And whatever the symbolic use to which Spenser put it, the well which heals the Red Cross Knight when wounded by the dragon, has surely something in common with the spring of healing which cured the Tuatha De Danann both of wounds and death when they fought the Fomorians at the battle of Moytura; though I do not suggest that wells or water of life are not common things both in legend and romance. In the Welsh *Dream of Rhonabwy* too, Arthur is a chief figure in a land of wonders.

It has been pointed out (Spence, *Fairy Tradition in Britain*), that the English fairy queens were not persons of much dignity. It was in Ireland that the old High King at Tara had his fairy counterpart with his queen in Kinvarraand Nuada, of whom the other fairy royalties were the tributaries.

It might be argued that the hostility of the Irish would have prevented them from telling their stories to their enemy. But apart from the evidence given in the *View* Spenser's relations with his immediate neighbours can hardly have been unfriendly. His acquisition of a second property as provision for his younger son, his family's remaining there after his death, his own evident love for Ireland and its scenery, all suggest those personally friendly relations which all those who have lived in occupied territory know can exist between people who are quite prepared to kill one another when circumstances change. The burning of Kilcolman was part of an organized rebellion, not an act of hostility against Spenser individually. Hence Gloriana's magnificence, her court and realm, may well have owed something not only to the queenly romantic figures found in Malory, or in stories like *Ogier the Dane*; to figures like the Lady of the Lake, or Morgan le Fay; but also to the High King and Queen of the Fairies of Ireland with their feudal realms and dependent royalties. Besides, the general practice of identifying the Olympian hierarchy, with its parallels in other lands, had brought a sunset glory of classical mythology to brood over the fairyland of that time, a glow in which the Diana character of the virgin-queen easily merged into that of 'the elf-queene and her joly companye'.

Fairy mythology in the British Isles distinguished two main types of 'fairy'; those like portunes and pixies and so forth, who are habitually smaller than men, even than children, and who appear in the popular stories of village and countryside, and those who, while able to change their size or shape, are usually thought of in terms of human dimension and appearance, even if bizarre. Their role in folk-lore and romance is more dignified. From them come the Huons, the Kinvarras and Gwynns, King Orfeo's black-haired enemy, or the queen who rode down Huntly bank. Oberon, as shown in *Huon of Bordeaux*, makes a sort of link. His small size, a relic of his dwarf origin, is attributed to malign enchantment, he should have been as tall as Huon. Shakespeare in fact makes him full sized, and supplied another link in the person of Puck.

Spenser's allegory makes him require mainly the second, romantic type. But it is clear that he was not ignorant of the first. Several of the knights are changlings, the work of the countryside fairies, and there is Mammon. He is akin to the metal-working dwarfs of the north; but also, and perhaps more closely, to the knockers of Cornish legend. His underground realm is specially suggestive of the stories of these mine-fairies, and so is his willingness to part with his riches. The vision of music and dancing figures which fascinated Calidore and vanished so quickly comes from no nearer Greece than the fairy ring in the English fields, however much the dancers may be called graces and the hill Acidale. The helpful animals of ballad and tales are represented, a little rationalized, by Una's lion, and the trees into which Fradubio and Fraelissa are transformed have literary parallels indeed, but also folk-lore ones. And Duessa, in the bath which betrayed her to Fradubio, was obeying the usual law of the witch.[1]

It is true also that Fairyland, as shown by many references, is already imagined as a place as well as a state. It is entered through hills or dark passages; it is that mysterious region where Thomas the Rhymer 'waded through red blood to the knee'; where King Orfeo found himself when he followed the fairy procession through the mountain; the Sidhe are hill dwellers; their Welsh parallels live in lakes, and Arawn's kingdom is underground. The elves too are material beings, not spirits, they may even die. They are not freed from space though they can play strange tricks with time. Their home is still part of this earth though permanently enchanted according to their wish or their condition. It is within these hills, under this ground, these thorn trees mark it, that well is an entry to it. It is not so long since a Sussex man explained his late return by saying he had had to go a long way round as the pixies were in the field he usually crossed. Spenser too distinguished Fairy land from, say South Wales, Britomart's country, and the land to which the Red Cross Knight and Artegall are to return, even though all England is also fairyland.

Bessie Dunlop was Spenser's contemporary and in 1576 she claimed to know a fairy man, a member of a local family, believed to have died in battle, but really carried away by the fairies. He came and went from somewhere near, where she too had been invited. She said she had carried his messages to his descendants, had healed by his directions, had revealed mysteries by his aid, and those for whom she had done these things did not deny having received these services. She claimed, besides, to have seen the fairy queen—no Gloriana, to have watched the fairy ride, to have seen comings and goings at the fairy thorn, where also she had recognized others whom her neighbours believed dead, and she herself till then. Perhaps she regretted that, for love of husband and children, she had refused these invitations to pass into the state which would have made all earth fairyland to her; for of all the commission of local gentry who heard her account

[1] Did Spenser, as suggested, get this from the romance of *Melusine*? He may have done; but there was no need to look so far.

of these things, there was not one who doubted that all was as she said, and for it she was condemned as a witch and duly burned.[1]

Modern superstition makes other mysteries, dealing in a world of rappings and table-turnings, materializations, astral bodies, strange voices, broken plates, and poltergeist tricks, a world much less rational than the realms of Oberon and Huon and ugly and vulgar to boot. But by citing those names I have already made a transition.

Whatever folk-lore origin there is for the figures of Oberon and Huon as they appear in the literature of Spenser's time, they belong not only to that dim otherworld, but also to the more definite existence of the story book. Popular literature of our day treats of rocket riding into space, of mysterious deaths, strange drugs, untraceable poisons, of careers in the modern world of entertainment which is unreal without being wonderful. Popular literature in Spenser's time treated of the *Seven Champions of Christendom*, the Twelve peers of Charlemagne, the deeds of Guy of Warwick and Colbrand his sword, of Guyron le Courtois, of Launfal, of Bevis of Hampton, of Sir Enyas the Swan-knight, the ancestor of the Beauchamps and the Staffords, to name only a few. And behind the luxury sport of tournaments, there lay a literature of such books as Caxton's *Order of Chivalry*. All this forms a background to the *Faerie Queene*.

Caution in assigning sources must of course be observed. Every coincidence is not a proof of indebtedness. In the widely read romance of *Lybeaus Disconu* the forest-bred hero is roused to desire the life of chivalry by the sight of armour on the dead body of a knight. It need not necessarily follow that this is why Tristram is similarly affected in Book Six of the *Faerie Queene*; for it is such a device as a writer might naturally think of. Other material is common to many romances, and great similarity of wording would be necessary to prove borrowing from any special one. Even the apparently individual detail of the distance within which the dragon may not approach, is found as exact in *Sir Bevis of Hampton* as in the *Seven Champions of Christendom*. And apparent similarities of language will not always be a sure guide,

[1] R. Pitcairn, *Criminal Trials of Scotland*, Edinburgh, 1833.

since two writers both dealing with the same theme will very likely resemble each other at times. But it still remains true that no one can read the *Faerie Queene* without being certain that the author knew the popular romances that formed the recreational reading of his time, and used them precisely as he has been shown to have used current historical works.[1] Indeed the whole question of literary 'borrowing' is much less simple than it is made to appear when it is light-heartedly assumed that certain authors 'copied' certain others.

Nothing can be more probable than that Spenser should have read the stories everybody read. It is even reasonable to suppose that when once he had conceived the general idea of his poem, he may have reread certain works which, as he already knew, contained useful material. For example, he could not make use of the legend of St. George and the Dragon, which is the foundation of the Red Cross Knight's story, without referring to the version in *The Seven Champions* and without following it rather closely at times. But, while this is so, nothing can be less likely than to suppose any process like a slavish 'lifting' of material. The confident ease with which Spenser carries on his narrative is very evident. That narrative is like the ship with which he is fond of comparing it, which tacks this way and that; but always in answer to the helm, and always moving in the right direction, if not by the straightest course. No doubt Spenser had read *Huon of Bordeaux*, *Arthur of Little Britain*, *Guiron le Courtois*, *Sir Ferumbras*, *Guy of Warwick*, *Bevis of Hampton*, *Sir Launfal*, the *Seven Champions*, and many more, just as he knew some of the Irish heroic poems. He had learned from this reading the form and the conventions of a romance, just as a modern novelist learns from his own reading the modes of his special genre, and his memory and imagination had been enriched by them. It is true to say that, with one exception, almost everything you can find in them is to be found somehow, and somewhere, in the *Faerie Queene*. He clearly meant to overgo the popular romances, as he meant to overgo the literary ones. These works, therefore, often throw light on the *Faerie Queene*, if only by bringing

[1] Cf. C. A. Harper, *Spenser's British Chronicle History*, monograph series, 1910, for a full discussion of this.

out the characteristic changes made by the poet in material common to both. For example, the hero of *Bevis of Hampton* rejoices when Josyan's presence tames the two lions that were about to attack, because this is a striking proof of her chastity. Una, however, is above such suspicion; it is the beauty of her goodness and truth which subdues the lion's lawless strength, though very likely Spenser may also have intended it as a passing comment on Archimago's accusation. Or again, the romance hero should have a special horse and a named sword. Spenser follows this convention when horse or sword have some natural connexion with the knight's quality, as Guyon's Brigadore, and Artegall's Chrysaor the sword of justice have. But he ignores it in other cases, Sir Calidore, for example, rescues Pastorella with a sword found by chance on the way.

Spenser treats his regular literary sources, the classics, Chaucer, Malory, Lydgate, Ariosto, Tasso, with exactly the same freedom, even when he translates. He does translate whole passages from the Italian. The curious reader may see Italian and English on opposite pages of Professor Praz's *Anthology*. He does this just as Shakespeare versifies whole pieces from North's *Plutarch*, or from Montaigne. But he transmutes such passages so entirely into his own style and mood, and procures it so chemical a union with its context, that the reader who did not know the original would not recognize them as borrowings at all. It is the same when he takes incidents or objects. Arthur of Little Britain had a white fairy shield, the mago Atlante had a magic diamond one, but Prince Arthur's dazzling shield has qualities unknown to either, and is very differently used. Bradamante's magic spear, given her by Astolfo, has suffered an almost sacramental change in becoming the ebony spear of Britomart. Alcina, tiring of Astolfo, transforms him into a tree, whose bough Ruggiero breaks as the Red Cross Knight breaks Fradubio's.[1] But the context, the reason, and the outcome, are all different. Indeed, so much is said about Spenser's debts to the Italians and fragments from Ariosto, in particular, are scattered over his pages as thick as blackberries, that it seems well to emphasize that when he has put

[1] And as Aeneas broke that of Polydorus.

all this treasure trove into position, the resulting story is very unlike the *Orlando Furioso*. I had at first contemplated noting these borrowings as they occurred. But it soon appeared that they were so numerous, that this procedure could only be a weariness both to writer and reader. But it also appeared that it would tend to make a false impression. Ancient Rome served as a quarry for the building of the medieval city, but that does not mean that the later structures resembled the earlier. Spenser used his Ariosto as a child uses his box of bricks when he builds to suit his own mind, a house that has no connexion with the highly coloured picture on the lid of the box. This does not mean, however, that Spenser did not owe a profound debt to Ariosto. He found in him a complexity of story, a system of breaking off and taking up again, of suspending finales, of flashing from one part of the pattern to another, of insetting stories, which served him well, for it gave him the whole structural pattern of the *Faerie Queene*. It is here, not in the superficial likeness of name, object, or episode, that the real influence of the Italians is to be found. Here Spenser was indeed the 'celestial thief' that Raleigh called him.[1]

Spenser's proper names are another proof of how widely he cast his net. One would guess that he must have collected likely names much as Dickens did. He does not usually invent names for those whose position in the story requires that they should be humanized, at least in some degree; but he is careful that they should be in a special way appropriate, though it does not follow that they designate quite the same sort of characters as those who originally bore them. Indeed, modifications are the rule. Britomart and Talus, for example, are classical; but Britomart originally was a virgin huntress like Belphoebe, rather than a 'woman knight' like, and how unlike, Bradamante or Camilla; and Talus, from being the bronze assistant of Minos, has become something more like an iron police-patrol car in human form. Tristram, except in being a hunter, has nothing in common with the lover of Iseult, even in his youth. The name of Ryence is given to Britomart's father, and the beard story, of which he is the

---

[1] Yet he could have learned the art of the inset story from the *Odyssey* or from Chaucer.

villain in Malory, is touched up and given to Crudor instead;
the Ollyphant of Spenser, Blandamour also, are very unlike
Chaucer's personages. Sometimes there seem to be too many
sources, of names, or of properties, or persons. If Josyan had
two lions, Guy of Warwick had one tame one, rescued from
a dragon; he even had a friend disguised as a palmer.
Friendly animals, however, hermits, palmers, and healing
wells, are all part of the common tradition of folk-tale and
romance. Names especially pass in a bewildering way from
one tale to another; sometimes changing sex on the way.
Florence, for example, is the heroine of *Arthur of Little
Britain*, and the hero of the continuation of *Huon of Bordeaux*
where, moreover, Gloriande is a fairy knight; but, in another
context, a fairy woman, and, in *Ogier the Dane*, a noble
princess. I have already given reasons for thinking that Guy
or Gyoun of Burgundy in *Sir Ferumbras*, may be in some
sort, the origin of Sir Guyon; but he appears once more in
Ogier, and if his palmer is in *Guy of Warwick*, other possibilities are suggested by *Guiron le Courtois*. It does indeed
seem possible that this latter may have contributed something to Book Six, if not Book Two, since it is of this romance
that Wieland remarks: 'The word courtois implies nobility
alike of mind, of manners and of birth.' It is likely enough
that when Spenser brought to mind a name such as would
suit, he neither recalled, nor troubled to think, where he had
originally seen it; though it can hardly be coincidence that
when he takes a name of strong associations, such as Tristram,
a thing he seldom does, he attaches it to a person of different
character and minor importance. At times it is clearly the
significance which is all important; though he could probably assume that few of his readers would still recognize that
Blandina's exactly appropriate name had first been that of
a virgin martyr of the early Church. This sovereign independence influences his use of larger borrowings. There is
something of Malory's Sir Gareth in the Red Cross Knight
and his story, and something of St. George and his adventures
in the *Seven Champions*; but his own stronger personality
dominates both these.

Spenser's later readings of classical authors entered an
imagination and visual memory already richly charged: the

wodwose and the satyr met and mingled in his poem as they met and mingled in his head. The most 'classical' of the books seems to be the second. If any of the knights resembles pius Aeneas, it is surely Sir Guyon, though presumably his part was meant to be principally taken by prince Arthur who, like Virgil's hero, is also the predestined seeker after a city. But Guyon illustrates much in this aspect of his character, and his palmer advises him like Anchises. The very character of his virtue, by which reason must always dominate feeling, has affinity to that of Aeneas, though Spenser was too wise to find any place for a Dido. It is Guyon who has the underworld journey, and Guyon who must cross the sea to reach his journey's end. But that sea voyage itself, like the description of his telling his story in Medina's castle, together with the character of Acrasia and her enchantments, modelled upon Circe, and of her final foiling, suggests the *Odyssey* rather than the *Aeneid*. But if these episodes hint at the *Odyssey* there are indications also of the *Iliad*. The very practice of suggestive names is Homeric, and one may doubt whether Spenser got his traitor Dolon's name from his knowledge of Greek, or from his knowledge of Homer's Trojan spy. The list of sea nymphs who are in company with Marinell's mother (iv. xi. 48 et seq.) closely resembles that in *Iliad* xviii, and the whole scene here recalls the mourning of Thetis and her attendants over Achilles, distressed for Patroclus. Achilles' shield too hung on his shoulders like the moon, as afterwards did Radigund's. Then, also, the epic similes derived from natural comparisons which Spenser uses so much, specially when describing fighting, are Homeric, though Spenser, who never borrows or uses blindly, makes his own variations, and serves his own purposes. I suspect we must blame Homer if we do not like Calepine's dodging of Turpine's spear; it seems ugly to us but Spenser, who has both to illustrate Turpine's cowardice and want of chivalry, and also to save Calepine, might well have thought that a lesser knight need not be more scrupulous than a Homeric hero when running away is concerned.

The likeness to Virgil is first in general; the *Faerie Queene* centres, on the factual plane that is, on Elizabeth I as the *Aeneid* does on Augustus and the destinies of Rome. This is seen in the chronicle histories which are made to lead up to her. Spenser was to be the English Virgil and this the national epic. But there are likenesses more inner than that. Spenser's knightly heroes, like Aeneas, are examples of vocation. They are each called to a task, and they cannot rest until it is accomplished, and though Spenser will not divide our sympathies by allowing any of them a Dido, the underlying temptation to abandon the path decreed and accept the worse alternative, is presented to most of them in one form or another, Fidessa, Philotime, Radigund. Britomart is again the exception. And surely in her there is more of Camilla than of Bradimante. There is also a profound difference between romance and epic. In Spenser there can be no Hector, no Turnus. Spenser's contests are of certain good against certain evil; there can be no conflict of right and right, of hero against hero. Hence there is both in Homer and in Virgil, an element of tragedy which is absent in Spenser. The vocation of his knights, too, is reasonable, because Christian, whereas that of Aeneas is fundamentally irrational.

Among other Latin poets Spenser seems to have been specially impressed by Lucretius. Mutability's argument is based upon Book V of the *De Rerum Naturae*, and the stanzas in canto X of Book IV, beginning: 'Great Venus, Queene of beautie and of grace' recall Lucretius' invocation. The conception the passage expresses, however, of Venus Genetrix, the genius of life reproducing itself, is integral to Spenser's whole treatment of love throughout the three books principally concerned with it.

Of course he also knew and uses the authors whose study had been an inevitable part of his own education, Ovid, Horace, Claudian: the industry of American scholarship has traced every possible reference to its source.[1] He made use too, as Warton long ago supposed, of the works of reference then available, such as the *Mythologia* of Natalis Comes. Pastorella's story when she is captured by the brigands, has much in common with that of Chariclea, also captured by brigands, and her lover Theagenes, which is narrated by Heliodorus, and which was well known in Spenser's England through the translation of Underdowne (1569). Of the

[1] Lotspeich, *Classical Myths in Spenser*, Princeton Studies in English, 1932.

influence of Aristotle and Plato enough, probably, has been
said; it is usually suggested that his neo-Platonism owed
something to the Italians and to Marsilio Ficino in particular. Yet one receives the impression that it was as much
Augustinian and medieval, as classical and Florentine. St.
Augustine was having a vogue at the universities at the time,
in those quarters which were interested in Calvin's use of
him, or were seeking him in reaction against St. Thomas
Aquinas. This book also assumes that, like many other
Anglicans of his type and time, he had inherited and not
rejected the moral and spiritual tradition from which sprang
that conception of life which it was the purpose of his poem
to express, and which he has refreshed through that famili-
arity with the Scriptures to which attention has been drawn
in various places. He assumes therefore, as did his contemporaries, the belief in an ordered universe where everything
had its due place in the hierarchy of being. When he raises
the question, as he does in the Mutability fragment, it is
only that he may lead to an affirmation of triumphant faith.

Among later writers Spenser himself makes special reference to Ariosto and Tasso, and I may add to what I have
already said of his ransacking of Ariosto, the further illustration of his having taken the whole of the tale of the Squire
of Dames from that source. From Tasso's poem he borrowed
less, though its temper was so much more congenial to his
own than that of the *Orlando Furioso*. Armida's garden no
doubt combined with those other poetic gardens that Spenser
knew, to furnish forth the Bower of Bliss, and Guyon's
guardian angel could claim kin with those whose ministry is
seen in the *Gerusalemme*. But Spenser's debt to Tasso is more
to the critic than the poet. The Italian poet composed three
Discorsi on the art of writing heroic poetry which have left
evident traces on the English poet's work. Tasso divides his
considerations under three heads: the material which is apt
to receive the more excellent form that the poet can give it;
the form itself which the poet should give; the decoration
which the form should receive and which should be the most
exquisite that the form allows.

In discussing the subjects proper to epic art, Tasso recommends something historical, because he regards truth,

comprising factual truth, as far more worthy of the poet's art
than invention. But to give scope to the poet's imagination,
and to provide picturesque and attractive adjuncts, the history should not be too recent, nor yet so remote that the difference of civilization should appear unsympathetic. The times
of Charlemagne or King Arthur are examples of the right
medium; especially because, again in the interests of 'true-
seeming', pagan subjects are excluded. The heroic poem
besides should not deal with tragedy; its purpose is not to
move pity or horror; it should have as basis, enterprises of
lofty courage, and comprise deeds of courtesy, pity, generosity, piety, religion, and in some of the persons there should
appear the total of all these virtues, the total that Spenser calls
Magnificence and attributes to prince Arthur.

The next point throws light on Spenser's treatment of
history. For what makes poetry different from history is the
poet's liberty to narrate things not as they were, but as they
should have been. Spenser pushes this liberty to a point which
Tasso would hardly have admitted. There follows an analysis
of the structure of heroic poems and their proper length.
Here Spenser would seem to have tried to reconcile both his
Italian models. Tasso argues that the heroic poem should be
of moderate length and simple form. The *Orlando Furioso*
was neither, but then, argues Tasso, it is not an epic but
a romance. Spenser seems to have arrived at the solution of
making the entire poem long and complex, like Ariosto,
while planning the single books more after Tasso's design.
He has his own way too with Tasso's chief problem, the
difficulty of having a sufficient element of the marvellous to
sustain the interest of readers without losing realism, *il
verosimile*, by using wonders of pagan origin. The Italian's
solution was to admit witches and fairies, which Spenser also
does with a difference, and to supply the rest by the religious
miraculous, by bringing in the direct intervention of God,
the angels, saints. Spenser rejects this as a general rule, in
part, probably, because his circumstances forbade; he could
hardly introduce saints and miracles without making his
poem definitely a Popish one; but still more because he had
a world synthesis which gave him a different solution. Like
Camoens he used the personages of classical mythology as

standing for powers of nature, so that, granting that the poem is in any case an allegory, Tasso's difficulty does not arise.

For Spenser's style, and the possible influence of Tasso's third discourse on this, the reader interested might care to refer again to chapter one where this is considered.[1]

I would myself urge that the strongest single influence on Spenser's work is that of the poet whom he himself repeatedly acknowledges as his master, Chaucer. 'Dan Chaucer well of English undefyled. . . .'

> 'in whose gentle spright
> The pure well head of Poesie did dwell.'

It has been suggested that the difference of language would have prevented Spenser from appreciating Chaucer as an artist. But by what magic is it, then, that no one should have written again with Chaucer's sweetness till Spenser? Actually the language difficulty would seem to have been greatly exaggerated. If the Elizabethans could read Langland's text, they could certainly read Chaucer's. Robert Crowley, introducing his edition of *Piers Plowman* in 1550, remarks that 'its Englishe is according to the time it was written in, and the sence somewhat darcke, but not so harde, but it may be understood'.[2] If this was true of *Piers Plowman* as its popularity seems to prove, still more would it be true of Chaucer whose dialect was that of Spenser's own London, and who is not so much more archaic than many ballads and romances. Moreover, the Elizabethans were not so ignorant of the older forms of the language as once was assumed. Archbishop Parker had a collection of Anglo-Saxon manuscripts, the Gospels were printed in 1571,[3] Verstegan studied that language in Oxford in the sixties of that century, William Lambarde, who wrote *Perambulations of Kent*, printed in 1576, knew something both of the language and the laws; Leland had studied Chaucer, and that Spenser knew Leland's work is suggested both by his antiquarian interests and connexions, and by the likeness in idea between his *Prothalamion*, and Leland's *Cygnes Cantio*, 1545, which

---

[1] pp. 14, 16.   [2] Skeat's ed. iii, p. xxii.
[3] Cf. T. D. Kendrick, *British Antiquity*, p. 115.

describes the Thames as seen by a swan swimming from Oxford to Greenwich.[1] It seems, then, safe to assume that if Crowley had some idea of Langland's alliterative principle, Spenser with his obvious linguistic talent, his exquisite ear and prosodical genius, understood Chaucer's versification sufficiently to realize how just were the praises he gave him. It is hard to believe that he wrote the fable in the February Eclogue in the *Shepherd's Calendar* without any knowledge of the sounding of the final *e* in Chaucer's poetry.

'Borrowings' on a large scale there certainly are; the *Merchant's Tale* gave the idea for that of Malbecco and Hellenore, the Legend of Friendship is Spenser's addition to Chaucer's half-told *Squire's Tale*, the figure of Nature in the Mutability fragment is referred by the poet himself to the *Parlement of Fowles* (VII. vii. 9), without any suggestion in the ironical phrase, to imply that he had himself troubled to take up Chaucer's own attribution to Alan of Lille. Melibee, Ollyphant, Blandamour, are names taken from the two tales which Chaucer himself claims to have tried to tell on the road to Canterbury, and several of the minor poems have a greater or less degree of dependence on Chaucerian models. Thus, both the title and the beginning of *Mother Hubberd's Tale*, to say nothing of the metre, are Chaucerian, and *Daphnaida* is connected with the *Book of the Duchess*. These latter have a likeness of form which is more important for my present contention than the use of episode and name in the *Faerie Queene*. But there is more in the *Faerie Queene* itself than that. I have more than once claimed that Chaucer and Spenser have the same type of lulling sweetness of melody. Here is now some proof; I take the quotations from the *Monk's Tale* so as to show the likeness between the two stanzas:

> Lordynges, ensample heerby may ye take
> How that in lordshipe is no sikernesse;
> For whan Fortune wole a man forsake,
> She bereth away his regne and his richesse,
> And eek his freendes bothe more and lesse.
> For what man that hath freendes thurgh Fortune,
> Mishap wol maken hem enemys, I gesse;

[1] Op. cit.

Here, from the *Parlement of Fowles*, are lines which show
that Acrasia's famous garden had a prototype nearer than
Italy:

> On every bow the bryddes herde I synge
> With voys of aungel in here armonye;
> Some beseyede hem here bryddes forth to brynge;
> The litel conyes to here pleye gonne hye;
> And further al aboute I gan aspye
> The dredful ro, the buk, the hert and hynde,
> Squrels and bestes smale of gentil kynde.
>
> Of instruments of strenges in acord
> Herde I so pleye a ravyshyng swetenesse,
>
> That God, that makere is of al and lord,
> Ne herde nevere beter as I gesse.
> Therwith a wynd unneth it myght be lesse,
> Made in the leves grene a noyse softe
> Accordaunt to the foules song alofte.

And now compare the later poet:

> The ioyous birdes shrouded in cheareful shade,
> Their notes unto the voyce attempred sweet;
> Th'Angelical soft trembling voyces made
> To th'instruments diuine respondence meet:
> The silver sounding instruments did meet
> With the base murmure of the waters fall:
> The waters fall with difference discreet,
> Now soft, now loud, vnto the wind did call:
> The gentle warbling wind low answered to all. (ii. xii. 71)

Such resemblance in difference is a proof of that unconscious
half-memory which is a far greater evidence of intimate
knowledge and understanding than direct imitation. Perhaps
a similar example is to be found in the *Book of the Duchess*, in
the few lines describing the cave of Morpheus.

> . . . he came to the darke valeye
> That stant betwixen roches tweye
> There never yet grew corn ne gras,
> Ne tre, ne (nothing) that ought was,
> Beste, ne man, ne noght elles,
> Save ther were a fewe welles
> Came rennynge fro the clyves adoun,
> That made a dedly slepying soun . . . .

This, however, is but the germ which was to flower into Spenser's stanzas. Spenser's irony is Chaucerian too, as witness Lucifera's courtiers prinking themselves; the people of Eden pushing round the dragon's body, very wise about it now, like Cambyuscan's courtiers pushing round the brazen horse; Paridell flirting with Hellenore, Hermes retreating with dignity when his wand does not frighten Mutability but, more than all, Braggadochio justifying his fright over Belphoebe by claiming an intuition about divine beings remarkably suggestive of Sir John's Falstaff's instinct for recognizing a true prince. The trees of the Wandering Wood are saplings from those that grew in Nature's garden on the feast of St. Valentine; Chaucer is with Spenser in his first canto and, with Nature herself, he is present in the last.

Of the other English classics as then considered, Skelton he clearly knew, since his favourite name for himself, Colin Clout, is Skeltonian, and the title of Skelton's morality play *Magnificence* may have been a fruitful seed. He also knew Lydgate and his adaptations from the French; in his *Falls of Princes* is a line that may well have struck a spark, a line about Arthur 'ycrowned in Fayrie', who would return 'Out of Fayrye and regne in Bretayne'. Among contemporaries, Sackville's *Induction* would clearly have been congenial and Sackville even has hints of Spenser's melancholy music. The *Gesta Romanorum* was still general reading, and King Ryence's magic mirror may have come from Virgil's in that, as easily as from the *Squire's Tale*.

So far, in trying to reconstruct something of the material which would have come to Spenser's mind and imagination from the outside world of his environment, and from his lighter reading, I have not alluded directly to persons. But the poet was always more or less in contact with learned persons interested in writing, like Harvey, or writers interested in learning and in the intellectual questions of their day, like Sidney Dyer, Raleigh; or with what the cant of today calls the 'intelligentsia', people like Ludowick Bryskett with his interest in Greek philosophy, and his faith in Spenser's guidance.

Spenser's letters show that he had played with Sidney's fancies about classical metres, though his good sense soon

led him to reject them, and obviously he did not begin a
romantic epic, experimentalist that he always was, without
studying that art of poetry which had awakened so much
contemporary interest and inspired so many brochures. His
early translations and imitations prove his knowledge of the
Pleiade, and no doubt he had read Ronsard's *Abregé de l'art
poetique français* which everyone read. Yet, apart from Tasso's
little book, one may doubt how far he was open to influence
in any matter that he held as serious. Harvey's views could
not put him off the subject of his *Elvishe Queene*, and his
pastoralism is largely his own. 'His vein', as Puttenham said
of his friend Raleigh, 'was most lofty, insolent and passionate', and, one might add, independent. Too large was his
ship, to use a metaphor he would have appreciated, to have
been moved by little winds. Yet this more technical reading
may well have confirmed him in the path he would have taken
any way. Perhaps he learned more from his study of actual
practice in, for example, Chaucer and Ariosto, than from
any theorizing, even Tasso's. And what of the science of the
day?

Spenser assumes for poetic purposes, and he can harmonize
it both with faith and philosophy in the magnificent synthesis
which forms an underlying pattern throughout his work, the
system of astrology, still much practised by his contemporaries, and envisaged both by them and by him, far more as
supplying the machinery to implement the divine decrees,
than as any argument for fatalism. It is Shakespeare's minor
and worser characters who assert themselves, like Mutability,
against the guidance of the stars, a concept which served the
imagination then, as the idea of the laws of nature does now.
Actually, except in the Mutability fragment, and perhaps
the notion that the planet-named gods were natural powers,
astrology as a concept seems to have been much less present
to Spenser's mind than to Shakespeare's. In his world of
faerie, of phenomena, there is far less room for it than on the
tragic stage.

There are also traces that Spenser's imagination had been
affected by the voyages and explorations which Raleigh's
interests, if no others, would have brought before him. The
strange world within his own mind might have been wide

enough for him without seeking further. Yet the frequent comparison of his narrative to a ship making a long voyage with only the stars for guide, and putting in for fresh supplies wherever a likely harbour offers; the figure of the Salvage Man, who, with the conditions of his life, is so vividly realized; Serena's enemies with their priest, their earthen altar, their ritual cannabalism, their doings half seen by flickering firelight; all these things suggest that fresh blood had flowed through the veins of older legend. But there is more positive evidence where the poet argues, at the beginning of Book Two, that if people should doubt the existence of his land of faerie, they might remember:

> That of the world least part to us is red;
> And dayly how through hardy enterprize,
> Many great regions are discovered,
> Which to late age were never mentioned.
> Who euer heard of th'Indian Peru?
> Or who in venturous vessell measured
> The Amazon's huge river now found trew?
> Or fruitfullest Virginia who did euer vew? (II. 2)

And he adds that later times will make still more discoveries.[1]

Among the various interests which are made manifest in the *Faerie Queene*, that in history is at times strikingly apparent. The casual reader might assume that the matter of Merlin's prophecies, and of the chronicles which Guyon and Arthur read, was simply made up to suit the occasion especially as the idea occurs in Ariosto, but, in fact, it had been carefully put together from historical sources. Harper, in *Spenser's British Chronicle History*, has carefully traced what these sources were. Geoffrey of Monmouth was, of course, the foundation both of Merlin's prophecy of the descendants of Britomart's marriage with Sir Artegall, the son of Gorlois of Cornwall, and hence Arthur's putative brother, and of the narrative read by Arthur in the House of Alma; but Spenser by no means depends on Geoffrey alone. Like Shakespeare, and all other Elizabethans, he was a reader of Holinshed; but also of Stow, Hardynge Grafton, Caxton. He knew Camden's *Britannia* and, one may fairly assume, Leland's biography of Arthur dedicated to Lord

[1] Cf. also IV. xi. 21. My attention has also been drawn to I. vi. 102.

Grey de Wilton; though it would not appear that he made much use of the latter. However, the point at issue here is not so much the proof of Spenser's interest in, and knowledge of, history, though this is most enlightening, as the fact that he treated his historical sources as he treated his literary ones, with extreme freedom and masterfulness, selecting, adapting, and arranging from the various sources as best suited his poetic purpose and, Kendrick points out (op. cit.), in harmony with the best historical thought of the day.

His use of the material taken from the *Orlando Furioso* is a striking illustration of this sovereign liberty. Critics have discussed his attitude to Ariosto, questioning whether in fact he recognized the satirical character which he ignored so completely. But Spenser was himself a satirical poet; he was familiar with other satires, such as *Sir Thopas* and the *Parlement of Fowles*,[1] and he was himself capable of passages of high comedy, even in the *Faerie Queene* where laughter, that potent solvent, had to be used with caution. It is to the highest degree unlikely that he who described Paridell flirting, and who created Braggadochio, who loved Chaucer, and who had written *Mother Hubberd's Tale*, should not understand Ariosto. But the fact is, the question hardly arises. When Spenser read for pleasure, he doubtless enjoyed Ariosto as he enjoyed Chaucer, and Malory, and *Lybeaus Disconu*, and *Huon of Bordeaux*, and *Sir Fierabras*, enjoying those better whose art was greater. But when he was working he treated them all as he treated the mythological collections of Natalis Comes; that is, as places where he could find what he wanted. Only, Ariosto was more useful because he could be translated at times, or whole stories could be made over. But what Spenser does not use out of the mass of material at his disposal, is even more enlightening than what he makes his own of it.

If one may judge both from antecedent probability, and from apparent parallels, Spenser knew a little book of Caxton's called *The Order of Chivalry or Knighthood*. The dedication gives a succinct account of that cosmological order which is the framework of the Mutability story: 'Unto

[1] Both Chaucerian.

the praysing and dyuyne glorye of God, which is lord and
souerayne kynge aboue and ouer alle Kynges celestyal and
worldly, we beginne this book of the Ordre of Chyualry; for
to shewe that to the sygnifyaunce of god, the prynce almyghty
whiche sygnoryeth aboue the seuen planettes that make the
cours celestyal, and haue pouer and sygnorye in gouerning
and ordeyning the bodyes terrestre and erthely, that in like-
wyse ouer the kynges princes and grete lordes to haue puys-
saunce and seynorie vpon the knyghtes. . . .'

The book opens with a meeting between a squire who is
making his way to a place where knighthood is to be conferred, and an old knight, now a hermit, who is so described
as irresistibly to recall the hermit, once a knight, who shelters
and heals Serena and Timias.

The laying down the qualities requisite in a knight, if we
allow for that elimination of whatever refers directly to
the Catholic religion, which we always find in Spenser, the
chapels, the Masses, the defence of the faith, the cult of the
Blessed Virgin, and so on, defines fairly exactly the character
of Sir Guyon, most impetuous, but also most gentle, retiring,
and compassionate, of all the knights. Indeed, his special
individuality is thus expressed, 'Vertue and mesure abyde in
the myddel of two extremytees.' Then, when it comes to the
symbolism of the knight's arms and armour, first on the list,
after sword and spear the knightly weapons, is the helmet
which signifies shamefastness. At once there flashes before
the memory that strangely vivid picture in the House of
Alma, Guyon confronted with the girl dressed in blue, the
colour of modesty, blushing and silent, and Alma's words:

> She is the fountain of your modesty
> You shamefast are—but Shamefastness itself is shee.

I have made this comparison to illustrate the essential
originality of Spenser. The more one realizes how his whole
text is graven all over by talismanic signs left by everything
that had interested him, the more one realizes with what easy
mastery he shapes this material to his own purposes. His
poem suggests a half, survived intact, of the last of one of
those series of buried cities which excavators find, Troy
below Troy, in which are relics of all that lies below, some-

thing of the Crusaders, the Romans, the Phrygyians or Phoe-
nicians, even in those days enriched with coin and pictured
seal, scarab, and statuette of a snake-entwined goddess,
brought from Egypt, Hatti, Mari, Ur. The comparison
would have pleased Spenser himself, for he was a great lover
of antiquities.

It has several times been remarked that Spenser makes
singularly little use of his seemingly obvious source, Malory.
There is a hint of the Gareth story, there are points of resemblance in the treatment of single combats, there is a certain
use of names, there is hardly even a debt of vocabulary, since
the language of chivalry was attainable from many other
sources as well. Even the Order of Maydenhede and the
twelve days' feasting:

> When every day brought forth a noble chance
> And every chance brought forth a noble knight

might have come to him from elsewhere, even if they did not.
The reason is probably in part to be found in the inextricably
Catholic character of Malory's narrative; but in part it is
bound up with his special use of the Arthurian legend itself.

If Spenser wanted to write a poem which, besides its
moral purpose, would be thoroughly national, as he did,
Arthur was inevitably indicated as the protagonist, as Milton
saw in after years. Arthur was equally a hero whether in the
English or the Welsh tradition, and the Tudor cult of 'the
Dragon of the great Pendragonship', had brought his name
forward as standing in the same relationship to Queen
Elizabeth I, as Aeneas did, in Virgil's intention, to Augustus
or as Tasso to the House of Este. Spenser, by his careful
manipulation of his chronicle material as well as by many
passing allusions, makes clear that he regards his poem as
also a sort of English *Aeneid*. Yet he has, evidently of a set
purpose, eliminated everything with which the name of
Arthur is usually associated, except the symbolic dragon on
his crest.

No name important in Arthur's personal cycle except
Merlin's, and that in quite another context, appears in the
Faerie Queene save where, at the end of Calidore's legend,

Spenser names some of Malory's best knights as failing in
after ages to check the Blatant Beast. Tristram, the most remote from Arthur of all his Round Table, who indeed
appears for a moment, does so in a character shared by persons of quite other romances, and he never comes into contact with Arthur himself. By placing the events in the time
before Arthur was king, Spenser has with one stroke eliminated the Round Table, the Holy Grail, Morgan le Fay, the
Lady of the Lake, Lancelot, Guinevere, Gawaine, Kay. His
horse is Spumadore, his sword Mortdure, his squire Timias,
his foster-father Timon. Of the Arthur of the Arthurian
cycle there remains the mysterious coming, the honoured
name, and the national symbolism going with the skill and
courage of the 'prowest knight of the world'. These Spenser
deliberately uses in a new context, to which a close association with Malory's text could only be an embarrassment.
Hence, even when Spenser took a very recognizable name,
he carefully disassociated it from its original context. It was
Lancelot who lived in Joyous Gard, but Malecasta's Castle
Joyous uses the name in a very different sense. Any well-
known figure receives only a minor role, and loses either his
name or his story. Brehus Sans Pité becomes Sir Sanglier,
for example. This applies even to the use of well-known
ballad material, such as the story of the Squire of Low
Degree. This shifting, we see it in Sir Blandamour whose
name comes from Chaucer, is so invariable, that it must be
deliberate. Some stock characters are of course inalterable,
whatever their names; the false woman whose favours
betray, is the same figure whether she be called Delilah,
Circe, Alcina, Armida, or Acrasia, but, familiar in many
contexts, she belongs to none in particular. Acrasia's garden
might be taken from either Ariosto or Tasso, but Spenser
needed neither poet to make Acrasia known to him. Phaedria
is equally a creature of experience, pretty, good-natured,
silly, meaning no harm, yet usually the occasion of it.
One may, indeed, doubt whether some borrowings that one
acknowledges, are so in fact. Ariosto suspends his stories,
but the whole structure of the *Faerie Queene*, with its irresistible forward flow, 'On such a tide as moving seems asleep',
required that all the affluents should be drawn into the main

current, and have no separate ending. This fact is emphasized by the parallel, contrasting, tale of Marinell and Florimell; for the untouched innocence of Florimell's beauty, though it ravishes everyone who catches a glimpse of it, does not belong to those involved in the struggle of our fallen nature, but to him who has known no other passion. Incidentally, the theory, repeated since the eighteenth century, that Florimell in the historical allegory, stands for the 'good side' of Mary Queen of Scots, seems most irrational. Even admitting that Spenser would have recognized a 'good side' in her; which, in view of Duessa, seems extremely unlikely, it is unrealistic to suppose that, in a poem designed under its national aspect, to glorify England-Elizabeth, he should have lavished such praises and such triumph on her rival. Even Arthur wishes that Gloriana were such as she. Loyal friendship might, and did, lead him to risk Elizabeth's anger and Burleigh's; but he had no motive for being a friend to Mary of Scotland. If Florimell must find a place in the historical allegory at all, it would seem more probable that, as the Red Cross Knight and Arthur both personify England under a particular aspect, religious or national, so Florimell might stand for the sceptred isle itself wedded, as Shakespeare too shows it, to the silver sea, typified by the sea-nymph's son, the Armada victor.

If one allows for the psychology of memory, it is probable that for some of his details Spenser himself could hardly have said if he had thought of them himself, or if they were flotsam and jetsam from ballad and romance read long ago. But one of the supreme examples of Spenser's sovereignty over his material is in what he rejects. Here is a self-confessed fairy story, drawing material largely from the Italian epics, Malory, the popular romances, the ballads, in all of which wonders are as thick as blackberries, and he leaves them all behind.[1] Those works depict an ordinary world into which things from elsewhere have intruded: ships that sail of themselves to their port when the appointed person boards; enchanted castles like that of Atlante, or Port Noys, or the Brosse, hippogriffs, journeys to the moon, the gift of wishing, unaccountable appearances and disappearances, monstrosities

[1] Cf., however, Tasso, op. cit.

like the transformation of the woman-knight, Huon's grand-daughter. Almost none of this is found in Spenser. He takes Cambell and Canacee from the *Squire's Tale*, for example, but not the magic horse. These wonders represent the unknown element in a known world. They take place in defined regions, Paris, Italy, Scotland, or at least the protagonist belongs somewhere; he is Sir Denys of France, Sir Guy of Warwick; he is linked with Charlemagne, or with wars, feuds, crusades, which had historical existence; in this way the events are even localized in time, they are happening, let us say, during the First Crusade. But the opposite is true of Spenser. His whole world is a marvel, a fayerye land, where space and time have no meaning, where known places, like South Wales, are left behind before the real story begins, where there are lonely castles and lonely huts, and savage tribes, but no place, except a transitory Arcadia, where men live together on the terms of this world's life. But in this world, which is itself a wonder, marvels are not brought in for their own sake, but as symbols, and they are usually the simplest kind of folk-lore marvel rather than literary elaborations. Monsters are not infrequent, but they are projections of the monstrous which is within the human heart. Pride, prostitution, unnatural lust, communism, are giants; but they are proportioned to the evils they represent. Busyrane has an enchanted castle, but it is a piece of fayerye, of illusion, depending on Busyrane's power which, again is only strong when his enemy is weak. There are good people and bad people, but there is on good 'maga' in the background to act as a *dea ex machina*; the only real magician is Archimago. He is seen working one spell, and flying on the north wind, but otherwise his magic is principally in his shape-shifting, the special attribute of the Celtic wonder-worker. Merlin has second sight, but one need only compare his prophecy in Spenser with that of the skeleton from the tomb in Ariosto to illustrate this, and the transformations of Malengin recall those through which Tamlane or Proteus passed; but no fairy queens, nor talismanic objects, are brought in to get the knights out of their difficulties without effort on their part. Their weapons may be better or more beautiful than others but, except for Britomart's spear and Arthur's shield, and his sword in one respect, they are not magic in the usual sense, and both these exceptions stand for heavenly grace. Bronze guards with flails appear in *Arthur of Little Britain*; but no other weapon could have been so appropriate to Talus with his special function. Guyon, it is true, meets a whole procession of strange appearances, psychologically quite justified, but these, again, are faerie illusion, and in form are taken from folk-lore rather than romance. Even the gods themselves are natural powers obedient to heaven and their own law, that of the stars in their courses. All that Spenser had read, seen, or imagined, passed through the furnace of his own creative genius and came out so transmuted that, when all his factual world has vanished, and even supposing all his 'sources' unknown, his ideal world still remains complete in itself.

In that world, things are seen sometimes in symbol, sometimes in act, sometimes in both, as we see Scudamour's adventures, while the unending series of contrasts are never quite simple; the Garden of Adonis, where Time is the only enemy, is contrasted with the Bower of Bliss not only as good with evil in general, but as the good originally created and intended, with the evil that has been brought into it by man's corrrupted nature. Had it not been for that, the Garden and the Bower would have remained identical and Acrasia would never have usurped the place of Amoret. Thus gradually when the poem is studied as a whole, incomplete indeed, but not mutilated, there emerges a pattern too large and intricate to be fully perceived with one glance, but all the more satisfying for that very reason, a pattern which sweeps into its vast synthesis even an occasional variation which has no part in the main scheme, like, perhaps, the Squire of Dame's Tale, but which is related to it as a man's passing fancies are to the real stuff of his mind. The comparatively narrow and formal plan, like the plot of a morality play, that Spenser himself defined in his letter to Raleigh, had come to life under the impulse of a creative shaping genius greater than perhaps he realized himself; so that what Shakespeare did for the outer world, in which men have to do with one another, Spenser did for the inner world, where a man's enemies are those of his own household. There is nothing in English more powerfully imaginative than the *Faerie Queene;* for in it the inward drama has been given an outward form by which it becomes conscious of itself. With a sweetness and splendour of verse in which he can excel even Shakespeare, with a spirit lofty and humane, impregnated with a compassionate understanding which Milton did not draw from like Biblical study, Spenser obeyed, as Sidney could never have obeyed, the command of Sidney's muse:

Fool, said my muse to me: Look in thy heart and write.

I would not be thought, in thus trying to reconstruct something of the poetic world, the mental climate, under the influence of which Spenser's poem was born and grew, to have done more than touch on the fringe of this subject. Obviously no complete treatment could ever be possible; since who could know what Spenser, commanding the languages he did, might not have read;[1] who could estimate fully the impact of his environment, part only of which I have hinted at, especially of that experience derived from his life as a public servant, on which the historical allegory must have largely depended. That his voyages to and from Ireland affected his imagination no one could doubt who has read his frequent allusions to the sea, and his love of the landscape of his Irish home is equally evident. But of that overwhelming 'love of nature' which has been esteemed so great a poetic virtue since the time of Wordsworth, there is less in Spenser than in Shakespeare, even though his subject might seem to call for it more. He loved beauty wherever he found it, he described beautiful things with truth and felicity whatever they were, but the beauty of inanimate nature is not more dear to him, nor more inspiring than any other form of beauty. Indeed he praises the natural beauty of sound, wind, wave, and bird song, by comparing it to that part singing which he evidently, like his fellow Elizabethans, found so peculiarly delightful; and no natural objects are described except where the action of the poem demands it. On the whole, he regards nature with the eye of a philosopher, more concerned to expose the secret of its working than to dwell

[1] Cf. Rathborne, *Meaning of Spenser's Fairyland,* for further suggestions.

on its appearance for its own sake, and he has throughout that mental disposition described in the quotation which begins the chapter on allegory, according to which outward things are valued more as pictures of what is within than for themselves. Even the factual occurrences of which he made his historical allegory, are such pictures, and this is the reason that they could be introduced without irrelevance into a poem whose main content is ethical and spiritual. In so far as they were pictures, they were useful; but they were 'faded out' whenever they ceased to represent the interior fact that Spenser had in mind. If I have concentrated attention almost exclusively on the moral allegory, it is partly for this reason; but also because the historical allegory has already been fully and adequately discussed, elsewhere; whereas, it has been my experience that new readers of Spenser require far more help with the moral allegory than Spenserian critics usually give them. This, besides the fact that I believe that the right understanding of this allegory in the light of the moral and spiritual conceptions usual at his time, removes many apparent obscurities, and discloses the underlying design on which the pattern of the whole poem depends.

Spenser, like most of our greatest poets, stood between two worlds. He was the last of the great medieval allegorists; the last in whom it would be natural and spontaneous that the outward world should appear as a picture of the world within, and should represent the struggle of the soul with its enemies. After him only Bunyan would look on the world with eyes like his. For good or for evil the old order was giving place, had almost given place in Spenser's time, to a humanistic order in which the picture would be considered the reality; the thing having worth in itself. Those very Amazons and other discoveries which Spenser himself had hailed, would prove so satisfying for the imagination that even the poet would not look behind them; though there would come those who would see both things together. Yet that Spenser belonged to that humanistic world as well is proved by the educational purpose he avows; he was preparing a gentleman or noble person for life in this world, not simply for the next; this manifests a far more profoundly humanistic attitude than the classicisms he shared with such as Gabriel Harvey. No one knew better than a man of Spenser's practical experience that the London tournaments were just a game, and that the images, through which he was telling his mind, no longer corresponded to any actual facts, and never would again. But this very thing made them the more suitable for his purpose, for their significance remained as unchanging as the past to which they now belonged. He had seized and fixed those figures, already of the past but not yet outworn, at the moment when the meaning he imposed upon them would preserve them for ever, and they it. By making his persons allegorical, he detached them from time, and thus, by a paradox, the humanity with which he also endowed them, has remained too. Keats was a true Spenserian when he claimed that the figures on his Urn, because they did not live at all, would live for ever; 'For ever wilt thou live, and she be fair.'

But Spenser's persons do not live only for this reason. His psychology of human feeling and conduct is singularly just and experiential. This is most clearly seen in Book One, where the relative simplicity and concentration of the story allow it to appear more clearly, as may be seen in the relations of the protagonist with Una. The Red Cross Knight, rudely shocked by his sudden loss of faith in Una's truth, is tempted to throw over belief altogether. But having defeated Sansfoy, he swings in reaction to the other extreme, and accepts Fidessa rather lightly. Yet, though he thinks he believes in her, he feels intuitively that she is not such as Una, and he treats her with much less respect. When his simple satisfaction and confidence in his achievement has been dashed by his defeat he falls into deep depression; but from that darkness there surges up anew his faith in Una whom, in his heart of hearts, in the region below superficial consciousness, he had loved all the time. When she reappears there is no reconciliation, no explanation, no apology. None was needed. Only his conscious mind had been deluded. Many a priest could illustrate that story from his own experience in reconciling those whom a sudden psychological event: 'a sunset touch, a fancy from the flowerbell—Someone's death' has brought back to a childhood's faith, abandoned and forgotten, apparently, for years. This is but one example.

This same observation, applied to the outer world, enables him to make his faerie land as realistic as Lilliput or Crusoe's island, and by much the same means. Malbecco's castle is marked on no earthly map; but the polite conversation there of well-bred strangers met by chance, could be paralleled in many an Elizabethan hostelry; so too Alma, tactfully feigning not to see Guyon's embarrassment, and Fidelia and Speranza gracefully excusing their sister's absence to Una. We seem to hear for a moment the voices of the Spencer sisters at Althorp, or of 'Sidney's sister, Pembroke's mother'. Even smaller, yet still vivid, touches of realism are the blistered fingers of the blacksmith, Care, the flies buzzing round Phantastes' room in Alma's castle, or the peasants running from Artegall and Burbon 'like squirrels'. Philotime's grand room is like a guild hall, and, delightful touch, Proteus, who lives in a cave, has an old nymph to do for him. So solid, so secure, was Spenser's world, where even Mutability had an appointed place.

The time was coming when the secure background of this order of being, harmoniously graded from the Uncreated to the least created thing, would pass from men's minds, and behind the brief human drama there would loom only a cloudscape, wild and whirling as the atoms into which the universe was soon to be resolved. He who conceived the giant of communism knew very well that forces had begun to work which would, at least might, disrupt the social order as hitherto understood. He used the genius of an artist to bear witness to the validity of certain concepts of human life and conduct, and to state in one unsurpassable form, values without which no human society can long exist.

I do not mean, of course, to suggest for a moment that Spenser formulated these ideas as definitely as this. I would not suggest either that the interpretation I have put upon his work might not at times seem to imply a mode of procedure which would hardly be likely to result in a great poem; as though he had composed a detailed moral and psychological system, and then electro-plated it, so to speak, with poetry, or rather, with poetic language. Creative composition is not done like that. Image and content were born together, grew together, developing under the poet's hand in

that strange partnership and interplay between creating
mind and created thing, in which, at times, the ruling intellect seems to lead, and, at times, seems to follow, as its doubly
contingent creature reveals the laws of its being and growth.
Concept, imagery, sound, and feeling, all react on one another, giving and taking, until the final result comes with a
certain shock of discovery even to the poet himself. That the
Faerie Queene should remain incomplete was inevitable from
the beginning, for Spenser had set himself a theme which
never could reach a conclusion in the earthly faerye land
where it began. That conclusion could only be the identification of the Cleopolis below with the Jerusalem above:

> Whose walls and towres were builded high and strong
> Of perle and pretious stone that earthly tong
> Cannot describe, nor wit of man can tell:
> Too high a ditty for my simple song . . .

Unfinished it was and must have been. But Spenser surely
it was who gave Sidney the vision of the ideal poet, who is
preferable to all the philosophers, because he knows all that
they know but, 'with a tale he comes to you, a tale that keeps
children from play, and old men from the chimney corner'.

CHRONOLOGY

OF SPENSER'S LIFE AND THE EVENTS THAT SPECIALLY CONCERN HIM

1552	Probable date of birth.	Northumberland Protector, Somerset executed.
1553–7	Childhood.	The troubles of Mary's reign. Accession of Elizabeth.
1569	Translations for Vander Noott's *Theatre of Worldlings*. Goes to Pembroke College, Cambridge.	The Rising of the North under Westmorland and Northumberland.
1570	Harvey becomes Fellow of Pembroke.	Elizabeth excommunicated.
1572		The Ridolfi plot.
1576	M.A. degree.	Leicester marries the Countess of Essex.
1577	Possibly in Ireland for Leicester.	Drake going round the world.
1578	Secretary to Young, Bp. of Rochester.	Alencon and Simier in London.
1579	In Leicester's household: *The Shepherd's Calender* published.	Desmond in rebellion in Ireland.
1580	Irish appointment: the Harvey correspondence.	Grey goes to Ireland; Smerwick taken from the rebels and Spanish allies.
1583	Living at New Abbey: Commissioner for Musters in Kildare.	Throgmorton's plot. Gilbert in Newfoundland.
1584		Raleigh's attempt in Virginia.
1585		Leicester's Netherlands expedition.
1586	In Dublin.	Sidney killed at Zutphen; the Babington conspiracy.
1587	Grant of Kilcolman.	Execution of Mary.
1588		The Armada. Death of Leicester.
1589	Clerk of the Council of Munster; Raleigh's visit.	Accession of Henry IV of France. Rise of Essex.
1590	In London, *Faerie Queene*, I–III, *Muipotmos, Mother Hubberd's Tale*.	Elizabeth grants the poet a pension.
1591	*Complaints, Daphnaida*. Return to Ireland, probably.	
1593		The Lopez plot.
1594	Marriage to Elizabeth Boyle.	
1595	*Colin Clout's Come Home Again, Amoretti, Epithalamion*.	

1596   In London again. *Faerie Queene,*
         I–VI, *Prothalamion, View*
         written but not published.
1597   Resigns Clerkship of Munster.
1598   Becomes Sheriff of Cork. Sack of   Burleigh dies and Philip II.
         Kilcolman. Mission to London.   In October the Irish rebel-
                                                   lion, Bagenal defeated.
1599   January, dies.   The Essex fiasco in Ireland.

A NOTE ON SPENSER'S TREATMENT OF HISTORY

THERE is a dispute among Spenserian critics about the way in which his historical allegory is to be interpreted. One group holds that the historical allegory in the *Faerie Queene* forms a continuous narrative, at least in Books One and Five, the figures corresponding throughout to the historical personages involved in that narration. The other group believes that the poet intends no more than occasional historical illustration, and that the personages, though corresponding from time to time with various historical originals, are introduced more as exercising certain virtues held as characteristic, than as actors on the factual scene.

The first school of thought is relatively modern, for though as early as 1693, Dryden had said in his *Essay on Satire*, that all Spenser's knights were represented in the court of Queen Elizabeth, it does not appear that he followed any tradition, or had any direct evidence beyond the ambiguously expressed dedicatory sonnets. It is not until the eighteenth century that Warton, in his *Observations on the Faerie Queene*, 1754, remarked that there existed an historical allegory of Elizabethan intrigue in it. But he does not attempt to reconstruct this. Four years later, in the notes to his edition of Spenser, Upton ventures on a number of historical identifications, many of which have held their ground until the present time. It is he, for example, who identifies the Red Cross Knight with Henry VIII. This opened a field for speculation which attracted various nineteenth-century critics, and they have been followed by many more in the twentieth century, especially in America. In *Notes and Queries* Ser. 3 and 4, in 1863, Howard, in an *Essay on the Historical Allusions in Spenser*, identifies Arthur with Essex (who was hardly so considerable a figure by 1590), the Red Cross Knight with Sidney, Archimago with Burleigh, and his son-in-law, the Earl of Oxford, with the three Pagan knights Sansfoy, Sansloy, and Sansjoy. But Scott, in his review of Tod's edition, had, with characteristic breadth of vision, envisaged a larger stage. For him Book One narrated the history of the Primitive Church: the fight with Error stands for the Arian controversy. Sansfoy stands for paganism, but with the reign of Constantine, worldly pride prevails in the palace of Lucifera, and a period of relaxation follows in which the church submits to the Pope and the Red Cross Knight is imprisoned by Orgoglio, until the Protestant Church is liberated from Mary

Tudor by the accession of Elizabeth. Thomas Keightley, too, saw a narrative of Church history (*Notes and Queries*, Ser. 4–7, 1871). For him Una's lion is the Count of Toulouse, Orgoglio is Charlemagne and his successors, while Una's satyrs are Waldenses, and Sansloy the Pope's adherents at the time of Simon de Montfort. Another interpretation associates Error's den not with Arius but with Pelagius; the three Pagan brothers are Spain, while Archimago's deluding dream becomes St. Augustine of Canterbury substituting Roman ritual for that previously in use among the monks of the Welsh Abbey of Bangor. But for Whitney (*Transactions* of the Amer. Phil. Assn. 1888), the Red Cross Knight is the English sovereign, *Fidei Defensor*, and Una is the true Christian Church, which is first represented by the Roman Church only, and then by the Protestant Church only. Henry VIII is then the Red Cross Knight, and his pride is Orgoglio: Una's parents are the Old and New Testaments, the episode with Despaire stands for Mary's reign; Archimago is equated with papal intrigue.

In fact, later critics have tended to abandon the Arians, Pelagians, and Waldenses, and to confine themselves to events arising from the Protestant Reformation. Whitney is followed, in 1911, also in America, by Philo Buck in *Political Allusions of the Faerie Queene* (Nebraska Studies 11), for whom the Red Cross Knight is the spirit of the English people, Arthur, the Earl of Leicester, Error the religious controversies at the end of Henry's reign, while Archimago's deception of the Red Cross Knight is taken as representative of Henry VIII's insistence that he was still a Catholic. Then Sansfoy is Henry II of France, who sought the alliance of Duessa-Mary Tudor, while Fradubio and Fraelissa become Guilford Dudley and Lady Jane Grey. It seems a hard heart that would give a name like Fraelissa to Ascham's honoured and heroic pupil; but so it is. The satyrs that were the Waldenses are now the 'Sea-Beggars' and the imprisonment of the Red Cross Knight suggests to the critic the capture of Calais; at which point Duessa becomes the Queen of Scots. Elizabeth comes to the throne in Canto VII, and the fight at the castle is Grey's battle at Leith against the regent of Scotland, Mary of Guise. For Lucifera's driving out to take the air with her ministers, the College of Cardinals, had already shown us Mary-Duessa, allied with Philip II, Guise, and Maximilian of Austria against heresy. By parity of reasoning Sansfoy becomes France, Sansloy is the Duke of Alva, Sansjoy, Philip II, and Orgoglio, François Duc de Guise.

Professor Padelford, an editor of the *Variorum Spenser*, though keeping to the Reformation period, does not wish to limit hypothesis unduly. Una's parents are the Old and New Testaments, or classical and Christian philosophy, or Natural and Revealed Truth, while Error is not Arius, or Pelagius, or Henrician religious controversy, but Henry's encouragement of Renaissance rationalism.

Those critics, however, who limit the historical narrative to the history of the Reformation, are nevertheless uncertain at what point this should be taken to begin; whether, that is, Henry VIII's reign should be included, or whether the accession of Elizabeth I, when English Protestantism became ascendant, should be considered the starting-point. This controversy principally affects Book One since in Book Five, by general agreement the most 'historical' of all, Spenser takes care to leave no doubt about the chief persons and events concerned, even though details may remain obscure.

Winstanley, the editor of Book One in 1915, sets out perhaps the most systematic statement of the extreme 'historical' view. She regards Mary Tudor's marriage with Philip II as the crisis of the book, and this is adumbrated in the Red Cross Knight's imprisonment, Orgoglio being Philip II, and his dragon the Marian persecutions. It was the disturbed condition of England at the end of Edward VI's reign which so weakened the Christian champion as to make him an easy prey. Lucifera is Mary Tudor too: the execution of St. Thomas More is to be seen in the fight with Sansfoy; though no part is found for Bishop Fisher. Cardinal Pole is Sansjoy, his exile being portrayed in the classical cloud in which the pagan knight is conveyed from the scene of conflict. Archimago is Bishop Gardiner, Bonner, that acute lawyer, is Ignaro, Henry VIII is Una's lion, and is killed by Edward Courtenay in the part of Sansloy, whose attack on Una stands for the Wyatt plot, in which Courtenay was to have married princess Elizabeth. The satyrs cease to be the Dutch 'Sea-Beggars', and become the common people of England. The parts of Fradubio and Fraelissa, which Buck had given to Guilford Dudley and Lady Jane Grey, are given by Winstanley to Cranmer and his wife. For rumour had said that the archbishop, having married before the new religion had made it lawful, had carried his wife from place to place in a wooden chest. But for Padelford, Cranmer, just now Fradubio trembling and wretched, is the gallant adventurer Satyrane who, for Buck, had been the Prince of Orange, and for Upton, Sir John Perrot, the Queen's unruly brother.

Other critics, doubting how far Henry VIII would have been considered a Protestant hero by his near contemporaries, have preferred to take Book One as beginning with the accession of Elizabeth; in which case persons and events move proportionately forward; Duessa can always be the Queen of Scots, Archimago is free to become Burleigh, and the fight with the dragon will vividly represent Sidney's letter to the Queen protesting against the French marriage (*Notes and Queries*, 1863).

To the other group of critics which seems to include many of the later English writers, it appears that this theory is altogether too rich in possibilities. A narrative so general that it can be interpreted of persons and trains of events so different, may perhaps have no continuous, particular significance at all. Or can Spenser, great poet as no one denies him to be, really have thought that the writing of a risky letter was like fighting a dragon to the death? Or would Arthur's momentary fall suggest to anyone, that is, but a critic, the attainder of the Dudleys after the Northumberland conspiracy? How St. Thomas More, Sansfoy to Padelford and Winstanley, was really regarded in Spenser's time is showed by the tragedy of *Sir Thomas More* in which Shakespeare's hand is seen. And is it not unrealistic to suppose that Cranmer, who was to Spenser and his Church, just such a martyr as St. Thomas More to the Catholics, could possibly have seemed to the poet to resemble Fradubio, or be shown by him telling Fradubio's story? Spenser's known attitude to Grindal and Young sufficiently confutes such an idea. When we are considering these points we must not forget that Spenser lived in the sixteenth century. I have so far spoken only of Book One in this connexion, because I wish not only to avoid confusion, but to try an experiment with Book Five that may help to decide Spenser's attitude to history by actual evidence.

First of all, the *View of the Present State of Ireland* forms a striking illustration that the poet was in fact a man of the sixteenth century and not the twentieth. It is quite evident in that treatise that the poet regarded Ireland, like his contemporaries, as the eighteenth century regarded America; that is, as a wild adventurous sort of place where an enterprising man might make his fortune. True there were natives, a savage uncivilized sort of people for the most part. The settlers needed protection against these, which their own country ought to provide. She, too, would benefit if her colonists succeeded in establishing order and agriculture where at present was neither the one or the other. If the Red Indians, or the wild Irish, rebelled, and especially if they called in the French, or the Spanish, they should be dealt with, and the settlers protected, just as, in the eighteenth century, the American colonists were protected. Spenser, if he could have known it, was reasoning in the *View* exactly as some 'opposite number' in an American colony in mid-eighteenth century would be likely to reason, or later on, in India or Africa. This point of view explains the attitude towards Ireland which he adopts in Book Five of the *Faerie Queene*.

In this book, 'the Legend of Justice,' Spenser really does take trouble to make it clear that he is dealing with actual historical events, at least in certain places. They are events which had taken place in his own lifetime, and his readers therefore could easily check his treatment of the facts against their own personal knowledge. He points out the events he is thinking of by his use of proper names: Irena for Ireland, Burbon and Flourdelys for Henry Bourbon of Navarre and France, Lady Belge and her seventeen sons, for the Netherlands. In fact, when Spenser intends to be clear no one can be clearer. He then tells the story of the dealings of Arthur and Artegall with these persons and places. Arthur undertakes the rescue of Lady Belge therefore he, at this moment, is Leicester. And now, what are the real facts? Leicester is placed in command of the expedition that Elizabeth had at last been reluctantly persuaded to send to the help of the Dutch insurgents. It is specially important that he should take and hold Antwerp. Leicester shows little aptitude for his task; but he almost assumes the throne which Elizabeth had refused, and bitterly offends her by so doing. He fights the battle of Zutphen, which is only remembered because Sidney was killed in it, dying as nobly as he had lived, and he eventually returns to England having accomplished nothing effective. Antwerp was not taken; the Netherlands were not freed; the Inquisition was not destroyed. Spenser tells us the exact contrary.[1] In Canto XI Artegall encounters Burbon, who has thrown aside the shield of faith in the hope of more easily obtaining his lady, Flourdelys. He rebukes him for his dishonesty; but persuades the lady of his real right and, by means of Talus, disperses Burbon's enemies. The aid which Elizabeth gave Henry of Navarre in 1591 certainly produced no such result; Henry IV did not owe his throne to any help he ever received from England. Neither Spenser nor his readers could have been under any delusions on this point.[2] Finally, in Canto XII, Artegall is shown eventually reaching the Salvage Island, killing Grantorto, freeing the grateful Irena, and establishing peace and good government, though not able to complete his reforms because of his recall. But neither does this correspond to the facts of Lord Grey's government, except that he was indeed recalled, at his own request, and he had defeated and slain the Spanish who were holding Smerwick fort. Yet in spite of this defeat, the Desmond rebellion was not effectively quelled, and Spenser, who had travelled with Grey's successor Norris, and who was Secretary of Munster, knew very well how little Grey had achieved.

Spenser's historical narrative when, by his use of proper names we can be sure he intended one, is just as ideal as all the rest of his story. It is more ideal; for Spenser's moral allegory is consistent both with the facts of the spiritual life, and with human psychology. There was no need of Bacon's 'imaginations as one would' in that field. But actual

[1] v. x and xi.
[2] No English expedition to France in Elizabeth's reign benefited either country.

events do not always follow the rule of virtue, and when that happened, Spenser corrected them.[1] What happens in his story is what ought to have happened in real life, what would have happened if all had gone well, and not as it did go. Spenser's first readers knew the facts too well not to understand what the poet was doing with them. It would be reasonable to infer that when the poet is deliberately more obscure, when he refrains from any hint by the use of names that he intends any specific persons or places, he in fact does not refer to particular instances. We can by no means assume that any historical events happened just as he narrates them. Book Five also throws some light on the question of chronology, historical sequence.

Since Spenser himself says, in his letter to Raleigh, that, in his second intention, Gloriana is Elizabeth, and Faerie land England, it will seem prudent to suppose that any historical allusions he does intend to be understood by the general reader will bear some reference to her career. If we examine Book Five from the point of view of the chronology of the real events he alludes to, in however manipulated a way, we get the following result.

The first date is the least certain. But de Selincourt,[2] and many prudent critics, hold it as certain that Artegall's imprisonment by Radigund in Canto V refers to a set-back in Grey's career resulting from his name having been found on Ridolfi's list of persons whose support could be reckoned on supposing the plot to free Mary and marry her to the Duke of Norfolk succeeded.[3] This would give the date 1572 for that canto. In the following one Britomart, hastening to his rescue, is deceived by Dolon, accepts his hospitality, and is nearly murdered in his castle. Afterwards the two sons wait in ambush for her. The motive assigned is the death of Guizor, whom Artegall had killed. Dolon's name means Guile, and the Dolon of the Iliad is a Trojan spy who betrayed his own side to the Greeks. All this hints at another plot, and the name of Guizor suggests France. Throckmorton's plot, in which the Duke of Guise appears to have been involved, together with the Spanish ambassador Mendoza, who had to leave England in consequence, may here be indicated. But now we get on to firmer ground. Artegall is freed in Canto VII. In Canto VIII Arthur kills the Souldan in his chariot and Artegall drives off his wife Adicia. The Souldan's chariot, his weapons, Arthur's inability to reach him, his final destruction through the bolting horses, all suggest to critics, Upton, followed by the others, that the poet here means the Armada, the runaway horses representing the wind which scattered the Spanish

---

[1] In so doing he goes far beyond the limits Tasso lays down in the *Discorsi*, op. cit.
[2] Cf. Introd. to the Oxford edition of Spenser, p. liii.
[3] Froude, *Reign of Elizabeth*, iv, 158, n. 1. Grey's name is nineteenth on the list.

fleet, and the combat taking place on land because Leicester was in command of the land defences. If so, the date is 1588. Canto IX contains, first, the foiling and death of Malengin, second, Mercilla's trial of Duessa. This latter event by general consent stands for the trial of Mary Queen of Scots, by Elizabeth. Indeed, there is some indication that it was so interpreted at the time, an unusual confirmation. The year then, is 1587. Some critics take the Malengin episode to stand for the Irish troubles and Irish plotting. But Artegall has not yet reached the Salvage Iland and the Irish unrest, with Maleger as a typical kerne, has already been described in a general way in Book Two in the attack on Alma's castle. The description of Malengin, and the context where the story occurs, would far more naturally suggest a conspiracy more definite, and having a connexion with the trial. This indicates the Babington plot, dramatically revealed in 1586. Malengin's changes of shape have enough literary parallels not necessarily to call for a special historical interpretation; yet, since Mary herself at her trial roundly accused Walsingham of rigging the Babington conspiracy, as Froude, not her friend, relates, and since Walsingham, as witness the citations of the same authority, gave a very fumbling answer (Froude, xii. 283), Spenser may well have known that the tangle of shifts, deceits, and counter deceits had been more complex even than usual. We must not credit the poet with knowing what only recent research has more fully revealed, but a public official can hardly have been unaware either of the methods of Burleigh and Walsingham, or of the web of domestic and international intrigue which periodically came to light in the exposure of plots and pseudo-plots.

In Cantos X and XI, where Arthur goes to the rescue of Lady Belge and her seventeen sons, Spenser makes it clear, by these names, that he is giving his version of Leicester's Netherlands expedition, which covered the years 1585-6. In Canto XII, Artegall at last reaches the Salvage Iland, defeats Grantorto, and rescues Irena. Lord Grey de Wilton arrived in Ireland in 1580. There the Desmond rebellion was going on, and its Spanish auxiliaries were holding Smerwick fort. Gregory XIII, regarding Ireland as a feudal appanage of the Papacy, had granted it as a fief to his nephew, Giacomo Buoncompacni. Whether Grantorto as an individual stands for Pope or nephew, or for Philip II, which is the critical tradition, or, in a more general sense, for the political and military power of either the Papacy or Spain, it is really immaterial to decide, since all these were involved together in the foreign assistance given to the Irish. The taking of Smerwick will be in any case the fact behind Artegall's single combat, there being no possible rival claimant.

It appears then, that even when Spenser makes it evident what historical facts he is dealing with, he not only changes them and their consequences to suit himself, and his moral allegory; but he even writes his history backwards with a consistency that cannot be indeliberate.[1] From this one may judge of the caution that may be needed when, with equal deliberation, he does not make it clear what, if any, historical facts he had in mind.

The only logical conclusion is that Spenser treats history as he treats romance, simply as a source of material for his moral allegory and his romantic epic. What is useful he uses, but the facts were subject to his imagination and his requirements. However, even when we admit that particular identifications will usually be extremely uncertain and transitory, it will remain true that Spenser does give at least a typical form to large historical movements or tendencies in which he saw the struggle of good and evil which was always his real theme. In this sense we may acknowledge, for example, that the poet sees the theme of Book One historically illustrated by the progress of the Protestant Reformation in England, culminating in the establishing of a national Church which had left Rome without joining Wittenberg or Geneva. Elizabeth was the historical heroine of his poem, and it is her settlement of the problem that he upholds.

In giving a generalized, typical, suggestion of this progress, hints of particular events or persons may be given in passing, but these cannot be pressed, or set in a chronological sequence. And here it may be well to touch on the theory that the poet was concerned with the possible marriage of Elizabeth with Leicester. What Harvey first saw of the *Elvishe Queene* had been written before 1580, when the Queen's marriage was still a real political issue, though, as she was already in her late forties, its consequences could hardly be other than political. But Leicester married the dowager Lady Essex, privately at first, about 1576. When Spenser first planned his poem, being still a member of Leicester's household, he can never have considered a marriage between Queen and Earl as even a remote possibility. But it would still have been the height of indiscretion to have given Arthur, whose quest for his fairy bride is the main romantic theme, any perceptible or constant political interpretation. If Professor Greenlaw is right, as seems extremely likely, in contending that in *Mother Hubberd's Tale* Spenser was satirizing Alençon and Simier, and had got into trouble with Leicester for doing so, it is not very likely that he would have

---

[1] The chronology is further complicated by the fact that only twelve days separated the beginning of the first story from the last, so that the times of each book are parallel, and when Arthur vanishes from one book it is because he is occupied in another. The Blatant Beast was flying from Calidore when he bit Timias and Serena.

burnt his fingers a second time.[1] When even the first part of the poem was published, not only was Leicester dead but Elizabeth's marriage was not even a political issue any more. Arthur could only be advanced as the romantic lover of Gloriana because, in fact, there was no political aspirant to the hand of Elizabeth with whom he could be identified. It is unrealistic in the same way to suppose that in the Radigund episode Spenser could be attacking the 'monstrous regiment of women'. Everyone knew that Elizabeth had never forgiven Knox for writing the book of that name in which he attacked female sovereignty, and even as poet, let alone as man of the world, Spenser, who had deliberately chosen to make a queen his romantic heroine, appearing under various aspects, and therefore figured by various persons, but all dominant characters, could possibly have intended to introduce an incident so discordant as such an attack. He does, however, suggest that others among the Amazons had erred by forcing themselves into masculine positions to which they had no claim. But he goes no farther. Elizabeth, however she might have chosen to disregard them in practice, had still notoriously shown herself sensitive to Mary of Scotland's rights as a queen.

Another instance of Spenser's intending to embody a whole historical movement or tendency in a typical symbolic form, is seen in the incident of the communistic giant.

The Protestant Reform among the peasants of Germany had quickly taken on a socially revolutionary character. The Peasants' Revolt, even though repudiated ultimately by Luther, had still been inspired by ideas taken from his teaching, and the rebels against the existing social order asserted the equality of all men and the sinfulness of claiming an absolute right to possessions on religious grounds. The social movement, however, became especially associated with the Anabaptists whose headquarters were in Holland, but who had passed into Germany and gained possession of the city of Munster (1534) where their doings under their leader Jan of Leyden, who was said to have sixteen wives, had sufficiently proved that their tenets were even more dangerous to civil society than to established religion. So Henry VIII had judged, so the ministers of Edward VI, so Mary, and so Elizabeth. All these proceeded with extremest rigour against any Anabaptist who fell into their hands. That the peril arising from their ideas had spread beyond the limits of their own sect, and was neither abstract nor remote, is proved by the fact that in 1530, Henry VIII condemned, among other propositions taken from the writing of Tyndale, in exile, but a Cambridge man, one of Cranmer's group, the tenets that bodily labour is commanded to all, that the rich may not dispose of their goods at will,

---

[1] Greenlaw, *Studies in Spenser's Historical Allegory*, chap. 3, pp. 115 et seq.

that only non-christians need submit to the secular power.[1] This was not mere theorizing. Robert Kett and his followers had made an armed attempt to put such beliefs as to property into practice no farther away than Norwich, and as recently as the regency of Somerset. And this had been purely a social rising. All this lay behind the incident of the giant of communism in Book Five. But that does not mean that he intends to portray any definite train of events; he is only interested in the principle involved.

Book Five itself is sufficient proof that Spenser's narrative, when it represents history at all, does so only in the sense of showing that ultimately good prevails over evil, even in this world, and he illustrates this thesis from actual facts only when they can be manipulated to show that victory. His historical allusions correspond to facts only when what he believed should happen did happen. And how often was that?

[1] P. Hughes, *History of the Reformation*, ii. 331–46.

INDEX

PRINTED IN GREAT BRITAIN
AT THE UNIVERSITY PRESS, OXFORD
BY VIVIAN RIDLER
PRINTER TO THE UNIVERSITY